AGRICULTURE AND EAST-WEST EUROPEAN INTEGRATION

Agriculture and East-West European Integration

Edited by
JASON G. HARTELL
JOHAN F.M. SWINNEN

LONDON AND NEW YORK

First published 2000 by Ashgate Publishing

Reissued 2018 by Routledge
2 Park Square, Milton Park, Abingdon, Oxon OX14 4RN
711 Third Avenue, New York, NY 10017, USA

Routledge is an imprint of the Taylor & Francis Group, an informa business

Copyright © Jason G. Hartell and Johan F.M. Swinnen 2000

All rights reserved. No part of this book may be reprinted or reproduced or utilised in any form or by any electronic, mechanical, or other means, now known or hereafter invented, including photocopying and recording, or in any information storage or retrieval system, without permission in writing from the publishers.

Notice:
Product or corporate names may be trademarks or registered trademarks, and are used only for identification and explanation without intent to infringe.

Publisher's Note
The publisher has gone to great lengths to ensure the quality of this reprint but points out that some imperfections in the original copies may be apparent.

Disclaimer
The publisher has made every effort to trace copyright holders and welcomes correspondence from those they have been unable to contact.

A Library of Congress record exists under LC control number: 99069526

ISBN 13: 978-1-138-71400-7 (hbk)
ISBN 13: 978-1-138-71373-4 (pbk)
ISBN 13: 978-1-315-19776-0 (ebk)

Contents

List of Figures	*vii*
List of Tables	*x*
List of Contributors	*xiii*
Preface and Acknowledgements	*xvi*
List of Abbreviations	*xviii*

1. The Implications of European Union Accession for Central and Eastern European Agricultural Markets, Trade, Government Budgets and the Macroeconomy
   Martin Banse, Wolfgang Münch and Stefan Tangermann — 1

2. Baltic Agricultural Competitiveness and Prospects under European Union Accession
   Klaus Frohberg and Monika Hartmann — 33

3. The Competitiveness of Czech Agricultural Producers in an Integrated European Market
   Tomáš Ratinger — 65

4. The Effect of European Union Accession on Poland's Agricultural Markets and Budgetary Expenditures
   Wladyslaw Piskorz — 85

5. Slovenia's Accession to the European Union: Implications for the Agricultural Sector
   Štefan Bojnec and Wolfgang Münch — 107

6. Integration with the European Union and the Competitiveness of the Bulgarian Agro-Food Sector
   Matthew Gorton and Sophia Davidova — 135

7. Agriculture and Integration: Trade Liberalisation Versus Migration
   Alexander H. Sarris — 171

8 From Central Planning to the Common Agricultural Policy:
   Analysis and Political Economy Aspects of Agricultural
   Policy in Central and Eastern Europe
   Jason G. Hartell and Johan F.M. Swinnen   187

9 Eastward European Union Enlargement and the Future of
   the Common Agricultural Policy
   Ewa Rabinowicz   215

10 The Impact of Central and Eastern Europe Joining the
   Common Agricultural Policy on Agricultural Protection in
   the European Union: A Political Economy Perspective
   Harry de Gorter and Ján Pokrivčák   247

List of Figures

Figure 1.1	Nominal protection rates in CEECs under the Nonaccession Scenario, 1989 to 2010 (per cent)	5
Figure 1.2	CAP Scenario: Absolute change of protection in CEECs during accession compared to Nonaccession Scenario	9
Figure 1.3	Agenda Scenario: Absolute change of NPRs in CEECs during accession compared to Nonaccession Scenario	10
Figure 1.4	Budget expenditure for market guarantees under different policy Scenarios in CEECs	14
Figure 1.5	Development of gross agricultural output in the Nonaccession Scenario	20
Figure 1.6	Development of GDP in the Nonaccession Scenario	21
Figure 1.7	Impact on gross agricultural output: CAP Scenario compared to Nonaccession Scenario	21
Figure 1.8	Impact on GDP: CAP Scenario compared to the Nonaccession Scenario	22
Figure 1.9	Impact on real exchange rates: CAP Scenario compared to the Nonaccession Scenario	24
Figure 1.10	Impact on total investment: CAP Scenario compared to the Nonaccession Scenario	24
Figure 1.11	Impact on GDP: Agenda Scenario compared to the Nonaccession Scenario	25
Figure 1.12	Impact on real exchange rates: Agenda Scenario compared to the Nonaccession Scenario	26
Figure 1.13	Impact on total investment: Agenda Scenario compared to the Nonaccession Scenario	26
Figure 3.1	Comparative advantage of Czech agricultural production - cereals (OECD prices)	76
Figure 3.2	Comparative advantage of Czech agricultural production - livestock (OECD prices)	76
Figure 3.3	Competitiveness of Czech agriculture, the Agenda 2000 Scenario with appreciated national currency	82
Figure 4.1	Differences in the level of human consumption of agricultural products in 2005 under CAP Scenarios	101

viii *Agriculture and East-West European Integration*

Figure 4.2	Differences in consumer expenditures for agricultural products in 2005 under different CAP Scenarios (compared to Nonaccession Scenario)	102
Figure 5.1	Nominal protection rates at the farm level	122
Figure 5.2	Nominal protection rates at the wholesale/processing level	123
Figure 5.3	Producer subsidy equivalents for the EU and selected CEECs	124
Figure 5.4	Market price support and other supports in the PSE, 1993-95 (per cent)	125
Figure 5.5	Development of agricultural and food protection under four policy scenarios (weighted average NPR, per cent)	128
Figure 5.6	Adjusted net budgetary spending for market guarantees under four policy scenarios	131
Figure 6.1	Spectrum of international integration	136
Figure 6.2	Bulgarian agro-food exports to the EU, 1992-97	141
Figure 6.3	Bulgarian agro-food imports from the EU, 1992-97	141
Figure 6.4	Bulgarian agro-food trade with CEFTA countries, 1993-97	154
Figure 6.5	Bulgarian farm prices in relation to EU institutional prices, 1995-97	158
Figure 7.1	Economy of an Eastern European country before and after opening to Western Europe	177
Figure 7.2	Economy of a Western European country before and after opening to Eastern Europe	178
Figure 7.3	Impact of Western European trade preferences on the economy of an Eastern European country	180
Figure 7.4	The economy of a Western European country after a decline in CAP support	181
Figure 7.5	The impact of investments in the nonagricultural sector of an Eastern European country	182
Figure 8.1	Average protection rates for CEEC agriculture, 1991-95	188
Figure 8.2	Aggregate per cent PSE, 1990-98	190
Figure 8.3	Per cent PSEs, selected CEECs and the EU, 1994 and 1996	190
Figure 8.4	Commodity level protection, 1991-93 and 1996-98	191
Figure 8.5	Decomposition of the PSE, 1991-93 and 1996-98	200

List of Figures ix

Figure 8.6   Agricultural support and economic development in
             CEECs, 1995   206
Figure 8.7   Agricultural support and value share of net agricultural
             exports in total agricultural production in CEECs, 1995   206
Figure 10.1 Examples of the price preferences for a net beneficiary
             of the CAP inside versus outside the EU   255
Figure 10.2 An example of the CAP resulting in higher price
             supports (analogous to the 'restaurant table' effect)
             assuming all 7 countries' agricultural sectors are of
             equal size   258
Figure 10.3 Size of production and the 'restaurant table' effect   259
Figure 10.4 Median price preferences and the accession of the
             CEECs   262

List of Tables

Table 1.1	Scenario assumptions	7
Table 1.2	CEEC-7 development of production under different policy options (million tons)	12
Table 1.3	Macroeconomic relevance of agricultural and food industry in the CEECs and the EU	16
Table 1.4	Trade balance of selected CEECs, 1995 (million USD)	16
Table 1.5	Impact of an adoption of the CAP on private households' welfare, 2003 (million USD)	27
Table 2.1	Key climatic and soil factors in the Baltics	38
Table 2.2	Production costs in ECU per ton, 1996	46
Table 2.3	Producer prices in ECU per ton, 1996	47
Table 2.4	Gross margins, 1996	48
Table 2.5	Comparative advantage based on the RTA, 1995-96	53
Table 2.6	Nominal and real effective exchange rates of the Baltic countries with their main trading partners, 1992-96	58
Table 3.1	Comparative advantage and effective protection - cereals, CZK per ton	77
Table 3.2	Comparative advantage and effective protection - livestock, CZK per ton	78
Table 3.3	Revealed comparative advantage: EU - CR trade	79
Table 3.4	Agenda 2000 Scenario - comparative advantage and effective protection, CZK per ton	80
Table 4.1	Nonpolicy scenario assumptions (per cent per annum)	88
Table 4.2	Scenario assumptions for Polish integration	90
Table 4.3	Polish agricultural production in the pretransition period, the base period, and in 2005 (million tonnes)	91
Table 4.4	Net trade of agricultural products in the pretransition period, the base period, and in 2005 (million tonnes)	94
Table 4.5	Market prices of agricultural products in the pretransition period, the base period, and in 2005 (PLN/tonne)	96
Table 4.6	Estimates of farm receipts under different accession scenarios (million ECU)	97
Table 4.7	Budgetary costs of different accession scenarios	98

Table 4.8	The impact of a 30 per cent increase in productivity of Polish agriculture on simulation results for the year 2005 (compared to scenario with zero productivity change)	99
Table 4.9	The impact of a 10 per cent PLN appreciation rate on simulation results for the year 2005 (compared to scenario with zero appreciation rate)	100
Table 4.10	Impact on agriculture of Poland's EU accession under an unreformed CAP (compared to Nonaccession Scenario)	103
Table 4.11	Simulated results for year 2005 for Polish agriculture, accession with an Agenda 2000-reformed CAP (compared to Nonaccession Scenario)	104
Table 4.12	Simulated results for year 2005 for Polish agriculture, accession with an Agenda 2000-reformed CAP (compared to Unreformed CAP Scenario)	104
Table 5.1	Social, economic and agricultural indicators for CEECs in comparison with EU-15	110
Table 5.2	Slovene exports and imports of food and agricultural products, 1995 (million USD)	111
Table 5.3	Production and marketing channels of agricultural products	112
Table 5.4	Comparison of Slovene and EU agricultural policy measures, 1996-97	119
Table 5.5	Nominal protection rates for Slovenia and the EU	121
Table 5.6	Projected change in Slovene real market prices by 2010 relative to 1994-96 under three scenarios (per cent)	127
Table 5.7	Projected Slovene production and net exports under four policy scenarios	130
Table 6.1	Comparison of policy instruments in the EU and Bulgaria	138
Table 6.2	Bulgarian exports of agricultural products, 1992-97 ('000 USD)	142
Table 6.3	Bulgarian imports of agricultural products, 1992-97 ('000 USD)	143
Table 6.4	Unit values of EU trade with third countries and Bulgaria for selected groups of agricultural products (ECU/tonne)	146
Table 6.5	Bulgarian tariff protection in the agro-food sector (per cent)	148
Table 6.6	Distribution of tariff rates in Bulgaria for agricultural products (8-digit)	149

Table 6.7	Distribution of the preferential tariff rates granted by Bulgaria to the EU without quantitative limits	149
Table 6.8	Commodity weighting index for Bulgaria	150
Table 6.9	EU share of Bulgarian exports index, 1996	151
Table 6.10	Bulgarian agricultural trade, 1993-97 (million USD)	153
Table 6.11	Share of Bulgarian agricultural trade with individual CEFTA countries, 1993-97 (per cent)	153
Table 6.12	Bulgarian farm prices, 1991-97 (ECU/tonne)	157
Table 6.13	Bulgarian retail prices, 1991-97 (ECU/kg)	158
Table 6.14	Nominal protection coefficients for selected farm products in Bulgaria, 1997	159
Table 6.15	Economic transfers in Bulgarian food supply chains at the farm level	162
Table 6.16	PSEs at the processing level in Bulgarian food supply chains	163
Table 6.17	Four-firm concentration ratios in Bulgarian and European food processing industries	164
Table 8.1	PSEs for selected commodities, 1998	192
Table 8.2	Summary of policy instrument developments in selected CEECs, 1998-99	196
Table 10.1	Importance of agriculture for the CEECs	251
Table 10.2	Intercountry balance of payments transfers due to the pre- and post-1992 CAP (billion ECU)	253

List of Contributors

Martin Banse holds a Ph.D. in agricultural economics from the University of Göttingen where he has also lectured. His specialization is in general equilibrium modeling and analysis of agricultural policies and has consulted for both the FAO and CEEC governments.

Štefan Bojnec is director of an independent institute in Ljubljana, assistant professor of agricultural economics at University of Ljubljana and visiting fellow at the Department of Agricultural and Environmental Economics at Katholieke Universiteit Leuven. He holds a Ph.D. in economics from University of Zagreb and has published extensively on agricultural and economic policy, privatization and restructuring, and European integration.

Sophia Davidova is lecturer in food policy for economies in transition at the Department of Agricultural Economics and Business Management, Wye College, University of London, United Kingdom. She hold a Ph.D. from Economic University, Sofia, Bulgaria, and has been senior advisor to the Bulgarian government.

Harry de Gorter is associate professor at Cornell University where his research focus is on the political economy and applied welfare economics of agricultural and trade policy. He has a Ph.D. from the University of California, Berkeley.

Klaus Frohberg is Executive Director of the Institute of Agricultural Development in Central and Eastern Europe (IAMO), in Halle/Saale, Germany and Head of the Division of External Environment for Agriculture and Policy Analysis. Prior to taking on this position he was with the Institute of Agricultural Policy, Marketing and Rural Sociology at the University of Bonn.

Matthew Gorton is lecturer in the Department of Agricultural Economics and Food Marketing, University of Newcastle upon Tyne, United Kingdom. He was previously employed as a post-doctoral researcher at Wye College, University of London.

Jason G. Hartell holds a M.S. from the Department of Agriculture and Applied Economics from the University of Minnesota and is currently pursuing a Ph.D. in agricultural economics at the University of Kentucky.

Monika Hartmann is Head of the Division of Agricultural Markets, Marketing and World Agricultural Trade at the Institute of Agricultural Development in Central and Eastern Europe (IAMO) in Halle/Saale, Germany. Prior to this position she was with the Institute of Agricultural Policy at the University of Frankfurt/Main.

Wolfgang Münch is currently pursuing a Ph.D in agricultural economics at the University of Göttingen, Germany. His research applies partial equilibrium models of market and trade policies in the EU and the CEECs to assess the agricultural implications of EU Eastward enlargement.

Wladyslaw Piskorz is agricultural counselor with the Mission of the Republic of Poland to the European Union. Previously he was head of SAEPR, the policy analysis unit in the Ministry of Agriculture in Poland.

Ján Pokrivčák is lecturer in the Department of Economics, Slovak Agricultural University, Nitra, Slovakia. He has a M.S. in Agricultural Economics from Cornell University and is pursuing a Ph.D. at the Department of Agricultural and Environmental Economics, Katholieke Universiteit Leuven, Belgium.

Ewa Rabinowicz is associate professor at the Department of Economics, The Swedish Agricultural University. She has written extensively on agricultural sector modeling, agricultural policy, political economy, and CEEC agricultural transition.

Tomáš Ratinger holds a Ph.D. from Charles University, Czech Republic. He is currently a senior researcher of the Research Institute for Agricultural Economics (VUZE) in Prague, and is heading the department of agricultural and rural development strategy.

Alexander H. Sarris is professor of economics at the University of Athens, Greece. He holds a Ph.D. in economics from Massachusetts Institute of Technology, USA. He has been advisor to several international organizations and governments on agricultural reform in CEECs.

Johan F.M. Swinnen is associate professor in agricultural economics and food policy and Director of the Policy Research Group at the Department of Agricultural and Environmental Economics, Katholieke Universiteit Leuven, Belgium. He has a Ph.D. in agricultural economics from Cornell University. He is currently on leave at the European Commission as economic advisor on CAP reform and eastern enlargement.

Stefan Tangermann is professor of agricultural economics at the Institute of Agricultural Economics, University of Göttingen, Germany. Previously he was a professor of economics at the University of Frankfurt/Main. He holds a Ph.D. in economics and has published widely on international agricultural trade, agricultural issues in the WTO, EU agricultural policies, and agricultural implications of EU Eastward enlargement.

Preface and Acknowledgements

This volume results from a research project on 'Agriculture and East-West European Integration', coordinated by Jo Swinnen and financed by the Phare ACE Programme of the European Union Commission. Two workshops were organized: in Ljubljana, Slovenia, on 17 May, 1997, and at the conclusion of the project in Prague, Czech Republic, on 24-25 January, 1998, when the individual findings and conclusions were reviewed and discussed.

Agricultural policy has been a major obstacle during the negotiations of many international economic agreements, e.g. the GATT Uruguay Round. Given the economic, social, and political importance of agriculture in both Eastern and Western Europe, this is also likely to be the case during discussions on the integration of the countries of Central and Eastern Europe (CEECs) into the European Union (EU). The principal objective of the research project was to assess some of the key uncertainties surrounding agricultural integration of CEECs with the EU, thus providing a basis for sound policy recommendations and strategies that would minimize adjustment costs and maximize the benefits of integration.

To provide insight into likely integration effects, the research papers in this volume: (1) analyze the comparative advantage of CEEC agriculture and its potential for growth under various accession policy scenarios; (2) compare the impact of current CEEC agricultural policies with EU policies and identify likely policy developments in both the CEECs and the EU based on economic, social, and political economy considerations; (3) provide an indication of expected economic effects and adjustment costs of CEEC-EU integration for the agro-food sector with emphasis on both efficiency and distribution impacts under these policy scenarios; and (4) seek to identify the most important constraints for CEEC-EU integration including policy convergence issues, the impact of various external commitments, and internal constraints such as budget implications and political opposition.

The volume brings together a number of timely and detailed country-specific and region-wide empirical analyses of current agricultural policies and likely production, welfare, budgetary, and other consequences of continued East-West integration. This analysis is further elaborated in a number of chapters that focus on the interaction and integration of price and trade policies between the CEECs and the EU and investigates the implications for trade, migration, and the development of the Common Agricultural Policy.

We are grateful to the EU Commission and the Phare ACE Programme for their funding of this research project. We thank Katrien Verhelst of the Leuven Center for Transition Economics (LICOS) for administrative management of the project. We also thank Ann Hartell for careful editing and Ria Uyttebroeck for assistance with formatting of the manuscript. Special thanks to Štefan Bojnec and Tomáš Ratinger whose excellent organization helped ensure the success of the workshops in Ljubljana and Prague, respectively. Finally, we would like to thank all the contributing authors of this volume for their dedication and hard work in meeting the project's objectives.

The views expressed here are solely those of the authors and not necessarily those of the sponsoring organizations, or the authors' affiliated institutions or universities.

Jason Hartell
Jo Swinnen

Leuven

List of Abbreviations

AA	Association Agreement
ACA	Accession compensatory amount
AMS	Aggregate measure of support
AP	Agricultural policy
ASAL	Agricultural structural adjustment loan
BFTA	Baltic Free Trade Agreement
CAP	Common Agricultural Policy
CEEC	Central and Eastern European country
CEFTA	Central European Free Trade Area
CEFTA-4	Hungary, Poland, Slovakia and Czech Republic
CES	Constant elasticity of substitution
CGE	Computable general equilibrium
CIS	Commonwealth of Independent States
CMEA	Council for Mutual Economic Assistance
CPI	Consumer price index
CR	Czech Republic
CSO	Czech Statistical Office
CZK	Czech crown
DK	Danish kroner
DRC	Domestic resource cost
EC	European Community
ECU	European currency unit
EFTA	European Free Trade Agreement
EPC	Effective protective rate/ effective protective coefficient
ESIM	European Simulation Model
EU	European Union
FDI	Foreign direct investment
FEOGA	Guidance Section of the European Agricultural Guidance and Guarantee Fund
FSU	Former Soviet Union
GATT	General Agreement on Tariffs and Trade
GDP	Gross domestic product
GS	General services
HN	Harmonised nomenclature

List of Abbreviations

HS	Harmonised system
IS	Input support
LFA	Less favored area
MFN	Most favored nation
NAFTA	North American Free Trade Agreement
NATO	North Atlantic Treaty Organization
NPC	Nominal protection coefficient
NPR	Nominal protection rate
OECD	Organisation for Economic Co-operation and Development
PLN	Polish zloty
PPP	Purchasing power parity index
PSE	Producer subsidy equivalent/ producer support estimate
RAS	Row-and-column-sum method
RCA	Revealed comparative advantage
RER	Real exchange rate
RMP	Relative revealed import penetration index
RTA	Relative revealed comparative trade advantage index
RXA	Relative revealed comparative advantage exports indicator
SAEPR	Agricultural Policy Analysis Unit
SEK	Swedish krona
SEM	Single european market
SMP	Skimmed milk powder
SNA	Standardized national account
UK	United Kingdom
USD	United States dollar
VAT	Value-added tax
VMPL	Value of marginal product of labor
WTO	World Trade Organization

1 The Implications of European Union Accession for Central and Eastern European Agricultural Markets, Trade, Government Budgets and the Macroeconomy

MARTIN BANSE, WOLFGANG MÜNCH AND
STEFAN TANGERMANN

Introduction

With their accession to the European Union (EU), agricultural policies in Central and Eastern European countries (CEECs) will change more or less dramatically depending on the nature of the future of the Common Agricultural Policy (CAP). These policy adjustments can clearly have significant implications for farmers and food consumers in CEECs, for market balance and trade in agriculture, for budget expenditures, and for macroeconomic conditions. Such economic effects will be relevant not only for the CEECs, but also for the EU. In particular, decisions on the future of the CAP will have to consider the market and budget implications of alternative future agricultural policies in the CEECs. This has become obvious in the vigorous debate about further reforms to the CAP stimulated by the Agenda 2000 proposals presented by the European Commission.

A rapidly growing literature, in part surveyed by Tangermann (1997), has analysed and discussed the agricultural implications of CEEC accession to the EU with much emphasis on the quantitative market and budgetary effects. This chapter is another contribution to this literature. What is the reason for adding one more set of quantitative projections to the existing body of knowledge? First, the economic environment and the policy situation keeps changing in both the CEECs and the EU, and with a moving base for projections there may well be changes in expected implications of future policy adjustments. In particular, agricultural policies in the CEECs changed from providing a mere safety net to more protective measures and world market prices increased to levels unknown in the past two decades. Moreover, a reform debate has started within the EU, centering on the Agenda 2000 proposals. All these developments justify a new effort to evaluate possible policy options for CEEC accession to the EU in the area of agriculture. The new starting point of the simulations presented here includes the latest data capturing recent developments. Additionally the Agenda 2000 proposals are explicitly considered in the policy scenarios analysed.

Second, there is no doubt that alternative agricultural policies can have significant implications for macroeconomic developments in the CEECs, given their large agriculture and food industry sectors. At the same time, involvement of the CEECs in the CAP, particularly in the 'financial solidarity' under the CAP and the resulting potentially large financial transfers between the EU and the individual CEECs, may result in noticeable macroeconomic repercussions. An appropriate analytical tool for studying such macroeconomic effects are computable general equilibrium (CGE) models, as used in this context, for example, by Orlowski (1996) and Weyerbrock (1997). However, one difficulty in using CGE models is that policy detail, like the many rather specific measures employed in the CAP, cannot easily be represented. We attempt to overcome this bottleneck by combining CGE analysis with analysis based on a partial equilibrium model of agricultural markets which includes a lot of policy detail. At the same time, this dual approach allows us to overcome one of the weaknesses of partial equilibrium models, i.e. their inability to consider the macroeconomic repercussions of the policies studied. To achieve this, we feed information on macroeconomic developments generated in the CGE framework, particularly exchange rates, into our partial equilibrium model.

The chapter is structured as follows. The second section is devoted to an analysis of alternative agricultural policy scenarios in selected CEECs in the framework of a partial equilibrium model, with subsections outlining policy scenarios, protection levels, market effects, and budget implications. The third section turns to the analysis in the CGE framework, and contains subsections describing the macroeconomic importance of agriculture in CEECs, the analytical approach adopted, and the results obtained. Finally, some conclusions are drawn.

Partial Equilibrium Analysis

Scenarios for the CEECs

This partial equilibrium analysis looks closely at the impacts three different CAP policy options may have on markets and government spending in the CEECs, compared with a continuation of CEECs' national policies. Recent developments from 1994-96 in agricultural markets, prices, and policies have been explicitly considered for the seven CEECs included in the analysis (Bulgaria, Czech Republic, Estonia, Hungary, Poland, Slovakia, and Slovenia). While the European Commission proposed (in the Agenda 2000), and the EU Summit of Luxembourg in December 1997, offered immediate accession negotiations to only five of these seven CEECs, the analysis will include all seven CEECs and assume that they accede to the EU jointly in 2003. We also assume that between 2000-02 the CEECs adjust their policies to EU levels regardless of World Trade Organization (WTO) constraints.

Four alternative policy scenarios merit particular attention and will be analysed. First, a continuation of the current national policies in CEECs, which will serve as a reference base, the Nonaccession Scenario. Second, accession without reform of the current CAP, the CAP Scenario. Although we analysed the two options in earlier studies (Tangermann and Josling, 1994; Tangermann and Münch, 1995; Münch, 1995), it is interesting to see what impact they might have on markets and budgetary spending in the light of a new starting point for the analysis. Third, accession under a new CAP as outlined in Agenda 2000 which we refer to as the Agenda Scenario. This Scenario takes into account the recent discussion which argues for not extending the compensatory payments for area and livestock to CEEC farmers. The main argument for this option is that these payments compensate EU farmers for price declines resulting from CAP reforms and since CEEC farmers generally would face price increases during accession, there would be no need to compensate them. Others argue that these payments are in part coupled to production and are not of temporary nature making them an integral part of CAP support to agriculture thus, withholding them would make CEECs 'second-class' members. Fourth, accession with an Agenda 2000 version which grants the unified area payments and payments for beef cattle and dairy cows to the new members, the Agenda Premium Scenario. In this Scenario crop payments are assumed to be totally decoupled as a result of the new form of implementation as proposed in the Agenda. Implicitly this assumes that, differing from the Commission proposal, the unified payments are also applied to protein crops and durum wheat.

CAP instruments generally aim at the first stage of wholesaling or processing. A crucial question for the CEECs is how their wholesale and processing sectors are able to vertically transmit prices to the agricultural producer. Marketing and processing has gained efficiency compared to the period of 1989-93 and will gain efficiency, especially as the countries accede to the EU.[1] While the development in 1994-96 has been recognised in model parameters, a further increase of efficiency has not been assumed.[2]

For all four policy options, market effects for twenty-seven agricultural products are analysed, i.e. the development of production, domestic use, net exports, and market prices, as well as budgetary expenditure.

During the earlier phase of transition, the CEECs liberalised their agricultural policies and markets. Protection decreased significantly and agricultural markets were freed from central planning. Institutions crucial for a market economy, such as private ownership and policies supporting competition, were established more slowly (Münch, 1994). This combination of restructuring and liberalisation resulted in domestic prices often at or even below world market prices and therefore far below EU prices. Also, during the first phase of transition in the CEECs, agricultural production became increasingly extensive, i.e. input use and investments dropped dramatically. Yields decreased as a result. Moreover, agricultural resources were left idle because of institutional problems and changing market conditions. In the second phase of transformation, which began in most countries in 1993, the economies gained stability and returned to sustainable growth. Despite these positive macroeconomic developments, our Scenarios do not assume that productivity catches up rapidly to pretransition levels. This assumption on productivity is taken throughout all Scenarios. Compared to previous analyses (see Tangermann and Josling, 1994; Münch, 1995) these Scenarios represent a lower bound of possible reactions and more closely resemble those used in Tangermann and Münch (1995).

Since roughly 1993 market-oriented agricultural policies have been continuously replaced by more CAP-like policies as the CEECs began to prepare for EU membership. However, the level of protection for agro-food products is still lower than that in the EU (Hartell and Swinnen, 1998; OECD, 1997a, 1997b). Figure 1.1 shows the development of nominal protection rates (NPRs) for the agricultural sector of the analysed countries.

These rates are weighted averages for twenty-two agricultural products including some processed goods which are all relevant for CAP instruments. These NPRs are calculated for the wholesale level and thus give the percentage difference between domestic and world market prices.[3] Apart from agricultural protection, they also include protection for parts of the downstream sector.

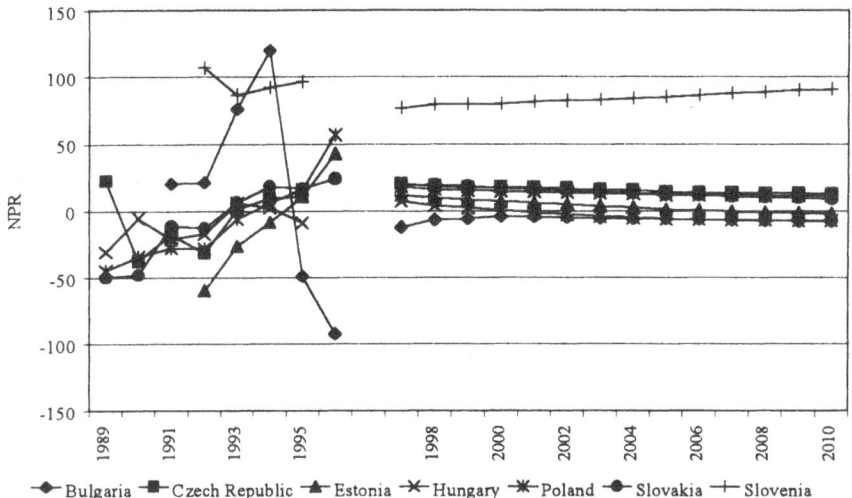

Figure 1.1   Nominal protection rates in CEECs under the Nonaccession Scenario, 1989 to 2010 (per cent)

During the base period (1989-96), strongly increasing NPRs are shown for Estonia and Poland. Since 1993 protection in Slovakia remained quite stable at around 40 per cent. In Hungary, the main exporter of agricultural and food products among CEECs, protection declined in 1995. Bulgaria and Slovenia are exceptions for these developments. While the former is in many respects at the beginning of transformation to a market economy, the latter never quite underwent the radical liberalisation of agricultural markets and has maintained a continuously high level of support for agriculture.

In the Nonaccession Scenario, developments from 1994-96 are the basis for assumptions regarding future development of agricultural policies.

Institutional prices are assumed to decline by an average annual rate of around 1 per cent in real terms. However, some products are subject to more intensive support than others. Intervention schemes or generous export subsidies exist for example, in all countries for dairy products and some grains. These aspects have been included regardless of potential violations of WTO constraints. Production quotas already exist in some countries, however they are generally less binding than in the EU. Therefore, only the sugar quota in Poland is included in the Nonaccession Scenario. For Bulgaria a special Scenario has been designed which allows domestic market prices to return to world market levels.

The assumptions explained above are kept constant in the Scenarios. The accession Scenarios only vary the policies, therefore the pure price policy effect is identified (table 1.1).

In the CAP Scenario the agricultural policies of the EU are implemented in the CEECs according to their current design, with production quotas and compensatory payments for area and set aside.[4] The latter has been set at the reference level of 17.5 per cent from 2000 onwards.

The Agenda Scenario, without compensatory and headage payments, simulates in a very detailed manner the recent proposals of the Commission (European Commission, 1997). In areas where the proposal is not clear some assumptions have been made. In this Scenario, compensatory payments and hence, set aside are not applied to the CEECs. Moreover, production quotas for milk are assumed to be abolished to analyse the pure effect of reduced intervention prices for dairy products.

The Agenda Premium Scenario makes the same assumptions as the Agenda Scenario, but headage payments and area payments are also granted in the new member countries. The unified area payments are supposed to be totally decoupled from production, i.e. they would have a budgetary but no production effect. However, headage premiums are coupled to production. Therefore, they do affect both production and budgets. Payment limits per farm are not considered here.

These Scenarios are analysed in a partial equilibrium model of agricultural markets in the EU, the CEECs, some other country groups, and the rest of the world. The European Simulation Model (ESIM) is a world model incorporating fourteen countries and twenty-seven products. It was originally developed by the USDA/ERS in cooperation with Tangermann and Josling (Tangermann and Josling, 1994) and has recently been extended (Münch, 1995; Banse and Münch, 1997).[5]

Changes in agricultural protection also affect macroeconomic developments. In a combined analysis with the CGE models for the CEECs outlined below, the comparative advantages of both general and partial equilibrium models are used. In a first round of analysis, NPRs

Table 1.1 Scenario assumptions

	Nonaccession	CAP	Agenda	Agenda Premium
Real exchange rates (RERs)	CGE results (for Estonia and Bulgaria constant RER)	CGE results (for Estonia and Bulgaria constant RER)	CGE results (for Estonia and Bulgaria constant RER)	CGE results (for Estonia and Bulgaria constant RER)
Real income growth	~3 % p.a.	~3 % p.a.	~3 % p.a.	~3 % p.a.
Return to pretransformation production potentials	No	No	No	No
Technical progress	Conventional rates with slightly higher rates from 1998 to 2002	Conventional rates with slightly higher rates from 1998 to 2002	Conventional rates with slightly higher rates from 1998 to 2002	Conventional rates with slightly higher rates from 1998 to 2002
Harmonization of price and trade policies with the EU-15 (prior to EU membership)	No	2000-02	2000-02	2000-02
Single Market and full member	No	2003	2003	2003
Set aside	No	17.5 % from 2000	No	No
Production quotas	Sugar quota in Poland	Sugar and dairy quotas	Sugar quota	Sugar quota
Compensatory payments	No	Compensatory payments for crops and set aside	No compensatory payments for area and no headage payments for dairy cows and beef cattle	Unified area payments headage payments for cows and beef cattle
CAP prices	As currently implemented	As currently implemented	Administrative prices decrease by : Cereals 20% Beef 30% Dairy products 10%	Administrative prices decrease by : Cereals 20% Beef 30% Dairy products 10%

based on ESIM simulations have been implemented into the CGE models for the CEECs. One important set of macroeconomic implications of changed agricultural policies, i.e. real exchange rates, has then been included in ESIM for the final analysis which generated the final results presented here.

In the policy Scenarios analysed here, exchange rates are found to revalue in real terms for Poland, Hungary, and the Czech Republic, as protection increases for agriculture during accession.[6] Only Slovenia faces real depreciation of its currency, the tolar, because protection declines significantly. Bojnec, Münch, and Swinnen (1997) showed the impact a real revaluation of exchange rates can have on protection and budgetary expenditure during accession: that the effects of implementing the CAP in the CEECs are reduced as the rise expected in output prices in the CEECs is dampened. This is exactly what our analysis implies for the cases of Poland, Hungary, and the Czech Republic. In the case of Slovenia, the price declines for outputs to be expected on EU accession (because Slovenia has higher protection than the EU) is less than it might be at a constant real exchange rate, due to a real currency devaluation. Hence, the exchange rate effect in Slovenia dampens the accession effects as well.

Accession Effects on Agricultural Protection

As figure 1.1 shows, in the Nonaccession Scenario protection in the CEECs remains stable because domestic policies remain unchanged until 2010. However, if accession to the EU and the CAP is assumed, protection in CEECs increases rapidly, by up to 80 percentage points in Estonia, assuming implementation of the current CAP. Slovenia is the only country where protection declines with accession (figure 1.2).

A pure application of the CAP prior to the integration of Slovenia raises protection. This is the case because Slovenia remains a net importing country and import regimes of the CAP provide even higher protection than the current Slovenian regulations.[7] Only the price equalising effect of the Single Market which allows for tariff free imports from the EU lets domestic prices decline in Slovenia. As a result Slovenian prices fall to those of the EU with integration into the Single Market. When the NPRs are broken down by commodity, the same effect can be seen. In the case of wheat in Poland, market prices are higher than in the EU during the harmonisation period prior to accession, because Poland remains a net importing country for wheat. This effect leads to distortions on markets, especially for animal feed as relatively cheaper feeds are substituted for wheat. All countries except Slovenia undergo increases of total protection for agriculture by 40 to 50 percentage points NPR (figure 1.2).

Agenda 2000 eases the situation regarding agricultural protection. The pattern of development of increased protection is largely the same, however, at a lower level than under unreformed conditions (compare figures 1.2 and 1.3).

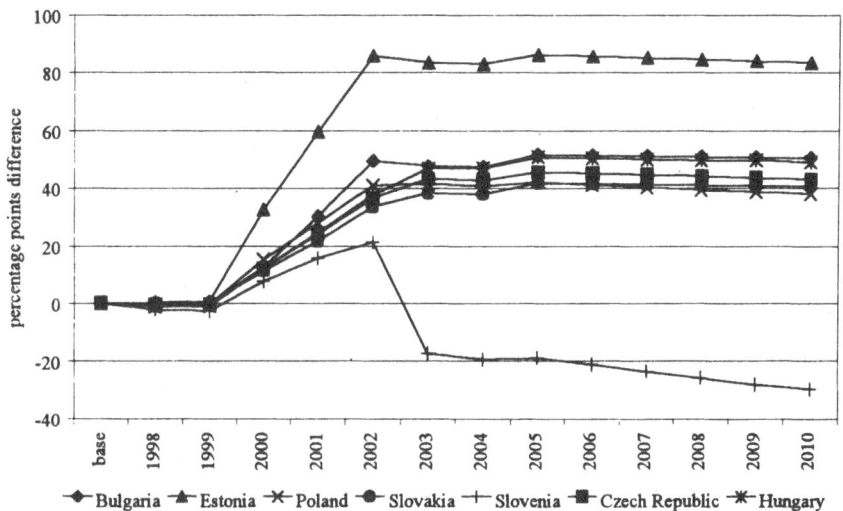

Figure 1.2 CAP Scenario: Absolute change of protection in CEECs during accession compared to Nonaccession Scenario

Although the same regulations are applied to the CEECs during accession, the level of protection for the agricultural sector is quite different. This is a result of different production structures in CEEC agricultural sectors. Estonia has a relatively large share of production of milk and beef cattle in total agriculture. Weighted average protection rises rapidly in Estonia during accession because the CAP provides intensive protection for these commodities. In crop-based agricultural sectors, especially wheat and corn, protection for agriculture increases less, as the CAP generally shields these commodities less than livestock products. Hungary has a large share of production in crops. Comparing these two countries, Estonia would be relatively more affected than Hungary due to their differing production structures. This demonstrates the differing impacts of accession on individual countries.

10 *Agriculture and East-West European Integration*

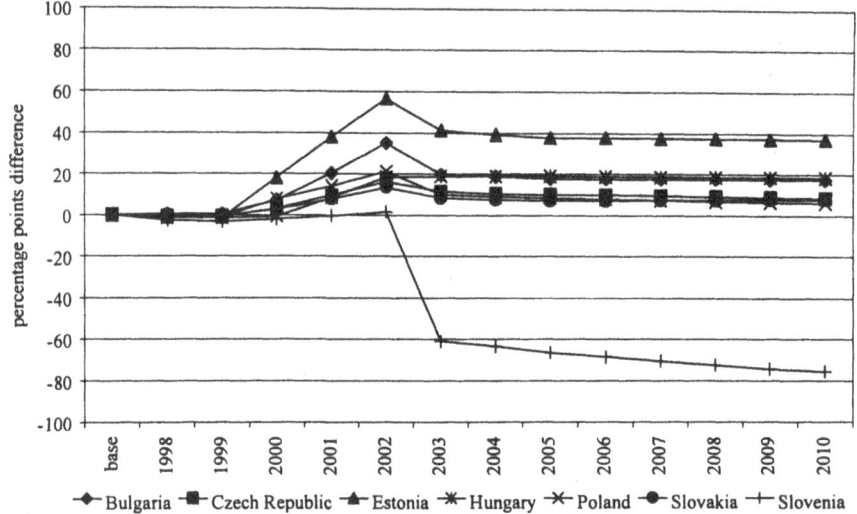

Figure 1.3 Agenda Scenario: Absolute change of NPRs in CEECs during accession compared to Nonaccession Scenario

The proposed Agenda 2000 reforms would also raise protection, i.e. market prices, but less so for sensitive products such as beef, some coarse grains, and dairy products. The decline of protection in Slovenia would be higher and the rise of protection in the other countries dampened compared to the CAP Scenario.

If the Agenda 2000 proposal had foreseen a stronger decline of dairy prices and a price cut for sugar, not only would protection and distortions on markets be less, but production quotas which are inhibitors of structural change could be removed from the CAP. Analysis of sugar markets shows that a price cut to 40 per cent of the EU intervention price for sugar would make the sugar quota redundant and result in welfare gains for the CEEC economies (Tangermann and Münch, 1997).

Compared to earlier analyses (Tangermann and Josling, 1994; European Commission, 1995; Münch, 1995), CEEC prices rise less in the Scenarios here presented. While most prices in the CEECs in 1991-93 were much lower than EU prices, the situation has changed significantly since then. High world market prices, increasing shares of imports, raised border protection, and better transmission of prices due to increased efficiency of markets are among the reasons for this. However, prices would still rise significantly during accession and it cannot be expected that CEECs could raise their protection to EU levels without conflicting with their WTO commitments (Tangermann and Josling, 1994; Bojnec et al., 1997; Twesten, 1997).

Market Effects

In the analysis of market reactions results are presented only for production and net exports of major products, and for the aggregate of all seven CEECs.

Crop production reaches the levels of early transition around the year 2003 in case domestic policies remain unchanged (table 1.2). Livestock production remains far below these levels, especially milk and beef production. However, production grows more quickly than domestic use which means that as an aggregate, the CEECs increase their net exports for most products by this time. Country results differ significantly: Hungary, the only country which is presently a net exporter of agricultural and food products, increases exports; other countries like Slovenia and, to some extent, Poland, still import main products.

During accession, strong incentives are given to producers while rising domestic prices inhibit use. This is especially the case for cereals. Despite production levels in the CAP Scenario being close to the Nonaccesion Scenario, cereals are less used in animal feeds. Net exports, particularly of coarse grains, which are strongly protected under the current CAP regime, rise to six million tons in 2003 and to 7.2 million tons in 2010. In the Agenda Scenario, production of cereals is even higher because the 17 per cent set aside in the CAP Scenario is not applied. However, this reform would remove much of the distortions produced by the current CAP. As price relations between coarse grains and wheat do not change to the extent seen in the CAP Scenario, production and use are less effected.

A clear, positive effect of compensatory payments on oilseed production is expected when accession takes place under an unreformed CAP, which is only dampened by the high set aside requirement. However, as other market price support for oilseeds are removed on accession, production is lower in the CAP Scenario than under the Nonaccession Scenario (current policies).

Milk and beef production get an extra incentive on accession under unreformed conditions. Production is lower than the pretransition level, nevertheless it rises significantly, by more than 30 per cent and 40 per cent respectively, as prices rise by 50 to 100 per cent in real terms. The milk quota becomes rapidly binding in the CAP Scenario and prevents milk production from exceeding 1990-91 levels.

Table 1.2 CEEC-7 development of production under different policy options (million tons)

	1990-91*	Base	2003				2010			
			Non-accession	CAP	Agenda	Agenda Premium	Non-accession	CAP	Agenda	Agenda Premium
Cereals	63.72	52.06	62.00	62.06	64.62	64.72	68.74	67.50	71.81	72.16
Wheat	26.73	22.22	27.01	24.72	27.84	27.88	30.16	27.04	31.42	31.51
Coarse grains	37.00	29.84	35.00	37.33	36.78	36.84	38.59	40.46	40.39	40.65
Oilseeds	2.97	3.08	4.15	3.43	3.28	3.34	4.64	3.39	3.67	3.75
Sugar	3.53	2.89	3.03	3.18	3.18	3.18	3.18	3.17	3.18	3.18
Milk	26.36	19.73	23.73	24.63	27.94	29.27	27.11	25.01	30.77	32.46
Butter	0.48	0.26	0.34	0.34	0.39	0.41	0.39	0.33	0.44	0.46
Beef	1.54	0.85	1.03	1.25	1.05	1.13	1.17	1.39	1.17	1.26
Pork	4.29	2.74	3.43	3.60	3.18	3.17	3.85	4.09	3.62	3.62

* Estonia not included in 1990-91.

Under the Agenda Scenario, prices for beef rise less and even fall more in Slovenia. Still net exports expand, although less than under unreformed CAP conditions. If headage premiums are granted as assumed in the Agenda Premium Scenario, production and net exports increase, remaining, however, below levels induced by an unreformed CAP.[8]

Under the Agenda 2000 proposals, price distortions would be removed for the benefit of CEEC consumers. On the other hand, production incentives are induced by the premiums which compensate some of the effects of price declines.[9] As a result, production of milk and beef in the Agenda Premium Scenario is higher than without the incentives. Milk production, which is not subject to quotas, increases in the Agenda Scenario and even more so if payments are granted to farmers in CEECs. The proposed intervention price cuts of 10 per cent for dairy products in the Agenda 2000 is too small to prevent production increases during accession.

Production of the less protected livestock products, i.e. pork, poultry, and eggs, does not expand like that of milk and beef in the Scenarios because rising feed prices compensate for much of the output price incentives during accession. In particular, for the five CEECs in the first wave of accession negotiations, pork production in 2003 is only 130 000 tons higher than without accession. In the Agenda and Agenda Premium Scenarios, production falls below the levels of the Nonaccession Scenario because EU-15 market prices would drop after any Agenda 2000 implementation. As a result the CEECs become net importers of pork.

In an accession under unreformed CAP conditions, the biggest market effects can be expected for beef, milk, and coarse grains. The Agenda 2000 reduces these effects, especially for beef and coarse grains. However, the headage payments as proposed in Agenda 2000 have positive effects on production when they are implemented in the CEECs. The proposed price cuts for dairy products is insufficient to reduce the production incentives.

Budgetary Effects

In terms of budget implications, ESIM generates projections only for net expenditure on trade measures, i.e. export subsidies minus tariff revenues, and compensatory and headage payments. To make the model results comparable to the Guidance Section of the European Agricultural Guidance and Guarantee Fund (FEOGA) spending, conversion factors have been applied to include spending for administration, storage, and other market regimes.

According to these calculations, market guarantee spending can be expected to rise significantly as a result of eastward enlargement. The largest increase takes place if an unreformed CAP is introduced in the acceding countries. Expenditure in the CAP Scenario reaches around 11 billion ECU for all seven CEECs, and 8.5 billion ECU for the five CEECs in the first wave of accession negotiations (figure 1.4). The most important part of the expenditure is direct payments, which would make up approximately 40 per cent of the spending.

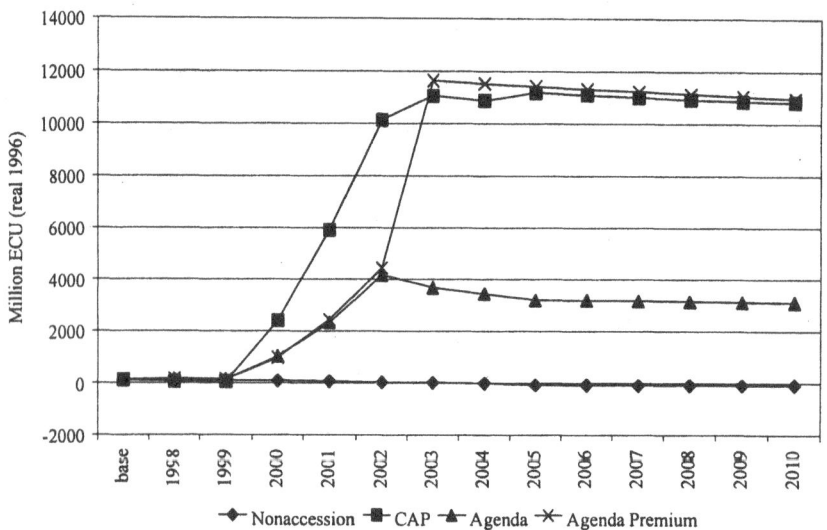

Figure 1.4 Budget expenditure for market guarantees under different policy Scenarios in CEECs

In the Agenda Scenario, expenditure on market guarantee is less, especially when no direct payments are transferred to CEEC farmers. Without direct payments, the additional FEOGA guarantee spending is roughly 3.5 billion ECU for the seven CEECs, and 3 billion ECU for the five CEECs in the first wave of accession negotiations. With headage payments for dairy and beef cattle, the additional FEOGA guarantee budget rises to 6.5 and 5.5 billion ECU respectively. The area payments add another 4.5 billion ECU for the CEECs and 3.5 billion ECU for the five CEECs slated for early accession. In this case the share of direct payments in total expenditure is 70 per cent. Interestingly, the Agenda Premium Scenario leads to expenditure roughly equal to that under an unreformed CAP. However, spending on export subsidies and other direct market support is significantly less than under unreformed CAP conditions. Moreover, CEECs consumers will suffer less from higher prices than they would under unreformed conditions.

General Equilibrium Analysis

Macroeconomic Relevance of the Agro-food Sector

The macroeconomic implications of introducing the CAP in the CEECs will depend heavily on the size of their agro-food sectors. Table 1.3 provides a rough description of the macroeconomic weight of the agro-food sector in selected CEECs. The share of agriculture and the food industry in total gross domestic product (GDP) as well as in employment is much higher than in the EU-12. Only in the Czech Republic does the agro-food sector have an economic relevance similar to that in the EU. In all other countries agriculture makes a much higher contribution to total income and employment than in the EU.

Private households in the CEECs spend relatively more income on food than an average household in the EU. Expenditure shares of food range from 14 per cent (in Hungary) to more than 60 per cent (in the Czech Republic) higher than the EU level.[10] Because of the high relevance of the agro-food sector, the introduction of the CAP in new Member States will have significant macroeconomic consequences on these sectors and other branches as well.

Table 1.4 presents the 1995 trade balances of the Czech Republic, Hungary, and Poland for both agro-food and total trade. All three countries have an overall trade deficit. While the Czech Republic is a net importer of both agricultural and food products, Poland has a negative trade balance in agricultural and a positive balance in food commodity trade. Hungarian agro-food trade shows a trade surplus of more than 1.9 billion USD. The Polish agro-food trade with the EU has a small deficit, but a surplus with the countries of the former Soviet Union (FSU). Hungary has a surplus in agro-food trade with the EU-15 and with the FSU. However these high trade surpluses in agro-food trade with the countries of the FSU fail to offset energy imports resulting in a negative balance of total trade.

Table 1.3 Macroeconomic relevance of agricultural and food industry in the CEECs and the EU

	Share of agriculture in total GDP (%)		Share of agro-food sector in total employment (%)		Household expenditure share of food (%)		Agro-food trade balance (mill. USD)	
Year	1989	1995	1989	1995	1989	1995	1989	1995
Czech R.	6.3	3.1	13.4	7.1	32.9	32	-658	-332.1
Poland	11.8	6.1	31.3	29.9	36.9	28.0	448	-475.2
Hungary	15.6	6.4	22.2	12.3	25.4	22.3[a]	1 557	1 922.6
Slovakia	9.4	6.1	n.a.	9.5	35.4	37.4	-117	-231
Slovenia	4.4	4.4	14.8	13.2	25.7	25.2[a]	-85	-374
EU-12	-	1.8	-	5.5[a]	-	19.6[b]	-	-7 091

[a] 1994 (only agriculture)
[b] 1992

Source: OECD, 1996; EU Commission, 1996; Statistical Yearbooks of CEECs.

Table 1.4 Trade balance of selected CEECs, 1995 (million USD)

	CEECs	EU-15	FSU	World
Poland				
Agricultural commodities	-108.8	111.1	49.4	-632.9
Food commodities	-25.2	-189.3	571.4	157.7
All products	-266.8	-2 540.8	-432.8	-6 058.8
Czech Republic				
Agricultural commodities	41.6	-61.1	5.2	-224.7
Food commodities	74.0	-171.4	81.2	-107.4
All products	190.0	-1 115.3	-1 038.1	-2768.3
Hungary				
Agricultural commodities	147.6	292.7	172.0	603.9
Food commodities	259.6	496.0	502.7	1 318.7
All products	232.7	-1 435.1	-918.4	-2 599.2

Source: OECD, 1997c.

The EU-15 is the most important trading partner in all three countries. Poland and Hungary receive more than 60 per cent of their total imports from the EU. Almost 70 per cent of total Polish and 63 per cent of total Hungarian exports are sold on EU markets. The smaller shares of trade between the EU and the Czech Republic are caused by the close trade relations between the Czech Republic and Slovakia.

Poland, Hungary, and the Czech Republic buy most of their imports of processed food commodities on EU markets. However, on the export side, EU markets are more important for raw products (agricultural commodities) than for processed food commodities. In each country, imports of EU agricultural commodities exceeds the share of food exports to the EU.

Comparing agricultural support levels in CEECs with support levels in the EU, all CEECs exhibit a support of agriculture which is far below that in the EU-15, as measured by the net percentage producer subsidy equivalent (OECD, 1997b). In 1996, agricultural support in the Czech Republic and in Hungary was only one-fourth of the EU-15 level, while Poland's farmers enjoyed support which corresponded to almost two-thirds of the support received by EU farmers. Therefore the implementation of the CAP in new Member States would lead to a dramatic increase in agricultural support. Because of the large economic relevance of the agro-food sector, one can assume that nonagricultural sectors would be strongly affected by the adoption of the CAP.

Assumptions for EU Accession

To analyse the overall implications of accession to the EU for the agro-food sector and for the rest of the economy, CGE models have been developed for four of the potential accession candidates from Central Europe, i.e. the Czech Republic, Hungary, Poland, and Slovenia.

These models are based on a model structure which had been developed by Adelman and Robinson (1978). The CGE models used for this study have been extended and further developed to include several country-specific elements. The models have a recursive-dynamic structure with a one period time lag for the instalment of new capital. They include only one type of labour which is perfectly mobile across eight sectors, i.e. heavy industry, agriculture, food, chemical, machine, consumable industry, construction, and services. Capital is assumed to be sector specific within each period.

Because of the complexity of CGE models, detailed policy instruments cannot be included in the same way as in the partial equilibrium model previously presented. Therefore the CGE model only includes *ad valorem* tariffs on imports and ad valorem subsidies on exports. Capital profits are taxed on a sectoral basis, while total household income (labour income and households' shares in profits) is taxed at a constant rate. Production is taxed or subsidised by sector specific, indirect rates of production tax or subsidy. In the CGE model all sectors are only modelled as a single firm/single commodity activity. Therefore commodity specific agricultural policy instruments such as set aside obligations, quotas, or compensatory payments which are included in the ESIM model are neglected in the CGE model.[11]

As in the partial equilibrium approach presented above, the CGE analysis compares EU accession with the Nonaccession Scenario. The Nonaccession Scenario (base run) simulates a situation where the four countries and the EU continue the reduction of their bilateral import tariffs which began under the rules of the Association Agreements. This complete liberalisation of trade with the EU covers all sectors except agricultural and food products. At the end of this base run, which covers the period from 1995-2008, all tariffs and export subsidies for nonagricultural products are set to zero. Moreover, it is assumed that all quantitative restrictions on trade-like import quotas are phased out.

The accession Scenarios analyse the impact of a gradual movement towards EU membership for the agricultural and food sector. It is assumed that the CEECs harmonise their agricultural policies with the CAP during an adjustment period, as assumed under the respective Scenarios. This gradual adoption of the CAP is modelled by a stepwise increase in import tariffs and export subsidies for agricultural and food products within a three year period beginning in 2000 and ending in 2002. During this adjustment period it is assumed that export subsidies will be financed by the national governments, with no financial assistance from the EU budget. This will increase the governments' budget deficit. On the other hand, revenue from import tariffs still flows into national budgets during the 2000-02 adjustment period. Full accession to the EU is assumed for 2003, when the principles of the Single Market and of the so-called 'financial solidarity' come into force. In other words, the distinction between 2002 and 2003 is that while trade prices, including tariffs and subsidies, are the same in both years, in 2003 all agricultural and food trade with the EU is completely liberalised and all revenues from agricultural import tariffs will flow into the EU budget while export subsidies on agricultural and food products will come from the EU budget.[12]

The data base for the four CGE models, used for calibration, are the most recent input-output tables and national accounts calculated on Standardized National Account (SNA). Therefore the base year for the Czech model uses data from 1992; for the Hungarian and Slovenian model, 1993; for Poland, 1994.[13] However, additional macroeconomic data such as foreign direct investments, foreign trade balances, government deficit, total labour supply, saving rates in private households, and sectoral investment shares are included in all four models until 1995. Therefore, in all four models investment decisions are set exogenously up to 1995. For the rest of the simulated time span, from 1996-2008, sectoral changes in capital stocks are derived endogenously in the CGE model.

The macroeconomic closure is defined by a given (exogenous) balance of payments. As a consequence, the exchange rate is endogenous. Government consumption in real terms is assumed to be exogenous, as is the savings rate of private households. The government deficit or surplus is determined as a residual, i.e. the total amount of saving is not affected by either government expenditure or investment decisions, hence, the whole model is savings driven.

For the Scenarios used in the CGE models, the level of protection for the agricultural and food industries is derived from the respective Scenarios of the ESIM model (previous section).

The protection level is calculated as the weighted average NPR for agricultural products in the Nonaccession, CAP, and Agenda Scenarios of the ESIM model. The difference in NPR resulting from the ESIM CAP and Nonaccession Scenarios is taken as an indication of the gap in agricultural prices between the acceding countries and the EU, (for the development of country-specific NPRs, see previous section). In the CGE models, this price gap is eliminated through an adoption of the NPR found in the EU, in the form of ad valorem rates of export subsidies and import tariffs for agricultural and food products for the period 2000-02.

Results of the General Equilibrium Models

In addition to analysing changes in sectoral prices and quantities, which can be compared to those for agricultural and food products resulting from the partial equilibrium model, the CGE model can serve as a tool to analyse the macroeconomic impact of an accession to the EU. Before the presentation of the results of different accession Scenarios, the development of gross agricultural output and GDP in the base scenario will be described briefly.

In all countries covered by this study agricultural output returns to its pretransition level within the simulated time span (figure 1.5). In all countries (except Slovenia) agricultural protection decreases within the base run (figure 1.1). Despite the reduced protection level, gross agricultural output expands by 2.7 per cent per annum in the Czech Republic and almost 3.7 per cent per annum in Hungary. However, the recovery of Czech and Hungarian agricultural output takes the entire simulation period. The increase in agricultural output can be explained by technical progress and by the increase of capital stock in agriculture.[14]

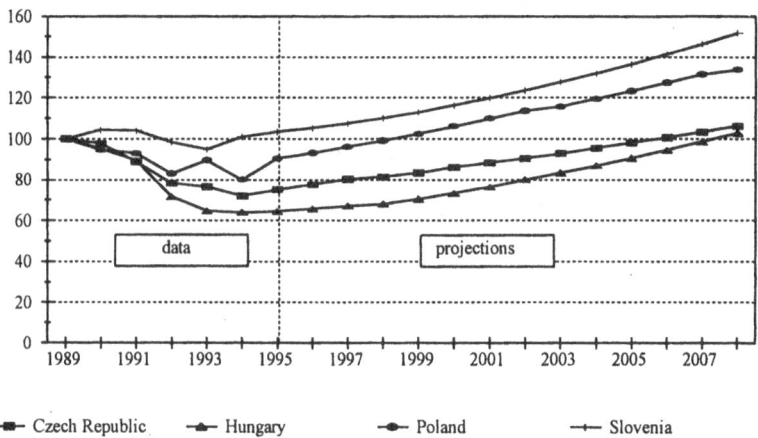

Figure 1.5 Development of gross agricultural output in the Nonaccession Scenario

Source: OECD, 1996.

In the base scenario, all countries show a positive development in their GDP. Figure 1.6 describes the historical values of GDP between 1989 and 1995 and the projected GDP until 2008. In line with high growth rates since 1992, Polish GDP increases by 40 per cent above the pretransition level under the base scenario.

If the CAP is adopted by the CEECs, agricultural output is stimulated by an increase of agricultural protection. Figure 1.7 presents the increase in gross agricultural output relative to the base run (figure 1.5). Czech agricultural output, which grows by more than 25 per cent relative to the base scenario, shows the strongest response due to the largest increase in agricultural investments and employment among all CEECs. Hungarian agriculture, which has very low protection rates in the base run, is stimulated by raising the NPR according to the CAP regime. Polish agricultural output increases by more than 8 per cent above the level of the base scenario. Only Slovenian agricultural output declines after joining the EU, and at the end of the simulation period agricultural production is about 5 per cent below the base scenario.

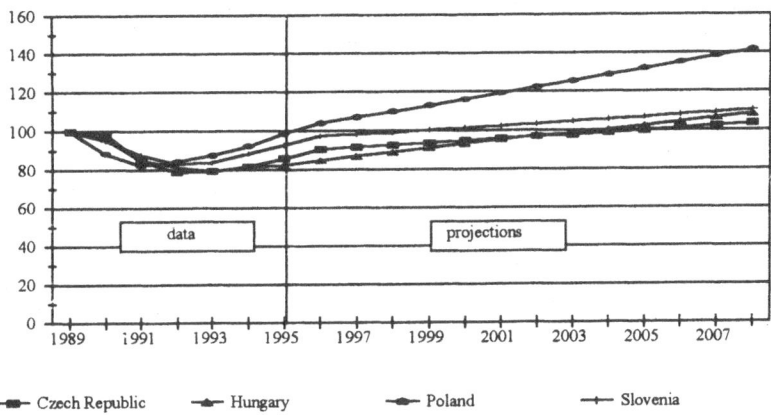

Figure 1.6 Development of GDP in the Nonaccession Scenario

Source: OECD, 1996; Statistical Office of the Republic of Slovenia, 1997.

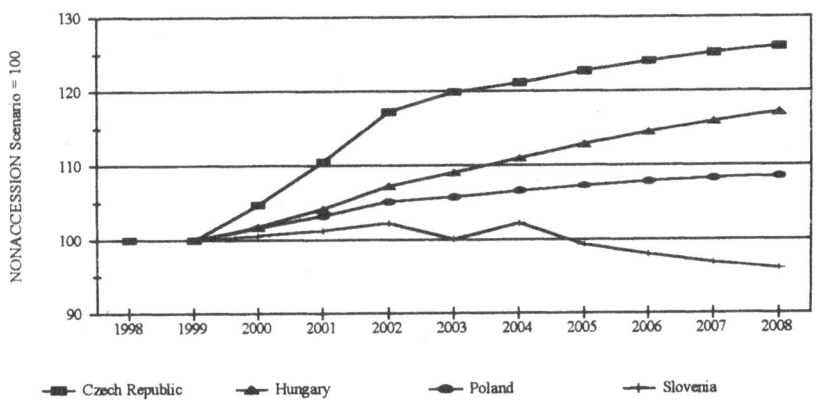

Figure 1.7 Impact on gross agricultural output: CAP Scenario compared to Nonaccession Scenario

While figure 1.7 focuses on the production incentives, an introduction of the CAP shows an even more dramatic impact on imports and exports. During the harmonisation period all four countries become net exporters in agro-food trade.[15]

During the harmonisation period of 2000-02, GDP of all four countries declines (figure 1.8). The negative GDP impact reflects the distortions resulting from an increase of agricultural protection as national policies are aligned with the CAP. While the reduction of the Slovenian GDP is only small, Hungarian and Czech GDP decline by almost 1 per cent relative to the base run. During the harmonisation period the level of Polish GDP is almost 2 per cent below the base run value. As full membership and 'financial solidarity' are established in 2003, the reduction of GDP relative to the base run is overcome. While Polish GDP increases by approximately 0.3 per cent it remains below the base scenario. Czech, Hungarian, and Slovenian GDP rise above the base scenario. The mechanism of 'financial solidarity' leads to an increase of more than 1 per cent in the Czech Republic and raises Hungarian GDP by more than 0.7 per cent.

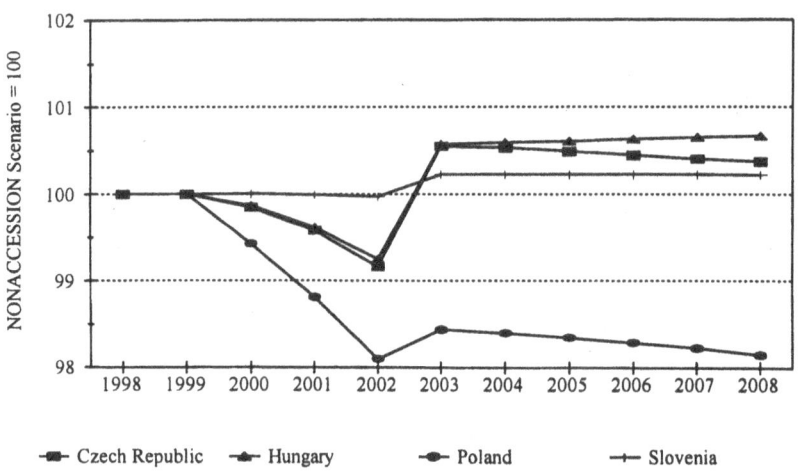

Figure 1.8 Impact on GDP: CAP Scenario compared to the Nonaccession Scenario

The main reason for the different macroeconomic effects between the acceding countries is based on the trade position of the agro-food sector. As mentioned above, all countries (except Slovenia) become net exporters of agricultural and food products. Even in the base run the Czech Republic changes its trade position to a net exporter in agricultural products. Apart from Slovenia, Poland is *the* net importing country in agro-food commodities in the base scenario. Therefore, the increase in the Slovenian GDP after 2002 is mainly due to a reduction in agricultural protectionism. During the harmonisation period the impact of an introduction of the CAP in the Czech Republic and Hungary is quite similar. After a increase of 1.2 per cent which is due to 'financial solidarity', Czech GDP remains almost unchanged until 2008. However, Hungarian GDP continues to increase, relative to the base scenario, even after the introduction of 'financial solidarity', which is due to an increase in Hungarian net exports of agricultural and food products in 2003-08.

While the introduction of the CAP raises the prices of agricultural products, reduces agro-food imports, and stimulates agro-food exports in all acceding countries (except Slovenia), the shift in the Polish agro-food trade position, becoming a net exporter, is the main reason for the almost 1.9 per cent decline in GDP in 2002. This reduction can be explained by two elements. The first is the attraction of labour and investments into the agro-food sector, which causes a decline of almost 1.3 per cent of total GDP. The second element is the loss of tariff revenues by the government. The 'financial solidarity', introduced in 2003, can only marginally ease this loss of national income. At the end of simulation period the Polish GDP is 1.8 per cent lower than in the base scenario.

In other words, introduction of the CAP itself is accompanied by a decrease of total income while these losses will be more than compensated by the macroeconomic impact of 'financial solidarity' in Hungary, Slovenia, and the Czech Republic. The changes in GDP beyond 2003 are caused by changes in national NPR of the agro-food sector.

Raising the level of agricultural tariffs and export subsidies results in an appreciation of the exchange rates of all currencies between 2000-02 (figure 1.9). The reduction of agricultural protection in Slovenia in 2003, caused by the Single Market effect in ESIM, leads to a depreciation of the tolar by almost 1 per cent relative to the base scenario.[16] In the remaining countries, the dominant effect is that of introducing 'financial solidarity', where tariff revenues are paid to the EU budget and export subsidies are financed by the EU. As 'financial solidarity' is introduced, there is a net financial flow from the EU to the CEECs, which leads to an additional appreciation of the Hungarian florint, Polish zloty, and Czech crown by around 1 percentage point in 2003.

24 *Agriculture and East-West European Integration*

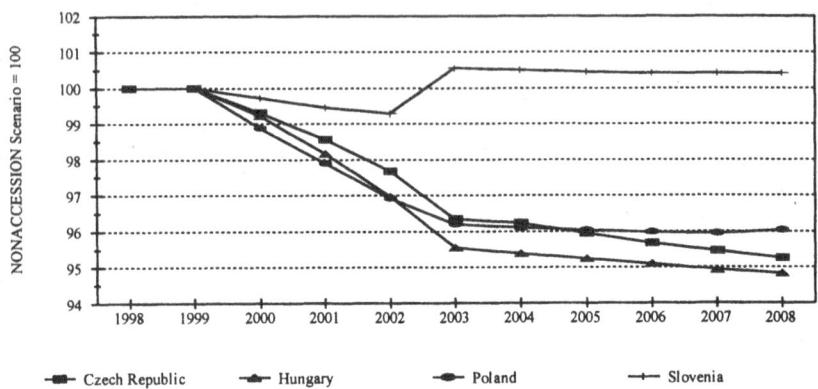

Figure 1.9 **Impact on real exchange rates: CAP Scenario compared to the Nonaccession Scenario**

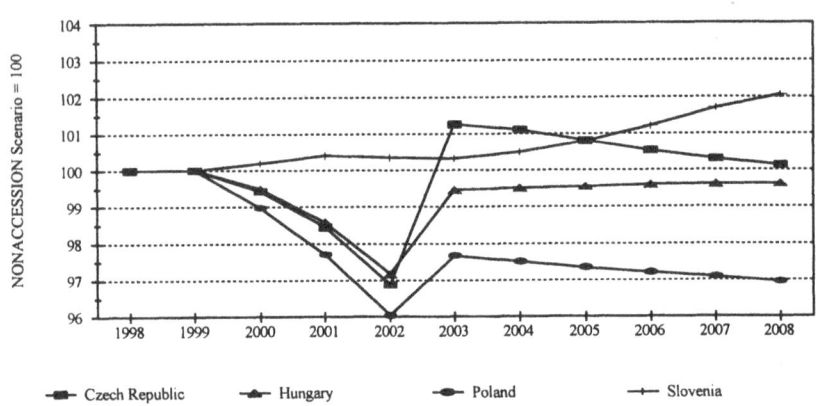

Figure 1.10 Impact on total investment: CAP Scenario compared to the Nonaccession Scenario

Note that the exchange rate is defined as units of national currency per unit of foreign currency. Hence a decline in the real exchange rate in figure 1.9 amounts to a revaluation from agricultural policies. The small surplus of the Slovenian government even grows from 2000-02 and leads to a small increase in total investment relative to the base scenario (figure 1.10). As a consequence of the increase in government budget deficit in the other three countries as they align their policies with the CAP, the total amount of savings and investments declines. Thus total Czech and

Hungarian investments drop by about 3 per cent between 2000-02 and total Polish investment declines by almost 4 per cent for the same period.

For net exporters of agro-food commodities, the system of 'financial solidarity' eases the government's financial burden and lowers the public deficit. Because total savings recover, total investments expand between 2002-03 by more than 4 percentage points in the Czech Republic and by more than 2 percentage points in Hungary.

The macroeconomic implications of an introduction of a reformed CAP according to the Agenda 2000 are presented in figures 1.11, 1.12, and 1.13. They are much smaller compared to the previous scenario. In 2000-03, GDP decreases in all four countries, from 0.1 per cent in Slovenia and 0.8 per cent in Poland. The mechanism of 'financial solidarity' reduces these economic losses in Poland. After 2003, Polish GDP is only 0.5 percentage point below the base scenario. GDP of all other countries is higher than in the base scenario.

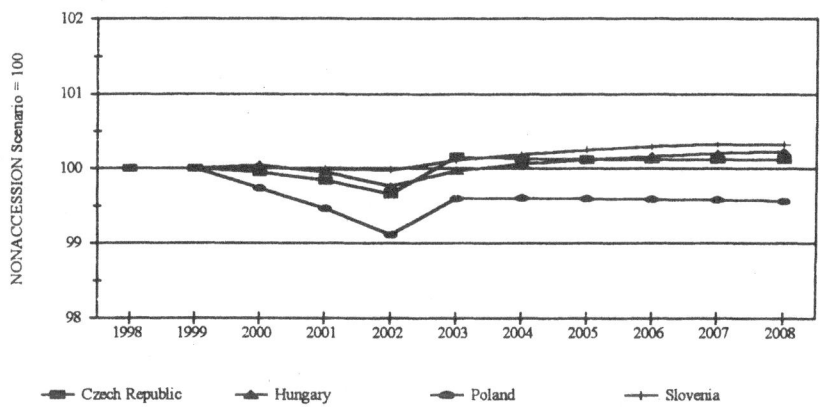

Figure 1.11 Impact on GDP: Agenda Scenario compared to the Nonaccession Scenario

As in the previous scenario, real exchange rates appreciate in all four countries due to an increase in agricultural protection. While the florint and the zloty continue to appreciate after the introduction of 'financial solidarity', the tolar depreciates between 2002-03 by more than 2 per cent compared to the base scenario. Lower EU protection levels caused this high depreciation.

26 *Agriculture and East-West European Integration*

As an effect of the reduced protection level, Slovenia becomes a net importer of agro-food commodities while the other countries remain net exporting countries. While Slovenia gains from the system of 'financial solidarity' under the previous scenario, the change in trade position leads to a net transfer to the EU. Therefore the total amount of savings and investments is 4 per cent lower than in the Nonaccession Scenario.

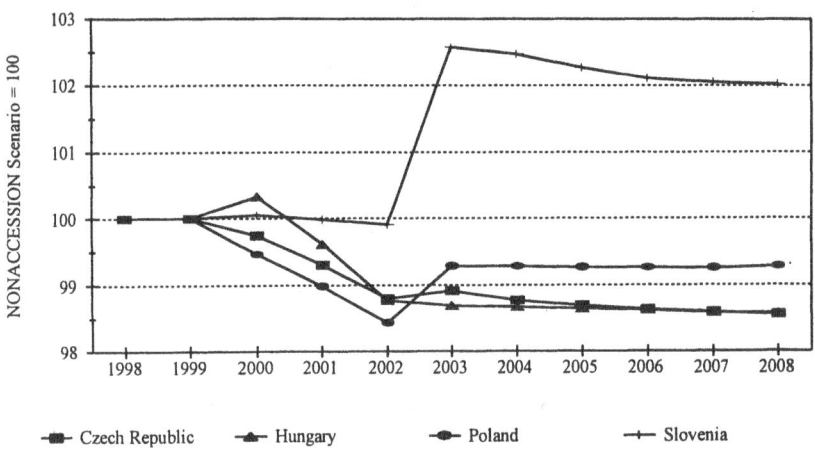

Figure 1.12 Impact on real exchange rates: Agenda Scenario compared to the Nonaccession Scenario

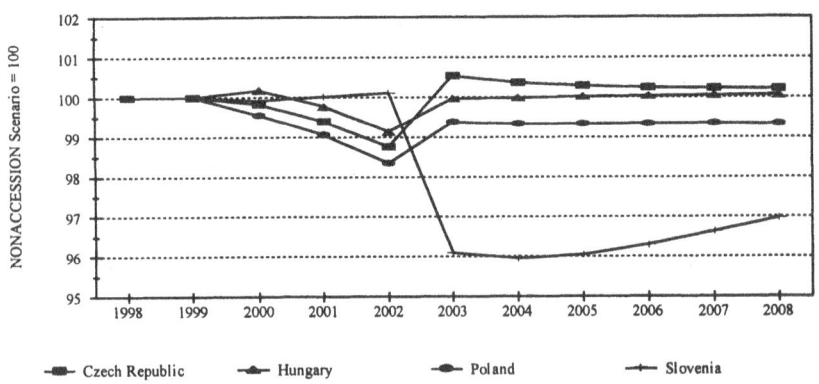

Figure 1.13 Impact on total investment: Agenda Scenario compared to the Nonaccession Scenario

The introduction of the CAP has far-reaching consequences for the welfare of the economies of the acceding countries. Table 1.5 presents the impact on private households' welfare in the four countries.[17] As shown above in table 1.3, households' expenditure shares of food in the CEECs are relatively high compared to the EU level. Therefore, higher food prices reduce consumers' welfare significantly. While agricultural producer welfare increases under an adoption of the CAP, producers of nonagricultural food commodities will lose.

Table 1.5   Impact of an adoption of the CAP on private households' welfare, 2003 (million USD)*

	Czech Republic	Hungary	Poland	Slovenia	Total
Unreformed CAP (CAP Scenario)	-31.4	-15.4	-948.8	2.2	-993.4
Reformed CAP (Agenda Scenario)	-27.2	-7.9	-252.9	5.6	-282.4

* Calculated on the basis of compensating variation.

Private households' welfare increases in Slovenia but decreases in the Czech Republic, Hungary, and Poland. The welfare of Polish consumers decreases by almost 950 million USD. As a consequence of the introduction of an unreformed CAP, total consumers' welfare in the CEECs covered here will be more than 990 million USD below the welfare in the base scenario. However, under an adoption of a reformed CAP, welfare would still be below the level of the base scenario, but the total loss in consumer welfare would be more than 70 per cent lower than under an unreformed CAP. The reduction in welfare of Polish households corresponds with the decline in GDP. However, welfare of Czech and Hungarian private households declines under accession, while GDP increases. This is mainly due to the fact that the increase in Czech and Hungarian GDP is caused by 'financial solidarity', which lowers public deficit and stimulates investment demand. Both parts of the GDP are not covered by measuring the welfare of private households.

Conclusions

The partial equilibrium analysis presented in this chapter shows that agricultural markets in the CEECs might react less dramatically during accession to the EU and introduction of the CAP than expected in earlier analyses which took 1991-93 as a starting point for projections. Also, if the recovery of CEECs' agricultural production from the transition shocks is expected to be slow (as in this analysis, contrary to our earlier projections), surpluses are lower than under more optimistic scenarios regarding the recovery speed of CEEC agriculture. Of course this also has implications for projections of future budgetary expenditure on agricultural market and price policies in the CEECs. In addition, the projections presented here are based on anticipated higher world market prices than those observed during 1991-93. As a result, projected CAP budget expenditure in the CEECs is further reduced compared with earlier estimates. Given this combination of 'cautious' assumptions of various aspects, the results presented here should be interpreted as the lower limit of possible accession effects regarding rising surpluses and budget expenditure. However, even under these conservative estimates, market effects and budgetary spending on market guarantee in the CEECs after their accession to the EU would be substantial if the CAP is not reformed.

Results of the general equilibrium analysis presented in this chapter confirm that an alignment of agricultural policies in the CEECs to the much higher prices in the EU under the current CAP is likely to result in a significant increase in agricultural production and exports. Moreover, the general equilibrium analysis shows that inclusion in the CAP may have major macroeconomic implications and noticeable effects on nonagricultural sectors in all acceding countries. Most currencies may exhibit a tendency towards appreciation, and total savings and investment may fall. Inclusion in the EU Single Market, and in 'financial solidarity' under the CAP, may have a positive impact on GDP in the CEECs. However, consumers and nonagricultural sectors in the Czech Republic, Hungary, and Poland are likely to suffer economic losses from extending the CAP to the CEECs. These effects would be less pronounced if the CAP were reformed (towards lower levels of price support and protection, in line with the Agenda 2000) before eastward enlargement of the EU.

Both types of analysis presented in this chapter show that, from the point of view of both the CEECs and the EU, eastward enlargement of the EU may require significant reform of the CAP. Reform elements, as those proposed by the Commission in the Agenda 2000, would be a big step in that direction.

Notes

1. For example, wholesale margins for wheat in Poland dropped from well above 20 per cent in 1991 to well below 10 per cent in 1996.
2. In reality, competition in the downstream sector is likely to increase as the CEECs are integrated into the EU Single Market. Moreover, foreign direct investment could rapidly alter production technologies in food processing. Both effects would increase vertical price transmission and result in higher farmgate prices and a positive supply response.
3. Note that NPRs are calculated by using world market prices as seen from the perspective of the EU.
4. As far as they were available, WTO commitments on export subsidies for dairy products have been taken into account for deriving possible milk quotas assumed to be set in the CEECs. Assumptions on sugar quotas have been made in the same way.
5. For a detailed description of the model see Nunnez-Ferrer and Buckwell (1997) and Lillard (1995).
6. Note that three of the countries included in the partial equilibrium analysis were not included in the CGE analysis (Bulgaria, Estonia, and Slovakia).
7. Note that the assumption for the adjustment period (2000-02) is that policies (rather than market prices) in the CEECs are aligned with those in the EU.
8. The payments are implemented as being coupled to production. Based on average yields per dairy cow and per beef animal they were calculated initially as additional payment for a ton of milk or carcass. Rising technical progress which increases yields and decreases the amount of payment for one unit of output has been directly implemented.
9. The effect of headage payments is accelerated by relatively low yields in the CEECs which means that the share of headage premiums in revenues respective to profits is even more important than in the EU.
10. The expenditure share in the Czech Republic includes spending on tobacco and beverages.
11. The CGE model used here does not have land as a separate factor of production.
12. This is technically implemented in the model by a complete removal of (the increased) export subsidies and import tariffs for agricultural and food products in 2003 and by an equivalent increase in c.i.f. and f.o.b. prices for these commodities in that year. Note that complete liberalisation of trade with the EU, and the implementation of 'financial solidarity', mean that trade prices are identical to domestic prices in the EU, irrespective of whether the acceding country trades with the EU or with third countries. An alternative approach to modelling the inclusion in the Single Market and the establishment of 'financial solidarity' which yields the same result, would be to maintain all agricultural tariffs and export subsidies in 2003, but to assume an equivalent exogenous change in the CEECs' balance of trade and government budgets as tariff revenues are transferred to the EU budget and expenditures on export subsidies are paid by the EU.

13 The most recent input-output table for Poland was published for 1990. However, final demand and value-added components were already published for 1994. The matrix of intermediate demand coefficients has been adopted for the year 1994 by using the Row-And-Column-Sum Method (RAS).
14 The annual rates of technical progress in agriculture are derived from ESIM and are between 1.6 per cent for Slovenia and 2.8 per cent for Hungary.
15 After 2002 Slovenia will return to being a net importer in agro-food products.
16 From 2000-03 all acceding countries adjust their national agricultural policies to the EU protection level without full integration to EU markets. Therefore, the 'Single Market' effect for Slovenia is a change from a threshold to an intervention price level for those products where the EU is a net exporter.
17 The change in welfare of private households is not comparable with the change in consumer welfare usually applied in partial analyses. In the general equilibrium approach, applied to this study, private households are both consumers and producers of goods and services.

References

Adelman, I. and Robinson, S. (1978), *Income Distribution Policy in Developing Countries-A Case Study of Korea*, Stanford.

Banse, M. and Münch, W. (1997), 'Auswirkungen eines EU-Beitritts der Visegrad-Staaten Eine Partielle und Allgemeine Gleichgewichtsanalyse', Paper presented at the Annual Conference of the German Association of Agricultural Economists (GeWiSoLa), Weihenstephan, 6-8 October 1997.

Berkum, van S. and Terluin, I. (1995), 'Accession of the four Visegrad countries to the EU', LEI-DLO Working Paper 545, Den Haag.

Bojnec S., Münch W. and Swinnen, J.F.M. (1997), 'Exchange Rates and the Measurement of Agricultural Price Distortions in the CEECs and of CEEC-EU Accession Costs', Working Paper 1/3, Joint Research Project *Agricultural Implications of CEEC Accession to the EU*, Göttingen, Germany.

Bojnec, S. and Swinnen, J.F.M. (1996), 'Pattern of Agricultural Price Distortions in Central and Eastern Europe. An Update : 1990-1995', Working Paper 3/2, Joint Research Project *Agricultural Implications of CEEC Accession to the EU*, K.U. Leuven, Belgium.

European Commission (1996), *Agriculture in European Community. Report 1995*, Brussels.

European Commission (1995), 'Study on Alternate Strategies for the Development of Relations in the Field of Agriculture between the EU and the Associated Countries with a View to Future Accession of these Countries', Agricultural Strategy Paper, Brussels.

European Commission (1997), *Agenda 2000*, vol. I and II, Brussels.

Hartell, J.G. and Swinnen, J.F.M. (1998), 'Trends in Agricultural Price and Trade Policy Instruments since 1990 in Central European Countries', *The World Economy*, vol. 21, pp. 261-79.

Lillard, P.P. (1995), *A Documentation of the Revised European Simulation (ESIM) Modelling Framework*, USDA/ERS, Washington DC.

Münch, W. (1994), 'Transformation und Agrarmärkte in den Visegrad-Staaten', Diplomarbeit am Institut für Agrarökonomie der Universität Göttingen, Göttingen, Germany.
Münch, W. (1995), 'Possible Implications of an Accession of the Visegrad Countries to the EU. Can the CAP do Without Reform?', Paper presented at the Agricultural Economic Society One-Day Conference, London, 13 December 1995.
Nunez-Ferrer, J. and Buckwell, A. (1997), *Using ESIM to Model Economic Impacts of Enlargement of the European Union to the Central and Eastern European Countries*, Wye, UK.
OECD (1996), *Agricultural Policies, Markets and Trade in Transition Economies: Monitoring and Evaluation 1996*, OECD, Paris.
OECD (1997a), *Agricultural Policies in OECD Countries*, OECD, Paris.
OECD (1997b), *Agricultural Policies, Markets and Trade in Transition Economies: Monitoring and Evaluation 1997*, Paris.
OECD (1997c), *International Trade by Commodities Statistics ITC*, HS Rev. 1 (1988) 1988-1995, Harmonized System, 1/1997, Paris.
Orlowski, W.M. (1996), 'Price Support at Any Price? Costs and Benefits of Alternative Agricultural Policies for Poland', Policy Research Working Paper No. 1585, The World Bank, Washington DC.
Statistical Office of the Republic of Slovenia (1997), *Statistical Yearbook 1996*, Ljubljana.
Tangermann, S. and Josling, T.E. (1994), 'Pre-Accession Agricultural Policies for Central Europe and the European Union', Study commissioned by DG I of the European Commission, Brussels.
Tangermann, S. and Münch, W. (1995), 'Agriculture in Poland, the Czech and Slovak Republics and Hungary and Possible Evolutions in the Medium Term-Using the ESIM Sector Model', Final Report of a study for the DGVI of the European Commission, Brussels.
Tangermann, S. (1997), 'Reforming the CAP : A Prerequisite for Eastern Enlargement', in H. Siebert (ed), *Quo Vadis Europe?*, J.C.B. Mohr, Tübingen.
Tangermann, S. and Münch, W. (1997), 'Sugar Markets in Central Europe and Eastward Enlargement of the European Union', Discussion paper of the Institute of Agricultural Economics University of Göttingen, Göttingen, Germany.
Twesten, H. (1997), 'Agricultural Trade Policies and Agricultural Trade in the CEECs. The Factual Situtation', Paper presented at the *Seminar on Regional Trade Arrangements and Agricultural Policies in Central and Eastern Europe*, 3-4 October, 1997, Tallin, Estonia.
Weyerbrock, S. (1997), *East-West Integration in Europe : A General Equilibrium Analysis of the Budgetary and Trade Implications*, Manuscript, Department of Food and Resource Economics, University of Delaware, Newark.

2 Baltic Agricultural Competitiveness and Prospects under European Union Accession

KLAUS FROHBERG AND MONIKA HARTMANN[1]

Introduction

The Baltic countries have substantially restructured their economies since gaining their independence. Changes were widespread and greatly affected agriculture. After initially contracting, the economies grew again; in Lithuania since 1993, Estonia since 1995, and Latvia since 1996. In all three countries a steadily increasing rate of growth could be observed during the last years. Forces behind these upturns are manifold: mainly a tight monetary policy, the implementation of institutions necessary for an efficient market economy, the effective privatisation and restructuring of a substantial number of companies, and the accompanying increase in competition.

In addition to the internal transformation process, all three countries signed trade agreements with and applied for accession to the European Union (EU) which required further adjustments. Pressure for changes are to be expected as well from external developments such as modifications in the Common Agricultural Policy (CAP) of the EU, from the Baltic Free Trade Agreement (BFTA) and the General Agreement on Tariffs and Trade/World Trade Organisation (GATT/WTO) agreement. Finally, all Baltic countries must prepare themselves for EU membership to make the process of accession as smooth as possible. This holds even though the EU Council of Ministers decided in December 1997 to select only Estonia from the Baltic countries as belonging to the first group of accession countries. Nevertheless, negotiations are expected to be initiated in the near future with the other two countries as well.

Given this state of change it seems difficult to obtain a clear understanding of the competitive potential of the Baltic agricultural sector following EU accession. This understanding, however, is necessary in order to effectively adjust to the opportunities and forces impacting on agriculture in the Baltic states. The relatively large importance of the agricultural sector in these countries underlines the relevance of the analysis provided in this study.

This chapter analyses the present competitive position of the agricultural and food sectors in the Baltics and the expected development of this position following accession to the EU. In order to realise this, it begins by discussing the main determinants of competitiveness and current conditions in the Baltic states. An ex post analysis of the competitive performance of the three Baltic countries is carried out in the following section utilising various indicators. Finally, some conclusions with respect to the methodology and the further development of the agricultural and food sector in these countries are drawn.

Competitive Potential

Competitiveness is the ability to supply goods and services in the location, form, and at the time they are sought by buyers, at prices that are as good as or better than those of other potential suppliers while earning at least the opportunity cost of returns on resources employed (Freebairn, 1986, p. 2).[2] The concept of competitiveness can be applied at different levels of product aggregation and spatial extension (see Frohberg and Hartmann, 1997). In addition, past performance (ex post) or the potential of competitiveness (ex ante) can be the focus of the analysis.[3] This section is concerned with analysing competitive potential, while in the following section the performance of the agro-food sector in the Baltic countries will be examined.

The competitive potential of agriculture, as of any sector, is influenced by a whole set of determinants. These include institutions and policies, factor endowment and climatic conditions, farm structure and management, input supply, processing and distribution, and scale and quality of consumer markets.

Institutions and Policies

Institutions and policies set the framework for private economic agents and have in general a profound impact on the international competitiveness of a sector. Since an effective transformation to a market economy requires the establishment of a whole new institutional framework ranging from constitutional guarantees (e.g. private ownership, freedom to engage in economic activity) to providing hygienic standards, current changes in the institutional and policy framework in these states might foster or hamper the competitiveness of their agricultural sectors.

With regard to the restructuring process in the agricultural and food industry, the following institutional arrangements are of major relevance: bankruptcy law and procedure, antitrust regulations, market and price information systems, as well as quality standards and controls. In addition, the adjustment of agricultural and macroeconomic policies plays an important role.

Bankruptcy law and antitrust regulations The implementation of bankruptcy law introduces full liability as an important constitutional principle of a market economy. Each entrepreneur is fully responsible for her/his activities. Government no longer covers or capitalises debts as it did in the centrally planned economy. Loss-making enterprises have to go out of business and the resources have to be allocated to those companies who can make better use of them. Each of the Baltic countries have passed bankruptcy laws. For fear of high social costs, governments in the first years of transition were reluctant to let enterprises go bankrupt but the laws are being increasingly applied.

Given the inherited monopsonistic and monopolistic structures in the processing and agro-service enterprises, antitrust regulations play an important role in enhancing competition. All three Baltic countries implemented antitrust legislation, to which all companies, including those of the agro-food sector, are subject. Antimonopoly committees were established in Estonia and Latvia to monitor the situation in the commodity as well as service markets and to enforce the antitrust laws. In recent years, competition has become stiffer due to both the legal framework and the emergence of many small scale private enterprises which compete with large scale companies for farmers' raw material and consumers' limited purchasing power.

Market and price information systems Since the beginning of transition to a market economy, a large number of small scale agricultural producers as well as new private companies in the up- and downstream sectors have entered the market. In addition, agricultural and food prices that were fixed over long periods during central planning were liberalised. Thus, information about market conditions became essential to economic agents in the agricultural and food sector. Yet, a lack of adequate information services in the Baltic countries led, in the beginning of transition, to a nontransparent agro-food market and was a major impediment to marketing efficiency. In the meantime, systems for regularly reporting on markets have been established in all Baltic countries. However, it seems that farmers still must make better use of these services. This remains an impediment for a more market-oriented agricultural and food commodity sector. In addition, the lack of market transparency can lead to regional market power (OECD/CCET, 1996d; p. 116; OECD/CCET, 1996b, p. 109; OECD, 1998, p. 158).

Quality standards and controls In the centrally planned economy, consumer satisfaction was mainly understood to be sufficient basic food at prices everybody could afford. One major problem in this regard was poor product quality. In order to enhance the competitiveness of Baltic food products since transition, many subsidies provided to agriculture are conditional on improvement of the quality of agricultural products and the use of high quality inputs. Stricter quality standards and sanitary controls have also been introduced. However, they are not yet adequate at all levels in the food chain as required for exporting agricultural and food products to Western countries. All three Baltic countries are in the process of harmonising their regulations with those of the EU. Yet more time is needed for these controls to be effective.

Agricultural policies After gaining independence, all three Baltic countries abolished most of the direct production and consumption subsidies introduced by the Soviet regime. Estonia has pursued the most liberal agricultural policy relying almost entirely on fuel excise tax compensation, credit interest, and investment support programs to improve and control product quality and to provide input support. In 1998 direct payments were introduced for cows, cereals, oilseeds, and flax which account for the lion's share of the agricultural budget (41 per cent). To qualify for this support a minimum level and quality of production is required. In general there seems to be growing pressure in Estonia to introduce more protectionism, including anti-dumping measures, to protect farmers' incomes and bring Estonian agricultural policy more into line with the CAP model.

Agricultural policies in Latvia and Lithuania are also relatively liberal compared to those in the EU, although to a lesser extent than in Estonia.

Particularly in Lithuania some reversal of the liberal policies occurred after the initial years of the transition process. In 1994 minimum farmgate prices and intervention purchases for specified quantities of main agricultural products were introduced. In 1997 the Lithuanian government implemented major reforms lessening state intervention. It revoked previously announced farm price increases and reduced the number of commodities subject to minimum prices and subsidies. In addition, the price support system has been reorganised to become more targeted toward higher quality of agricultural output. The remaining agricultural policies are relatively less distorting and rely primarily on indirect support measures such as reimbursement of excise tax for fuel as well as other input subsidies. Latvia has policies quite similar to Lithuania.

Credit policies play an important role not only in Estonia, but also in Latvia and Lithuania. Due to a lack of clearly defined property rights farmers cannot provide collateral. In addition, a rural financial system that would enable saving and financing has not yet been organised. This is regarded as a major impediment for providing sufficient working and investment capital to agriculture, thus hampering the progress of the agricultural sector. To overcome these obstacles all Baltic countries have implemented some form of credit subsidy schemes. Support is given to agricultural producers in the form of interest rate subsidies covering part of the investment costs and/or providing collateral.

Tax concessions serve as another significant indirect support to agriculture, especially to family farming, in all three Baltic states. These include exemption from land tax and tax concessions on personal income and corporate profit tax. In Lithuania farmers and agricultural companies involved in primary farming also enjoy reduced road tax rates as well as reduced tariffs for electricity and natural gas.

There is no separate social security system for farmers in Estonia, Lithuania, and Latvia. However, in Lithuania, farmers enjoy reduced rates of financial contribution to social insurance and health insurance funds.

Factor Endowment and Climatic Conditions

Standard trade theory stresses the importance of a country's factor endowment to its competitiveness. New approaches, however, do not just consider a nation's stock of basic production factors such as labour, land, capital, natural resources, and infrastructure as crucial for its competitive position but also more important qualitative aspects. Human capital is sometimes considered to be the most important production factor for gaining and maintaining international competitiveness (Porter, 1990, p. 80; Gahlen, Rahmeyer, and Stadler, 1986, p. 141; Horn, 1985, p. 327).

The much higher ratio of land to inhabitants can be seen as an advantage for agriculture in the Baltics compared to the EU. In terms of hectares of agricultural land per capita, these countries have almost a 200 per cent higher resource capacity than the EU-15. While this ratio is equal to 0.96 in the Baltic countries it equals 0.37 in the EU. With respect to arable land this relationship is even more favourable (0.65 in the Baltic states compared to 0.21 in the EU).

Besides size, land quality also affects the competitive position of a nation's agricultural sector. In all three Baltic countries soil quality is rather poor (table 2.1). In Estonia about 80 per cent of agricultural land, all but the central part of the country, is shallow and stony, and about 60 per cent of it is drained. Most soils in Lithuania are also not highly fertile. About 45 per cent of them have pH values of less than 5.5 and require periodic liming. Outdated and wasteful cultivation practices have led to a further deterioration of soil fertility, increasing weed incidence and plant disease, and a rising susceptibility to wind erosion (Boruks, 1996).[4] In Latvia soil fertility is also relatively poor.

Climatic conditions in the three Baltic countries vary, also contributing to differences in the structure of agricultural production. Table 2.1 reveals that, besides soil quality, climate conditions are also not very favourable for intensive agriculture. The short growing season especially presents a sizeable problem for reaching high yields of grains, forage maize, and fruits and vegetables. This problem is especially pronounced in Estonia while it is of less relevance in Lithuania.

Table 2.1 Key climatic and soil factors in the Baltics

	Latvia	Estonia	Lithuania
Aggregate active temperatures, above 10° C, on average	1850	1780	2150
Vegetation period (days/year)	180	176	190
Uneven surface (% of total area)	33	6	30
Eroded soils (% of total area)	15	4	13
Drained land (% of total reclaimed land)	86	47	78

Source: Data from Boruks, 1996.

To reiterate, the Baltics enjoy a relative abundance of land which is, however, countered by relative low soil fertility and disadvantageous climate conditions.

Farm Structure and Management

Restitution was the main instrument for reestablishing private property rights in agriculture in the Baltics. If the original property could not be handed back or was not desired by former owners, compensation was offered instead. Transfer of equivalent physical property or payment in form of vouchers did not take place. However, full property rights are not yet restored in any of the Baltic countries. Finishing registration and providing titles will require additional time.

In Estonia only about 25 per cent of agricultural land had restitution claims due to low incentives. Land is not of high value while costs of restitution were rather high. As of 1 January 1998, 80 per cent of this claimed land is registered in the cadastre and received a title. Thus a significant part of Estonia's agricultural land is still property of the state and waiting for final disposition (Loko and Sepp, 1998, p. 28). Currently, it is leased on short term contracts.

In all Baltic countries, most agricultural land is cultivated as family farms and household plots, specifically 52.1 per cent in Estonia, 84 per cent in Latvia, and 64.7 per cent in Lithuania as of 1 January 1996. The emerging farm structure is rather mixed. Farms are especially fragmented in Lithuania, where the average size of family farms was 7.8 ha in 1996. In Latvia and Estonia, this number was 20 ha and 21 ha, respectively. So far, Estonia in particularly has avoided excessive land fragmentation. About 60 per cent of agricultural land is operated by farms of more than 100 ha. A much better utilisation of economies of scale will, therefore, be possible in Estonia compared to the other two Baltic countries and also to most farms in Western Europe. This may stimulate productivity growth and increase Estonia's international competitiveness.

One of the major structural deficiencies having quite some negative impact on competitiveness of agriculture in the three Baltic countries is the lack of a well functioning land market. The transfer of full property rights is still hampered due to the previously mentioned bottleneck in the restitution process. Leasing land, however, is somewhat easier.

Input Supply, Processing, and Distribution

An important determinant of competitiveness of a given industry is the existence of internationally competitive up- and downstream sectors (Porter, 1990, 100ff.). In the former Soviet Union, the downstream sector was the weakest link in the whole food chain, receiving the least amount of investment resources. This, in turn, led to poor quality of processed foodstuffs. Moreover, both up- and downstream industries were characterised by monopolistic structures.

Unlike primary producers, suppliers of agricultural inputs, food processing enterprises, and the food distribution sector were mostly privatised by tender, by public or restricted auction, or by a public offer for sale of shares through the stock exchange. Cooperatives formed by those who use inputs produced by the upstream sector or who produce agricultural products for processing were given preferential treatment in the acquisition of up- and downstream enterprises.

In the agricultural upstream sector there has been a growing trend towards specialisation of services. Together with an increase in the number of firms, enhanced competition has resulted in inputs being offered to farmers which are cheaper, more diverse, and of better quality. Progress is especially pronounced with regard to machinery and equipment inputs but also in crop varieties and livestock breeds. Likewise, farm managers are becoming better skilled and more market oriented. Nevertheless, more effort in this regard is still needed before Baltic agriculture will be competitive with that of the EU, because the advantages of low labour and energy costs are expected to slowly decline.

In Latvia and Estonia, the privatisation of the food processing industry is almost complete and has led to an increasing number of firms and contributed to the improved competitiveness of this sector. The method of privatisation applied in the Baltics which preferred producer cooperatives for most primary food processing companies is likely to have a negative impact on improving efficiency of these firms. Farmers lack the capital to develop their own farms. How can they be expected to invest money into cooperatives they jointly own? In addition, they generally do not have sufficient technical, marketing, and business skills to make the necessary long term decisions regarding development of these companies. Moreover, this privatisation method may also have contributed to the lesser amount of foreign investment in this sector. Other factors which indicate a relatively low level of competitiveness of these sectors are the increasing labour costs,[5] use of outdated technology, and considerable overcapacities due to the sharp decline in demand for food. This results in negative consequences for upstream agriculture in the Baltic countries.

Marketing infrastructure was poorly developed in the former Soviet Union. In general, agricultural products were supplied directly by farms to the food industry. The distribution of processed products was managed by state owned companies (see e.g. OECD/CCET, 1996b, p. 64). After 1990 the food trading system was completely overhauled in the Baltics both in regard to ownership structure and the range of products traded. Particularly in Estonia, a great variety of enterprises emerged such as discount shops, purchasing associations of independent retailers, franchises, and cash-and-carry stores. In addition, methods of distribution have improved considerably. Liberalisation, especially of the food retail sector, opened up opportunities for many new private entrants leading to less concentration. However, although the total number of traders is in many cases very large, the sector is often dominated by a few leading companies (see e.g. OECD/CCET, 1996b, p. 86). High processing and distribution margins, especially in Latvia and Lithuania, indicate that the distribution network is not yet sufficiently developed (e.g. too few wholesale markets). Institutions providing services for entering export markets are also still missing or insufficient.

The land-based transportation systems need improvement (OECD/CCNM, 1998, Table III.2.2). Road density is low and their quality suggests inadequate maintenance in the past. Although there is no shortage of trucks they usually are not adequate to haul perishable goods over long distances which leads to excessive losses. In addition, rough road surfaces cause excessive wear on vehicles. The railroad system is also in desperate need of investment. All these factors translate into high shipping costs which impede agriculture's competitiveness.

Scale and Quality of Consumer Market

Demand conditions in the Baltic states negatively influence the competitiveness of agriculture and the food sector. This is due to two factors. First, the size of the domestic market hampers the improvement of static efficiencies. The quantity of products domestic markets can absorb is relatively low because of the small number of consumers and their low purchasing power. This causes suboptimal static efficiencies. Secondly, dynamic efficiencies determined by quality of domestic demand is disadvantaged. A critical and anticipatory home market often induces innovations which, in turn, improve the competitive advantage of those firms supplying it. The little attention paid to consumer preferences during the socialist period still affects consumer behaviour in these countries. This, combined with low income levels make retail demand in the Baltic countries less sophisticated compared to those in Western European countries.

However, future demand is expected to improve both in quality and quantity which will very likely enable the processing sector to better utilise economies of scale in the future. Three reasons back up this expectation: First, all three countries are on an accelerating path of growth in real gross domestic product (GDP). This trend is anticipated to continue. Second, the BFTA has enlarged the markets. Third, the EU accession will increase Baltic markets even further.

The discussion so far reveals that agriculture in the Baltics is faced with both opportunities and deficiencies. To simply level them off is not possible since relative and not absolute changes affect international competitiveness. Thus, a quantitative assessment is necessary to better understand which factors are important in shaping the international competitiveness of the Baltic countries' agricultural and food sectors. This is provided in the following section.

Ex Post Analysis of Competitive Performance

Several approaches are used for analysing the past performance of competitiveness. The most important ones are accounting methods like production costs or gross margins (profitability), market share indicators, foreign direct investments, and real exchange rates. They differ widely in their methodology and their data requirements. This section summarises some results with respect to those four indicators.

Profitability Indicators and Costs of Production

Profitability of producing a commodity is one way to measure competitiveness. This indicator utilises the quantities of all inputs and outputs as well as their prices. This provides detailed farm level information which offers useful insights with respect to future developments of competitiveness.

Although valuable in many respects, this approach has serious shortcomings and problems (Frohberg and Hartmann, 1997). Among others, these include assessing the value of those fixed factors for which market prices are difficult to obtain and selecting appropriate farms and technologies. If the comparison of farm level indicators of competitiveness is to be a useful exercise, these measures must be representative of all those farms for which the comparison is valid.

Gross margins are commonly used as profitability indicators. Furthermore, production costs are often compared to get an indication of the competitiveness of farms across countries. In this study, both production costs and gross margins of type II and type III are discussed. They relate to each other in the following way:

    Total returns, in ECU per animal or ha
- Total operating costs, in ECU per animal or ha
= Gross margin type I, in ECU per animal or ha
- Labour costs, in ECU per animal or ha
= Gross margin type II, in ECU per animal or ha

and

    Gross margin type I, in ECU per animal or ha
÷ Labour requirement, in hours per animal or ha
= Gross margin type III, in ECU per hour.

In agriculture, production activities often yield more than a single output. Gross margins are calculated for such processes. Alternatively, one might contrast revenues and total production costs of only the most valuable output of a production process. The latter concept is also used in this analysis. One of the advantages of this approach is that it can be compared to prices received by farmers. Total production costs of a main output are derived as follows:

    Operating costs
+ Labour costs
+ Fixed costs
= Total costs of the production process
- Value of by-products
= Total production costs of the main commodity.

Profitability indicators only measure competitiveness at the farm level. Since primary commodities must also be marketed and transported, competitiveness is likely to be affected by these downstream activities as well.[6] Sometimes transportation costs to the port of exit are included in these analyses if the product is exported. These indicators do not account for activities adding additional value to the primary product. Processed goods are not included.

Calculation of profitability indicators for the Baltic countries assumes that production technology and yield levels are the same as those adapted by the most efficient quarter of farms in the mid-1990s. Currently, average production costs might be somewhat higher and gross margins somewhat lower than those shown in this study. An appropriate choice of farms for which profitability indicators are to be calculated is very difficult in transition economies because of rapidly changing farm structures. The data used in the calculations for Estonia and Latvia refer to 1996. Lithuanian data are from 1995.

For comparison, production costs are also provided for Poland, Hungary, and Germany. Finland and Sweden are also added to contrast producer prices and gross margins of the Baltics with two northern countries of the EU. For Finland, the calculations describe the gross margins of family farms in southern Finland (Association of Rural Advisory Centres, 1996) and for Sweden of family farms in the Stockholm region (Agricultural University of Sweden, 1996). Farm subsidies and value-added taxes were not taken into account in the calculations. This is likely to introduce some bias since transfer payments represent a substantial share of farm income, especially in Finland. In 1997, 42 per cent of total returns to Finnish agriculture consisted of such payments.

A detailed description of the numerous assumptions made in the data collection and calculations is beyond the scope of this chapter. (The interested reader is referred to Kämäräinen et al., 1998.) Only the most important assumptions are stated here. In milk production, a typical feed ration was chosen. Considerable differences exist in milk prices received by farmers. For example, in Estonia the price small farms commonly receive is approximately 30 per cent lower than received by large farms. In this analysis, the price large farms receive was used. Another problem arises regarding quality differences in milk. For Estonia, an average milk price was determined assuming 85 per cent was graded premium quality, 14.5 per cent first quality, and 0.5 per cent second quality. An average quality was assumed for the other two Baltic countries. Fixed costs have been calculated assuming a herd size of 40 cows in a new cow shed. Depreciation of the cow shed has been calculated so as to write off the book value over fifteen years. Appliances considered include milking machines, air conditioning, and manure removing systems.

Profitability calculations for beef production are carried out for a male animal of a dairy breed. The calculations describe relatively extensive husbandry consisting mainly of pasture feeding. The period of fattening is about fifteen months. In Estonia and Lithuania, beef cattle are grown to 225 kg slaughter weight; in Latvia to 240 kg.

Profitability indicators for pork production are calculated under the assumption that the operation is set up for one hundred fifty pigs to be fattened. The feed ration is a combination of fodder grain and protein concentrate. In Estonia and Latvia, pigs are fattened from 12 kg live weight to 70 kg slaughter weight. In Lithuania, they are fattened from 12 kg live weight to 80 kg slaughter weight.

In crop production, fixed costs consist of land tax, insurance, management, as well as overhead costs. Tractor and harvester costs are evaluated according to custom work rates. Consequently, operating costs include those for labour involved in tractor and harvester work. Thus, these activities are not part of labour costs. For profitability of potato production, it is assumed that 67 per cent of output is used for human consumption and the remaining fraction for animal feed. Labour is valued according to an average salary of farm workers which includes social security payments and taxes (33 per cent of the average salary in Estonia).

Table 2.2 depicts production costs for the Baltic countries. For comparison, those of Poland, Hungary, and Germany are added. In Latvia the cost of milk production is 30 per cent higher than in Estonia and Lithuania which may be explained by differences in milk yield. Producer prices of milk exceed production costs only in Estonia but not in the other two Baltic countries. When compared with production costs in Poland and Hungary, milk production in the Baltics has a slight competitive advantage. The main reason for this result is low fodder costs, especially for pasture rent (Kämäräinen et al., 1998). Production costs of milk are also not met by the price farmers received for milk in Poland and Germany. If all transfer payments, however, were included in determining revenues, this result might be different.

Table 2.2   Production costs in ECU per ton, 1996

Product	Estonia	Latvia	Lithuania*	Poland	Hungary	Germany
Milk	136	170	143	150	180	330
Beef	1390	1570	1220	750	920	1980
Pigmeat	1330	1070	960	790	740	1170
Wheat	76	86	57	130	60	100
Rye	88	100	88	150	-	120
Barley	73	86	63	150	50	110
Oats	68	88	61	-	-	-
Rapeseed	132	180	128	230	130	210
Potatoes	102	53	110	30	130	110
Sugar beet	24	16	14	30	20	30

* 1995 data for Lithuania

Source: Data from Kämäräinen et al., 1998; Miglavs and Snuka, 1997; Wissenschaftlicher Beirat beim Bundesministerium für Ernährung, Landwirtschaft und Forsten, 1997, table 3.8.

As can be seen from table 2.2, both Poland and Hungary are more cost efficient in beef and pork production than the Baltic countries. Furthermore, Poland is the cheapest potato producer among all countries considered. This holds for Hungary with respect to barley. The ranking of all other products is not so clear. Interestingly, the Baltics produce sugar beets more cheaply than Poland and Hungary, excepting Estonia where costs exceed those of Hungary. A similar pattern emerges for rapeseed. Production costs of all Baltics are below those of Poland, and Lithuania's costs are even slightly below those of Hungary. Based on production costs, Germany hardly has a competitive advantage among these countries. Only with respect to Poland, Germany seems to be more competitive for some crops.

In the Baltic countries, producer prices of beef are only half that of Finland and Sweden (table 2.3). In Estonia, the producer price is roughly equal to production costs, whereas in Latvia beef production is not profitable. In Lithuania, the producer price exceeds production costs.

The producer price of pigmeat in Latvia is higher than in any other country included in the comparison. Production costs exceed the producer price in Estonia whereas in Lithuania and especially Latvia, production of pigmeat is profitable.

Table 2.3 Producer prices in ECU per ton, 1996

Product	Estonia	Latvia	Lithuania*	Finland	Sweden	Poland	Hungary	Germany
Milk	186	150	117	321	373	145	187	309
Beef	1360	1240	1338	2610	2750	1471	1470	1253
Pigmeat	1260	1630	1174	1480	1440	1142	1160	1142
Wheat	116	138	86	140	140	148	128	129
Rye	116	111	67	141	129	-	-	109
Barley	103	103	67	112	129	112	119	164
Oats	97	103	76	114	126	-	-	115
Rapeseed	194	168	153	208	-	246	191	170
Potatoes	162	73	153	106	-	45	-	146
Sugar beet	29	36	27	58	-	27	24	49

* 1995 data for Lithuania

Source: Data for Finland and Sweden from Kämäräinen et al., 1998; for remaining countries see source note, table 2.2.

Table 2.4 depicts gross margins for the Baltics, Finland, and Sweden. Labour costs for Finland and Sweden also include tractor and harvester work which are not included as part of the operating costs crop production in the Baltic countries. Consequently, the gross margins of type III are not comparable and are not listed for Finland and Sweden.

Among the Baltic countries, type II gross margins are highest in Estonia for almost all products with the exceptions of pork and sugar beets in Latvia and Lithuania, wheat in Latvia, and beef in to Lithuania.[7] A comparison with Finland is not very indicative since its margins are negative except for milk and oats.[8] For the former, Estonia enjoys higher margins than Finland, and the other two Baltics lower ones. Lithuania has negative gross margins II for milk. For oats, all Baltic countries have higher margins than Finland. Sweden enjoys higher type II gross margins for almost all products than any other country considered.

Gross margins of type III reflect the difference between total revenues and total operating costs and are based on a working hour. Most are positive for nearly all commodities and countries shown in table 2.4. Negative values are found for rye in Lithuania, beef and pork in Finland, and pork in Sweden. For six out of ten commodities, Estonia enjoys higher type III gross margins than both Latvia and Lithuania indicating higher labour productivity. For livestock products, Finland and Sweden enjoy higher type III gross margins than the Baltic countries except for beef and pork in

Finland and pork in Sweden where operating costs are not covered by total revenues.

In comparison, production costs reveal a competitive edge better than gross margins. This is due to the widely different farm prices prevailing in the countries in this study. Therefore, a policy change may rather drastically alter rankings based on gross margins. In general, the comparison indicates that milk is the product for which the Baltics reach the highest level of competitiveness.

Table 2.4   Gross margins, 1996

Product	Gross margin II, ECU per animal or ha				
	Estonia	Latvia	Lithuania*	Finland	Sweden
Milk	359	113	-19	280	445
Beef	29	-43	48	-349	102
Pigmeat	8	46	32	-23	-10
Wheat	171	288	131	-26	215
Rye	108	82	-58	-162	58
Barley	113	105	18	-49	139
Oats	109	87	59	49	103
Rapeseed	123	3	50	-	-
Potatoes	1 122	201	1 066	-	-
Sugar beet	155	852	539	-	-

	Gross margin III, ECU per hour				
	Estonia	Latvia	Lithuania*	Finland	Sweden
Milk	5	3	1	11	21
Beef	2	0	3	-3	23
Pigmeat	2	9	5	-14	-10
Wheat	58	98	41	-	-
Rye	37	29	-18	-	-
Barley	39	37	7	-	-
Oats	37	31	21	-	-
Rapeseed	42	3	18	-	-
Potatoes	141	27	134	-	-
Sugar beet	10	52	33	-	-

* 1995 data for Lithuania

Source: Data for Finland and Sweden from Kämäräinen et al., 1998; for remaining countries see source note, table 2.2.

Market Share Indicators

A host of different indicators are used in the literature to measure competitiveness based on market information. To those belong production and export and import shares for the agricultural and food sectors in total and/or for selected agricultural products. These very simple indicators seem to be less appropriate to measure competitiveness since competitiveness is a relative measure. Absolute production and market shares say little about the competitive position of a sector/subsector in an economy unless calculated relative to other sectors. This is done in more comprehensive measures of international competitiveness (see e.g. Balassa, 1989; Vollrath, 1991):

- The Relative Revealed Comparative Advantage Exports Indicator (RXA)
- The Relative Revealed Import Penetration Index (RMP)
- The Relative Revealed Comparative Trade Advantage Index (RTA)

The RXA and the RMP are calculated:

$$RXA_{ij} = (X_{ij} / \sum_{l,l \neq j} X_{il}) / (\sum_{k,k \neq i} X_{kj} / \sum_{k,k \neq i} \sum_{l,l \neq j} X_{kl}) \qquad (1)$$

$$RMP_{ij} = (M_{ij} / \sum_{l,l \neq j} M_{il}) / (\sum_{k,k \neq i} M_{kj} / \sum_{k,k \neq i} \sum_{l,l \neq j} M_{kl}) \qquad (2)$$

In equations (1) and (2), X and M refer to exports and imports, with the subscripts *i* and *k* denoting product categories, while *j* and *l* denote country categories. The numerator is equal to a country's exports or imports of a specific product category relative to exports or imports from the rest of the world of this product. The denominator reports the exports or imports of all products but the considered commodity from the respective country as a percentage of all other countries' exports or imports of all other products. The level of these indicators shows the degree of revealed export competitiveness/import penetration. Values for RXA or RMP which are above 1 suggest that the country has a comparative advantage in the exported commodity (a high level of import penetration). Similarly, RXA or RMP values below 1 indicate a low level of export competitiveness or import penetration of the considered product.

While the RXA and RMP indexes are calculated exclusively on the basis of either export or import values, the RTA considers both export and import activities:

$$RTA_{ij} = RXA_{ij} - RMP_{ij}.$$

It is the difference between the RXA and the RMP: values below 0 indicate a competitive trade disadvantage; values above 0 indicate a competitive trade advantage.[9] This indicator implicitly weights the revealed competitive advantage by calculating the importance of relative export and relative import advantages, and it is thus not dominated by extremely small export or import values of a specific commodity. From the point of view of trade theory, this seems to be an advantage. Due to the growth in intraindustry and/or entrepot trade, this aspect is becoming increasingly important (Frohberg and Hartmann, 1997). Thus, to make sure that a high competitive advantage/disadvantage is indeed prevalent, the RTA was also calculated.

Besides the structural problems these indexes have, they should be interpreted with care because of numerical problems (e.g. in the extreme case that trade in one product is carried out by only one country the index is undefined). A further problem arises with interpreting unbounded indexes. The RXA is not bound from above, the RMP is not bound from below. The RTA is unbounded both from above and below.

Finally, market share indicators measure competitiveness only on the grounds of observed, and possibly distorted, market data. Thus, when interpreting the indicators such intervention needs to be taken into account. Especially in the agro-food sector, trade is considerably hampered by tariff and nontariff trade measures with the effect of reducing, and distorting exchange between countries.

RXAs, RMPs, and RTAs have been calculated for all three Baltic countries and the EU-15 for thirty-nine raw and processed agricultural products/product groups. All merchandise trade excluding the respective product has been used as the reference product group in the analysis. The reference country group is the world, excluding the respective country. Strong statistical irregularities were prevalent at the beginning of the transition period. These were very likely still present in 1994. For this reason table 2.5 summarises the results of the RTA only for 1995-96. The discussion concentrates on the RTA since this index implicitly covers the other two.

The RTA values show quite a heterogeneous but not unexpected picture. Table 2.5 reveals that for most animal products the indicator is higher than for crops or for processed crop products. This very general result is due to the unfavourable climatic and soil conditions in the Baltic countries. Therefore, crop production has a natural comparative disadvantage; e.g. in Estonia the poor climatic conditions limit the production of certain crops and the quality of some others. In the past, most grains were of only feed quality and less suitable for human consumption in Estonia and Latvia (OECD/CCET, 1996c, p. 102). This has changed for Latvia due to the introduction of new varieties, although low quality grain production still persists in Estonia.

Particularly high positive RTA values are revealed in table 2.5 for milk products in all three Baltic countries. This can be explained by the high share of pasture in total agricultural land. The negative, albeit small, value for fresh milk and high positive values, especially for such processed products as dry milk and butter in Estonia, suggests that this most northern country imports fresh milk that is processed by the local dairy industry.

This indicates that the Estonian dairy industry must be very competitive compared to the respective industry in the neighbouring countries. The EU also possesses a revealed competitive advantage for milk and processed milk products. This latter result is mainly the outcome of the high protection for this product in the EU.

In the Baltic countries, beef and veal are mainly by-products from the dairy industry. For dairy cattle, as well as beef and veal, positive RTA values were calculated for all Baltic states in the years 1994-95, but for Latvia only in 1995.[10] However, in 1996 the RTA values for beef and veal turned negative in Estonia. Low prices for beef combined with high feed prices have forced farmers in Estonia to slaughter newly born male calves. In general this is done at the age of a few weeks so that the hide of the animals can be used. Thus, in 1996, of the three Baltic countries only Lithuania reveals positive RTA values for dairy cattle (0.6) as well as for beef and veal (2.6). Lithuania also seems to be competitive for other livestock, meat, and meat products. Small negative values are revealed only for pigmeat. The revealed trade advantage is less pronounced for Estonia and Latvia except for sausages. All Baltic countries seem to be highly competitive in the production of this product. The EU also shows positive

RTA values for most livestock, meat, and meat products. In the case of the EU the only exception is live sheep and goats as well as their meat.

For the year 1996, table 2.5 shows that the RTA values are negative for all crops except for rapeseed in Estonia and Latvia. The extreme difference in the RTA values for rye in Latvia for 1995-96 is surprising. The explanation for these numbers is as follows: In 1993, large amounts of rye were imported from Finland on a concessionary basis. Consequently, huge stocks were accumulated and the rye price dropped. However, rye stocks could not be used for food requirements and thus were reexported from 1994-95. Due to the decline in prices, domestic production of high quality rye decreased leading to a deficit on the domestic market in 1996, thus rye had to be imported that year. Given the small quantities of rye traded internationally, this development has resulted in a large positive RTA value in 1995 and an even higher negative number in 1996.[11]

With respect to crops the results are rather mixed for Lithuania. The analysis suggests that Lithuania possesses a revealed comparative advantage for rye, potatoes, sunflower seeds, rapeseed, and apples while a lack of competitiveness seems to be prevalent for all other crops.

The EU shows a comparative advantage for all considered grains, sugar, and tomatoes while the examination indicates a lack of competitiveness for soybeans and sunflower seeds. While the RTA values are also negative for all oilcakes in the EU, positive values are revealed for processed oil and margarine products. The latter result might have two causes. First, in this sector tariff escalation is a fact in the EU, thus the nominal and effective protection rates increase with the degree of processing. Second, productivity in the oil processing industry seems to be quite high.

In Lithuania the RTA values for 1995-96 also hint at a competitive advantage in the production of vegetable oil and margarine (table 2.5). However they were negative in previous years. What is the explanation for this result? First, the protection level for oilseeds production is relatively high in Lithuania. While in 1996 (1995) the producer subsidy equivalent amounted to 14 per cent (6 per cent), the respective figure for oilseed was 41 per cent (39 per cent) (OECD/CCET, 1997b). In addition, in 1994-95 one oilseed crushing plant was modernised with the help of foreign direct investments and another one was newly built, improving the processing capacities in Lithuania thus providing an additional incentive to farmers to grow oilseeds (OECD/CCET, 1996d, p. 99; Girgzdiene and Kuodys, 1998).

Table 2.5 Comparative advantage based on the RTA, 1995-96

	Estonia 1995	Estonia 1996	Latvia 1995	Latvia 1996	Lithuania 1995	Lithuania 1996	EU-15 1995	EU-15 1996
Live Animals								
Dairy cattle	0.1	0.0	-0.4	0.0	0.6	0.6	0.6	0.4
Sheep & goats	0.1	0.1	0.0	0.0	0.0	0.0	-0.2	-0.2
Pigs	0.7	0.3	-1.1	0.0	0.4	0.3	0.2	-0.1
Meat and Meat Products								
Beef & veal	0.3	-2.2	-0.1	-0.1	1.6	2.6	0.1	1.9
Mutton & goat	0.0	0.0	0.0	0.0	0.0	0.0	-2.0	-2.3
Pigmeat	-0.5	-4.0	-0.6	-1.9	-0.1	-0.2	1.4	0.3
Bacon & ham	0.3	-0.1	-0.2	-0.6	0.0	0.0	2.9	4.7
Sausages	2.5	2.7	2.1	6.9	3.8	1.2	2.2	1.0
Meat, prepared	8.4	-1.2	5.2	0.1	1.9	3.7	0.5	0.3
Poultry meat	-0.9	-3.1	-0.2	-0.3	0.8	0.5	0.2	0.0
Eggs in shell	-0.1	0.9	-0.1	0.0	4.0	2.7	1.1	0.9
Milk and Milk Products								
Milk, fresh	-0.4	-0.1	2.0	1.7	1.1	0.9	9.4	5.0
Milk, dry	13.0	17.8	0.2	0.5	22.3	21.5	1.7	1.5
Butter	15.7	19.3	2.3	3.9	18.2	15.6	1.5	0.0
Cheese	1.7	2.7	2.1	1.5	4.3	3.4	3.8	3.9
Crops								
Wheat	-0.1	-0.2	-0.7	-1.8	-0.5	-0.3	0.2	0.2
Barley	-2.5	-7.4	-0.4	-2.3	-2.2	-1.2	1.2	0.9
Rye	-5.2	-3.4	11.7	-21.7	1.9	1.4	9.6	11.0
Potatoes	0.6	-0.5	-0.6	-0.5	0.2	0.3	0.2	-0.1
Sugar	-1.9	-2.4	-1.6	-2.3	-1.5	-1.1	0.2	0.1
Tomatoes	-1.5	-1.5	-0.9	-0.3	-0.2	-0.1	0.0	0.6
Onions	-1.6	-1.2	-4.2	-1.7	-2.0	-0.5	-0.1	0.0
Apples	-2.0	-2.3	-2.5	-1.3	0.9	0.2	-0.4	-0.7
Grapes	-0.9	-1.4	-0.8	-1.0	-0.5	-0.5	-0.3	-0.4
Rape/mustard seed	1.8	2.8	0.3	0.2	2.6	0.8	-0.8	0.1
Soybeans	-0.1	-0.2	0.0	0.0	0.0	0.0	-1.5	-1.2
Sunflower seed	-0.2	-0.8	-0.9	-0.9	0.2	0.5	-3.6	-3.7
Processed Crops								
Wheat flour	-5.5	-7.1	0.0	-0.1	0.1	0.2	1.8	1.7
Soybean oil	-0.4	-0.6	-0.1	-0.2	0.0	0.0	0.2	0.3
Sunflower seed oil	-1.4	-0.8	-4.8	-3.5	2.4	1.8	0.2	0.4
Rape/mustard oil	-8.7	-11.7	-3.8	-6.1	3.4	3.5	2.2	1.9
Margarine	-9.1	-13.3	-4.4	-3.7	12.8	10.2	1.9	1.7
Soybean cakes	-0.5	-0.3	-0.4	-0.1	-3.0	-1.6	-1.4	-1.3
Sunflower cakes	-4.1	-8.3	-0.6	-1.1	-3.3	-1.7	-5.3	-6.1
Rapeseed cakes	0.0	0.0	0.0	0.0	0.0	0.0	-0.8	-0.8
Wine	-1.8	-2.2	-0.9	-0.4	-1.5	-0.2	6.2	4.5
Beer	-1.4	-2.0	-0.9	-0.5	-1.7	-1.1	1.7	1.8
Chocolate	-0.9	-2.8	2.0	1.1	8.2	6.7	2.9	2.2
Other Agric. Products	-0.7	-1.3	-0.1	-0.4	-1.2	0.3	-0.2	-0.3
Non Agric. Prod.	0.1	0.2	0.7	0.9	-0.7	-0.7	0.2	0.1

Source: Data from FAO, 1998.

The situation is somewhat different in Estonia and Latvia. Since there is a lack of oilseed pressing plants in both countries, the raw products are generally exported for refining (e.g. to Finland or Denmark), and the processed products are then reexported.[12] Competitiveness is thus revealed in the analysis for the raw product rapeseed while the opposite holds for vegetable oils and margarine. With respect to all other processed crop products a lack of competitiveness is also revealed for Estonia and Latvia. An exception is chocolate in Latvia. This can be explained by the success of the well-known chocolate company LAIMA in Latvia. In Lithuania the results are again rather mixed. For the EU, competitiveness can be detected for all processed crop products except for oilseed meals.

It should be emphasised that the Baltic countries are in a transformation process which still implies strong shifts in competitiveness, potentially even from year to year. The results presented in this section thus have to be interpreted with caution and can only be indicative of the competitive position of the Baltic agro-food sector in 1995-96. This becomes obvious when looking at the coefficient of variation of the RTA values from 1994-96. While the average coefficient of variation over all thirty-nine agricultural product groups analysed amount to 0.4 for the EU, this coefficient equals 2.7 for Estonia, 1.6 for Latvia, and 2.8 for Lithuania.[13]

Foreign Investments

Foreign direct investment (FDI) is important not only as a source of capital but also as means of transferring foreign experience, technology and management skills. With regard to competitiveness, FDI can serve as an indicator of the attractiveness of a country of internationally mobile production factors (Horn, 1985, p. 326).[14]

Estonia has attracted the most FDI among the Baltic states and ranks second after Hungary among those countries of Eastern Europe that have signed Association Agreements with the EU (United Nations, 1998, pp. 271-88). In 1996, it reached a ratio of FDI stock to GDP of 19 per cent which is only slightly higher than that of Latvia (17 per cent), but almost five times larger than that of Lithuania (4 per cent). Indeed, the ratio of FDI stock to GDP in Estonia and Latvia considerably exceeds the world average of 11 per cent in 1996. With respect to FDI stock per capita the difference between Estonia and the other two Baltic countries is even more pronounced; in 1996, 551 USD in Estonia; 335 USD in Latvia; and only 80 USD in Lithuania.[15] As measured by the percentage of gross fixed capital formation, FDI ranks very high in Estonia reaching 23 per cent in the period 1994-96.

Interestingly the smallest of the three Baltic countries has attracted the bulk of FDI.[16] In general, the small size of a market is seen as a substantial impediment for attracting FDI. Obviously, favourable external conditions compensated for this disadvantage. Together with the Czech Republic, Hungary, Poland, and Slovenia, Estonia is seen as having achieved the most progress in restructuring its economy (United Nations, 1998, p. 273). Macroeconomic stability, favourable taxes, and well-managed privatisation tenders thus might be very important attractants or attractors of FDI, especially in the smallest of the three Baltic countries.[17] However, considerable progress in this respect has also been achieved in recent years in the other two Baltic countries. This is reflected not only in high GDP growth rates but also in high growth rates of FDI inflows in the period 1995-97: 125 per cent per annum in Lithuania and 35 per cent in Latvia (United Nations, 1998, p. 277).

In the Baltic countries, agro-food has also been among the sectors attracting a large share of foreign investments. During 1992-97 16 per cent of total FDI went into this sector in Lithuania, 11 per cent in Estonia, and 8 per cent in Latvia.[18] The bulk of these investments has been directed into the food processing industry, while the share going into the primary sector was negligible (OECD, 1998, p. 168-69).

In general, sectors producing high-value finished products, such as tobacco, alcoholic beverages, confectionery and soft drinks have attracted the bulk of FDI in the Baltic food industry, while other subsectors of the food industry, such as meat processing, the milling industry and the dairy sector, have received little foreign capital (OECD, 1998, p. 170; EU Commission, 1998, Lithuania, p. 35; Latvia, pp. 55-6). One reason for the low foreign involvement in the latter sectors is the type of privatisation that was pursued. In the privatisation process, agricultural producers were given preferential treatment in the sale of shares of the enterprises in these subsectors. In Estonia, for instance, Article 32 of the Law on Privatisation virtually excluded Estonian and foreign investors, other than producer cooperatives, from tenders involving meat and milk enterprises (OECD/CCET, 1996b, Estonia, p. 84).

Real Exchange Rate and Purchasing Power Parity

When discussing the development of competitiveness in the real sphere of the economy, the real exchange rate is often referred to. In its most widely used definition, the real (bilateral) exchange rate (E_r) is equal to the nominal (bilateral) exchange rate (E_n) multiplied by the ratio of the appropriate price deflator for the foreign currency (P_w) to the appropriate deflator for the domestic currency (P_d):

$$E_r = E_n * \frac{P_w}{P_d}.$$

In another definition, the real exchange rate represents the relative price of two sets of goods, tradable and nontradable. This relative price may also be interpreted as the domestic production costs determined by nontradables. An appreciation of the real exchange rate indicates an increase in production costs caused by nontradables and, therefore, a loss in competitiveness.[19] Changes in prices of tradable inputs, it is implicitly assumed, affect all countries alike if prices are fully transmitted from the world to the domestic market, i.e. if trade barriers do not exist.

The nominal bilateral exchange rate is a measure of the price of one currency in terms of another. If the analysis concerns the impact of the exchange rate on trade, a multilateral rate is more appropriate. For this purpose the effective exchange rate is usually used. This indicator is a weighted average of all exchange rates of the most important trading partners. For the current study the geometric mean is taken using the simple average of shares in agricultural trade during 1995-96 as weights. Rather than including all countries in the calculation of this composite exchange rate, only those with high trade volumes which add up to about 90 per cent of total volume traded in these two years were included. Using this procedure, eleven trading partners were selected for each of the Baltic countries.

To adjust nominal exchange rates for price differentials among countries, the purchasing power parity index (PPP) is widely used. The PPP is the ratio of an index of a basket of goods at domestic prices to an index of the same of goods at foreign prices. In this analysis real exchange rate is arrived at by dividing the nominal exchange rate by the PPP. Since calculating the PPP requires a vast amount of information which is not widely available, it is often approximated by using some kind of relative price index, e.g. the ratio of the domestic consumer price index (CPI) to that of the foreign country. Instead of employing domestic and foreign CPIs, corresponding food price indexes may be used if one is interested in competitiveness of agriculture.

The major difference between using the PPP and the ratio of CPIs of two countries is that the former uses the same basket of goods in the numerator as well as in the denominator while the latter does not. The CPI is always based on a typical basket of consumption goods of the country for which it is calculated. Hence, if one takes the ratio of the domestic to the foreign CPI as a deflator, one uses index–each of which is aggregated using different weights. Again, an average of the inflation rates of the countries included in the calculation of the real effective exchange rate is needed. This may be done using an arithmetic or a geometric average. For the current study, a geometric mean of the foreign consumer price indexes were calculated using the same weights as for determining the nominal effective exchange rates. It is common to hold the weights constant over time to obtain the real effective exchange rate for different years (e.g. Poganietz, 1998). This procedure was taken here as well since the necessary data determining the weights for each year were not easily available.[20]

Table 2.6 shows the result of these calculations for each of the three Baltic countries. The deflator used is the ratio of the CPI in the corresponding Baltic country to the geometric average of the CPIs of all trading partners considered. According to these calculations, the effective exchange rates of the Baltic countries appreciated in nominal and real terms over the period 1992-96. This happened in spite of the fact that each of the three countries fixes its currency against another currency or set of other currencies. Estonia pegs its currency to the German mark, Latvia to the Special Drawing Rights and Lithuania to the US dollar. Nevertheless, the differences in the development among these countries are quite strong. Latvia experienced the largest nominal appreciation for 1992-94 which was 2.5 times that of Estonia and 1.3 times that of Lithuania. The real appreciation of the effective exchange rates are also quite substantial. For Latvia, this even exceeds the nominal rate because of unfavourable inflation rates. The real effective exchange rate of Latvia in 1996 was nearly ten times that of 1992 which amounts to an average real appreciation of more than 50 per cent a year. This is twice the increase in Lithuania and 3.5 times that in Estonia.

Table 2.6 Nominal and real effective exchange rates of the Baltic countries with their main trading partners, 1992-96

Year	Estonia Nominal	Estonia Real	Latvia Nominal	Latvia Real	Lithuania Nominal	Lithuania Real
1992	100.0	100.0	100.0	100.0	100.0	100.0
1993	189.0	143.0	278.9	370.0	219.2	290.4
1994	247.5	182.6	528.2	628.9	386.4	391.0
1995	325.3	232.3	806.6	848.5	565.0	448.1
1996	329.0	261.5	834.5	944.9	614.7	497.0

Source: Data from DIW Kooperationsbüro Osteuropa-Wirtschaftsforschung, 1995; ZMP, 1995; IMF, 1995; EU Commission, 1995; OECD/CCET, 1995; Statistisches Bundesamt, 1995; OECD/CCET, 1997a; Deutsche Bundesbank, 1997. Data collection and calculations by Drs Mienlschmidt and Poganietz of IAMO.

Given these strong appreciations, price competitiveness of the Baltics steadily weakened, providing favourable conditions for imports and impeding exports. It should also be noted that keeping the weights constant for geometric averaging introduces a certain amount of bias. If varying weights were applied the results would be different. Especially during times when trade shares vary considerably from year to year, the latter approach might have advantages. However, to calculate trade shares as weights for different years is very labour intensive and often the data are not available. Therefore, this approach is rarely followed. Frohberg and Glauch (1998) provide such indicators of adjustments in the exchange rates which are based on the 'currency basket method' in which the necessary statistics are available only after long time delays.

Another aspect of calculating changes in exchange rates is that averaging over all trading partners might not reveal all peculiarities. It is not unusual that the development of bilateral, real exchange rates among trading partners diverges. Price competitiveness might, therefore, be differently affected. This is also the case with the Baltic countries (Frohberg and Glauch, 1998). Their bilateral real exchange rates with EU member states and some countries of central Europe appreciated while at the same time depreciating against other central European countries and especially Russia, Belarus, and the Ukraine. These divergent developments of the exchange rates had considerable impact on the development of trade. While the trade balance with the EU became negative, it improved with the members of Commonwealth of Independent States.

Conclusions

In this paper the major determinants of competitiveness in the agricultural and food sector in the Baltic states are discussed. Some empirical measures and indicators are also provided.

The results reveal that although the amount of agricultural land is very favourable in these countries, many other determinants such as quality of soil, climatic conditions, input supply, quantity as well as quality of processing and distribution facilities, and the scale and quality of the consumer market impede international competitiveness. Though Estonia is most hampered by unfavourable natural conditions among the Baltic countries, it was rather successful in providing the necessary institutional framework for a speedy transition of the whole economy which has also benefited agriculture.

According to the RTA, milk production seems to have a competitive advantage while crop production appears to be less competitive in the Baltic states. This general result might be due to the unfavourable climatic and soil conditions for growing grains, oilseeds, and sugar beets in these regions. Profitability indexes partly support these results showing that, in comparison to Germany, production costs in the Baltic countries are low for milk and beef production, while for some other products such as pork they are higher. The picture is less clear with respect to the gross margins.[21]

An extrapolation of the results presented can be done only with caution since restructuring in the Baltic states is ongoing and thus considerable intra- and intersectoral adjustments in the allocation of resources are taking place. The annual variation in production and trade still exceeds that in other countries such as those in the EU. Although these limitations have to be taken into account, the figures presented can provide a first indication with respect to the level of competitiveness in the different product markets in the Baltic states. Competitiveness of the agricultural and food sector in the future very much depends on the development of relative prices and technological changes as well as on price- and technology-induced adjustments of production. Those changes might occur with the prospect of EU accession.

After joining the EU, it can be expected that the ratio of output to input prices in the Baltic states will initially rise. Prices of inputs traded freely on world markets will not change. However, those which are generally determined by internal factors may rise, particularly labour costs. In the mid-1990s, the wage rate in Estonia, Latvia, and Lithuania was less than 10 per cent of that in Germany. As time passes, labour costs are expected to increase from their current low levels toward those prevalent in the EU.[22] The explanation for this adjustment is provided by the Heckscher-Ohlin factor price equalisation theorem. If this is going to happen, labour intensive production techniques will gradually be replaced by those requiring a relatively high share of capital input. This will lead to an adjustment of production techniques toward those used in the EU.

The change in crop and livestock prices will largely depend on the adjustments in the EU agricultural policy prior to accession. However, given the fact that protection of nonruminant meat in Latvia and Lithuania exceeded the level in the EU in 1996 and 1997, prices for these products might decline rather than increase (see OECD, 1998; OECD/CCNM, 1998). In Estonia, the same could be observed only for poultry meat. In all Baltic countries, grain prices might rise if the CAP is reformed, thus putting a second source of relative disadvantage on nonruminant meat products as feed grains make up about 45 per cent of total production costs of these commodities. During the initial period of EU membership starchy crops might dominate feed rations, but with rising labour costs this is expected to become too costly and a gradual shift toward a larger share of feed grains in the feeding ration can be expected.

Increases in prices of ruminant meats and milk can be expected in the Baltics even if the EU lowers price incentives to produce beef, milk, and sheep meat. This holds in Estonia and Latvia where beef and veal are taxed but will be slightly smaller in Lithuania where these products already receive some protection. Also, protection of milk is, compared to the EU, relatively low in Estonia and even negative in Latvia and Lithuania (see OECD, 1998; OECD/CCNM, 1998). Thus an increase in the production of milk products in the Baltic states is very likely. Given soil and climatic conditions, ruminant production is expected to have a comparative advantage in the future, providing an additional impetus for production growth.

With respect to changes in relative prices of crops, a rise in grain prices is anticipated relative to other crops. However, this is not expected to lead to a drastic increase in production since climate conditions are not favourable for intensive grain production and already a large share of agricultural land is devoted to grain.

Finally, it has to be noted that the competitiveness of agriculture in the Baltic countries crucially depends on the quality of their products and the efficiency of the processing as well as distribution sectors. Thus, additional production incentives due to an eastward EU enlargement would be severely reduced if the Baltic states are not successful in improving the quality of their food products and in reducing the inefficiencies in their food industry and wholesale markets.

Notes

1. The authors would like to acknowledge support from the PHARE - ACE Programme through the project P95-2198-R. Thanks are also due to our partners in this project with whom we have jointly undertaken the research. Parts of this chapter draw heavily on the final report of this project which was jointly written. Responsibility of this chapter, however, remains with the authors.
2. There is in fact no single definition of competitiveness in the economic literature. The difficulties in defining competitiveness are due to the various dimensions of this concept. The above definition, however, seems to be widely accepted in the economic literature. Its main advantage lies in that it not only considers the output markets but also considers factors of production.
3. For an overview on measures of competitive potential and competitive process, see Porter (1990) or Fanfani and Lagvevik (1995).
4. For example, large tracts of agricultural land in the Baltic states were drained. At least partly due to the current fragmentation of land ownership, delays with the land title registration process, and the slow development of land market, maintenance and reconstruction of drainage systems as well as other land reclamation activities have become difficult to carry out.
5. One major problem in this respect is overstaffing; many food processing enterprises were not able to reduce their labour force to the same extent as their output declined (OECD/CCNM, 1998, p. 163).
6. Transportation costs account for a substantial share of production costs. In countries which are spatially large and land locked, efficient transportation systems are an especially important factor for determining competitiveness.
7. Some of the gross margins of type II are negative in Latvia and Lithuania.
8. Again, as mentioned earlier, this is largely due to the fact that transfer payments are not included in the revenues.
9. If the RTA is greater than 0, this does not imply relative export advantage. It can very well be that RXA is smaller than 1, pointing to a relative export disadvantage while the RTA is greater than 1. This has to considered in the interpretation of the indicators.
10. However, numbers for 1994 are not revealed in table 2.5 due to the general data problems discussed for the years up to 1994.
11. The positive value for 1994, when the bulk of these exports took place, was even higher, leading to a RTA value of above 100.
12. Latvia has no oilseed crushing plant while Estonia has one plant that is suitable only for basic processing (OECD/CCET 1997b, p. 194).
13. The competitiveness of the agricultural and food sector in the Baltic countries after accession to the EU very much depends on the similarity or complementary structure of agricultural trade advantages of these states and the EU as well as in the other

acceding CEECs. For a detailed discussion and analysis of the similarities in trade advantage between these countries and regions, see Bergschmidt and Hartmann (1998).

14 However, one needs to differentiate with respect to FDI. If a large part of investments are used primarily as a means to accessing foreign markets that can perhaps not be accessed through exports due to trade barriers, they mirror competitiveness of the donor country and not necessarily of the recipient country. Unfortunately, it is generally difficult to distinguish which of the two causes dominates.

15 Total FDI stocks in 1997 (1996) amounted to about 1148 USD (886) million in Estonia, 901 USD (679) million in Latvia, and 1041 USD (647) million in Lithuania.

16 Due to the establishment of the BFTA, the market for foreign investors has increased which might result in an additional incentive for investment in all three Baltic countries.

17 For a discussion of the main factors that can inhibit FDI flows, see Dimelis and Gatsios, 1996, pp. 145-47.

18 Unpublished data of the United Nations reveal somewhat smaller numbers. In this source the 1996 share of the agro-food sector in overall FDI stock is 11.3 per cent in Estonia, 13.6 per cent in Lithuania, and 10.2 per cent in Latvia.

19 At this point, a note regarding the interpretation of the real exchange rate should be given. Changes in this indicator can be either a reflection or the cause of improved or deteriorated international competitiveness. If enterprises gain shares in domestic and foreign markets this will ceteris paribus, result in an appreciation of the domestic currency which will be reflected in the appropriate movement of the real exchange rate. The intensity of variations in the real exchange rate is indicative of the extent of improvement or deterioration in international competitiveness. However, experience gained over recent decades reveals that changes in real exchange rates are very often more influenced by capital movements and their impact on the nominal exchange rate than by changes in basic conditions of the nonmonetary part of the economy. Thus, relating changes in the real exchange rate to modifications in international competitiveness is correct only if the causes of the variations are known (Sachverständigenrat, 1988, p. 101; Horn, 1985, p. 326).

20 Another reason often put forward for using constant weights is to ease the interpretation of effective exchange rate indexes. Keeping the weights constant reduces the causes of changes in such effective rates to only alterations in exchange rates (Turner and Van't dack, 1993, p. 14). However, the authors of this paper do not agree with this reasoning since by using a changing weight it would be possible to divide the total real exchange rate effect into a structural and a performance effect, which would provide some additional and quite interesting information.

21 It should be pointed out that the comparision of the results of the profitability indexes between countries, although desirable, is quite difficult. This is due to the fact that the base year and the methodology used in the different studies on profitability differ. It is even more difficult to make a comparison of the profitability indexes to the RTA values obtained, because of differences in the level of processing and marketing of the products considered. In addition, and possibly most important, the reference country/region differ. The profitability results are compared to Germany while the

reference country group with respect to the RTA is the world excluding the considered country.
22 Nevertheless, there is some evidence that factor prices and especially wages will not adjust to the same extent as commodity prices. In the EU-15 there still exist large differences in wages.

References

Association of Rural Advisory Centres (1996), 'Mallilaskelmat', Gross Margin Calculations for Finland, Helsinki.
Agricultural University of Sweden (1996), Gross Margin Calculations for Sweden, Uppsala.
Balassa, B. (1989), *Comparative Advantage, Trade Policy and Economic Development*, New York and London.
Bergschmidt, A. and Hartmann, M. (1998), 'Agricultural Trade Policies and Trade Relations in Transition Economies', IAMO Discussion Paper No. 12, Halle, Saale.
Boruks, A. (1996), 'Common Agricultural Market in the Baltics', in *Lauku avîze*, 17 September 1996.
Dimelis, S. and Gatsios, K. (1996), 'Trade with Central and Eastern Europe: The Case of Greece', in R. Faini and R. Portes (eds), *European Union Trade with Eastern Europe. Adjustments and Opportunities*, Centre for Economic Policy Research, London, pp. 123-66.
Deutsche Bundesbank (ed. 1997), Monatsbericht Februar 1997, Frankfurt / M.
DIW Kooperationsbüro Osteuropa-Wirtschaftsforschung (ed. 1995), Wirtschaftslage und Reformprozesse in Mittel- und Osteuropa - Sammelband.
EU Commission, DG VI (1995), 'Agricultural Situation and Prospects in the Central European Countries', Summary Report and various country studies, Brussels.
EU Commission (1998), 'Agricultural Situation and Prospects in the Central and Eastern European Countries', various Country Reports, Brussels.
Fanfani, R. and Lagnevik, M. (1995), 'Industrial Districts and Porter Diamonds', Discussion Paper Series No. 8 of the concerted action project on Structural Change in the European Food Industries.
FAO (1998), FAOSTAT, Rome.
Freebairn, J. (1986), 'Implications of Wages and Industrial Policies on Competitiveness of Agricultural Export Industries', Paper presented at the Australian Agricultural Economics Society Policy Forum, Canberra.
Frohberg, K. and Glauch, L. (1998), 'Stand der Transformationsbestrebungen in den mittel- und osteuropäischen Ländern', *Agrarwirtschaft*, vol. 67, no. 3/4 pp. 135-46.
Frohberg, K. and Hartmann M. (1997), 'Comparing Measures of Competitiveness: Examples for Agriculture in the Central European Associates', IAMO Discussion Paper No. 2, Halle, Saale.
Gahlen, G., Rahmeyer, F. and Stadler, M. (1986), 'Zur internationalen Wettbewerbsfähigkeit der deutschen Wirtschaft', *Konjunkturpolitik*, 32. Jg, Heft 3, S. 130-50.

Girgzdiene, V. and Kuodys, A. (1998), 'Lithuania's Food Processing Industry in Transition', in M. Hartmann and J. Wandel (eds), *Food Processing and Distribution in Transition Countries. Problems and Perspectives*, Kiel, forthcoming.

Horn, E.-J. (1985), 'Internationale Wettbewerbsfähigkeit von Ländern', in *WiSt*, Heft 7, Juli, S. 323-29.

IMF (1995), 'International Financial Statistics Yearbook 1995', Washington DC.

Kämäräinen, J., Martikainen, J., Ala-Orvola, L., Laurila, I.P. (1998), 'Maataloustuotannon kannattavuus Virossa – vertailu Suomeen ja Ruotsiin' (Profitability of agricultural production in Estonia: A comparison with Finland and Sweden), Agricultural Economics Research Institute, Working Papers 1/98, Helsinki.

Loko, V. and Sepp M. (1998), 'Structural Policies and Privatisation in Estonia', in OECD/CCNM (ed), *Agricultural Policies in the Baltic Countries*, Paris, pp. 28-37.

Miglavs, A. and Snuka, R. (1997), 'Profitability Indicators for Latvia', unpublished paper, Latvian Institute of Agrarian Economics, Riga.

OECD/CCET (1997a) *Short-Term Economic Indicators Transition Economies 1/1997*, Paris.

OECD/CCET (1995, 1996a and 1997b), *Agricultural Policies Markets and Trade in the Central European Countries, Selected New Independent States, Mongolia and China*, Paris.

OECD/CCNM (1998), *Agricultural Policies in Emerging and Transition Economies. Monitoring and Evaluation 1998*, Paris.

OECD (1998), *Agricultural Policies in OECD Countries. Measurement of Support and Background Information 1998*, Paris.

OECD/CCET (1996b), *Review of Agricultural Policies: Estonia*, Paris.

OECD/CCET (1996c), *Review of Agricultural Policies: Latvia*, Paris.

OECD/CCET (1996d), *Review of Agricultural Policies: Lithuania*, Paris.

Poganietz, W.R. (1998), 'Wechselkurs und Wettbewerbsfähigkeit des Agrarsektors - Eine komparative Analyse fünf ausgewählter Staaten Mittel- und Osteuropas', in A. Heissenhuber und W. von Urff (eds), *Land- und Ernährungswirtschaft in einer erweiterten EU. Schriften der Gesellschaft für Wirtschafts- und Sozialwissenschaften des Landbaues e.V. Band 34*.

Porter, M.E. (1990), *The Competitive Advantage of Nations*, London and New York.

Sachverstandigenrat zur Begutachtung der Gesamtwirtschaftlichen Entwicklung (1998), 'Jahresgutachten 1988/89', *Arbeitplatze im Wettbewerb, Teil C: Die Deutsche Volkswirtschaft im Vergleich*, Stuttgart, pp. 101-18.

Statistisches Bundesamt (1995), *Statistisches Jahrbuch für das Ausland 1995*, Wiesbaden.

Turner, Ph. and Van't dack, J. (1993), *Measuring International Price and Cost Competitiveness*, Basle.

United Nations (1998), *Word Investment Report 1998: Trends and Determinants*, Geneva.

Vollrath, T.L. (1991), 'A Theoretical Evaluation of Alternative Trade Intensity Measures of Revealed Comparative Advantage', *Weltwirtschaftliches Archiv*, vol. 127, no. 2, p. 265-80.

Wissenschaftlicher Beirat beim Bundesministerium für Ernährung, Landwirtschaft und Forsten (1997), 'Die Entwicklung der Landwirtschaft in Mitteleuropa und mögliche Folgen für die Agrarpolitik in der EU', *Schriftenreihe des Bundesministeriums für Ernährung, Landwirtschaft und Forsten*, Reihe A, Heft 458.

ZMP (1995), *Agrarmärkte in Zahlen. Mittel-und Osteuropa '95*, Bonn.

3 The Competitiveness of Czech Agricultural Producers in an Integrated European Market

TOMÁŠ RATINGER

Agriculture and European Union Accession

In the fall of 1997, the Czech Republic (CR), one of six chosen Eastern European countries, was invited to start negotiations for future membership in the European Union (EU). The Czech government and population understand this act as recognition of the historical importance of the Czech nation to the Western and Central European community as well as a recognition of the success of recent economic and social reforms. However, the start of negotiations brings with it many doubts about the readiness of the country for accession and consequently doubts about the Czech government's awareness of the extent of accession problems.

Among the serious questions which confront the EU and countries applying for membership, three seem to be crucial: existence of the political will and overall consensus for integration, similarity of long term policy goals, and compatibility of policy instruments for achieving these goals. There are probably no doubts that policy instruments cannot be fully compatible since plenty of measures remain from the previous regimes in Central and Eastern Europe. While political consensus and similarity of policy goals have been considered to be implicitly fulfilled at the national levels for the Central and Eastern European countries (CEECs) since the political changes in 1989, this has not been necessarily true at the sector level.

When comparing agricultural policy priorities between the Common Agricultural Policy (CAP) after MacSharry reforms and the Czech agricultural program (MA CR, 1993), it becomes obvious that short term transition goals of the Czech agricultural policy did not fit with the long term goals of the EU. Additionally the long term policy goals declared by the Czech government in 1993 were not in full accord with the CAP. The Czech government has never held income parity of agriculture with nonagricultural sectors as a high priority, rather policy measures have been introduced as response to fears of total disruption of the farming sector during transition. The essential difference between current Czech and EU agricultural policies is that the CAP has been designed to compensate for comparative disadvantage of the farming sector by price support while the Czech policy has tended to moderate the socioeconomic impact of restructuring the inefficient industry that developed under autarky. In light of this, the Czech policy has been more ad hoc and, in some respects, less transparent. A common feature of both policies has been the accent on common (nonaddressed) measures.

Besides the pressure of large suppliers of agricultural commodities on the world market, the perception of increasing surpluses and substantially higher budgetary outlays when the EU enlarges eastward has called for further reforms of the CAP (European Commission, 1995). The demanded change in the CAP toward the integrated development of rural areas of the EU includes economically efficient farming in a stable economic environment as well as plenty of nonagricultural activities, mainly services, carried out by various agents (Buckwell et al., 1997). Such reform would definitely lead to an introduction of new measures or an expansion of already adopted approaches that are largely anchored in individual (addressed) responsibility and benefits (e.g. environmental contracts).

On the other hand, there have already been doubts as to whether EU Member States are willing and able to forsake the farm income policy priority for integrated rural development which directs support to other sectors as well as farming. And thus, the CEECs have concentrated more on speculating what the EU farm income policy will be at the time of enlargement instead of focusing on their own policy priorities. Since Agenda 2000 confirms a continuation of debate regarding the priority of future EU policies towards newcomers, the CEECs' governments should play a more active role in opening discussion about long term CAP goals and actively spell out their own interests (Ahner, 1997).

Definitely, two benefits of integration into the EU are expected: benefit from the trade of products, and benefits from a larger mobility of factors—labor and capital. Concerning agriculture, who will benefit from the enlarged custom union depends mainly on whether lower protection of the CEECs or higher price support of the current EU members is adopted. In the former case it would be Western consumers who benefit, while in the latter case it would be Eastern agricultural producers.

Integration itself will increase the rating of the CEECs for investors and together with a reduction of barriers for capital mobility it will increase the capital flow to CEECs. Consequently, capital costs can be expected to drop and the capital/labor cost ratio should improve (decline). It will probably lead to a large substitution of labor by capital. On the other hand, one might expect a tendency toward an increased inflow of labor into the EU from the new associates. This will push up labor cost in the integrated CEECs and again improve the capital/labor cost ratio. Hence, large structural changes in the CEECs that join the EU can be expected during which only those who will adjust employment of factors to the new ratio will be able to survive.

However, even before accession, continuing transition and stabilization policies will tend to improve the capital/labor ratio. According to the macroeconomic forecast, the capital/labor cost ration will decline by 45 per cent between 1996 and 2005 (Kraus et al., 1997).

Factor market development will definitely affect the competitiveness of agricultural products. The preaccession agricultural policy will format the choice of technology and allocation of resources, and hence, competitiveness at the moment of EU accession.

This chapter analyzes the current state of competitiveness of Czech agricultural products in relation to the EU, examining one possible accession scenario, and drawing implications for policy design under the assumption of fixed technology with no substitution between factors. The next section introduces a concept for assessing competitiveness. The third section examines current experience with the Association Agreement (AA) with the EU. The fourth section presents calculations and the last section sums up the analytical results.

Methodology

Competitiveness is one of the most debated issues in the topic of integration between Eastern and Western Europe. Competitiveness is usually understood to be the ability to supply goods and services at the time, location, and form sought by buyers at prices as good or better than those of the other potential suppliers while earning at least the opportunity cost of returns on resources employed (Freebain, 1986). Competitiveness is closely linked to comparative advantage. The only difference between the two concepts is that competitiveness includes market distortions while comparative advantage does not (Frohberg and Hartmann, 1997).

Measuring Comparative Advantage

Let us consider the following ratio for an agricultural commodity (Safin, 1995):

$$\frac{\text{Value added at domestic prices}}{\text{Value added at world prices}}, \qquad (1)$$

in which value added equals the difference between the value of output sales and value of tradable input purchases. Evidently, if markets are not distorted, value added at domestic prices can be equivalently expressed as the sum of the costs of nontradable inputs and factor incomes:

$$\frac{P_i - \sum_{j=1}^{k} a_{ij} w_j}{P_i^b - \sum_{j=1}^{k} a_{ij} w_j^b} = \frac{\sum_{j=k+1}^{n} a_{ij} w_j}{P_i^b - \sum_{j=1}^{k} a_{ij} w_j^b}. \qquad (2)$$

where w_j, w_j^b are the domestic and border prices of traded inputs $j \leq k$, domestic prices of $k+1 \leq j \leq n$ are nontradable inputs or factors, and P_i, P_i^b are the domestic and border prices of traded outputs.

If domestic markets are distorted, the value added (more precisely the sum of factor incomes) is distorted and might substantially differ from its valuation at the social (opportunity) costs. The left hand side of equation (2) with the numerator evaluated at actual prices reveals effective protection of the commodity in question, while the right hand side with the numerator calculated at social opportunity costs reveals comparative advantage. In both cases, value added at world prices is considered to be the proper benchmark. The former ratio is often called the effective protective rate or the effective protective coefficient (EPC) (Corden, 1974), and the latter the domestic resource cost coefficient (DRC) (Brent, 1990). A value of the DRC higher than one will suggest that the commodity subsector does not have a comparative advantage with respect to the world market. On the other hand, whenever the DRC coefficient is smaller than 1, the subsector should expand. Similarly, if EPC is larger than 1 the commodity sector is effectively protected while if EPC is lower than 1 the sector is effectively taxed. It is vital to notice the equivalence between these two coefficients in the sense that an EPC larger than 1 usually implies a DRC larger than 1 since protective measures have been introduced to offset the comparative disadvantage.

The ratios defined in equation (2) do not incorporate any substitutions when prices change (Bureau and Kazlaitzandokanes, 1995). Therefore, having DRCs or EPCs for two countries (e.g. the EU and the CR) will yield only a small amount of information about the competitive or protective position between them, unless production technologies and border prices (representing world prices) of inputs and outputs are assumed to be the same.

An option to overcome this problem is to use the price pattern of one country as a benchmark for stating DRC or EPC of the other. This is a particularly rational and justifiable approach when assessing a country's trade position with respect to a customs union. To distinguish between usual notations and the bilateral coefficients we suggest including the measured and benchmark country in the superscripts as follows:

$$DRC_i^{r,s} = \frac{\sum_{j=k+1}^{n} a_{ij}^r w_j^r}{P_i^s - \sum_{j=1}^{k} a_{ij}^s w_j^s}, \qquad (3)$$

$$EPC_i^{r,s} = \frac{P_i^r - \sum_{j=1}^{k} a_{ij}^r w_j^r}{P_i^s - \sum_{j=1}^{k} a_{ij}^s w_j^s}, \qquad (4)$$

where r respective s denotes the country of interest with respect to the benchmark country. Since the questioned country is always the CR, we simplified the notation to DRC(EU) and EPC(EU) whenever the benchmark market is the EU.

Coefficients defined by equations (2) through (4) incorporate a one-way view of the problem. It means that we are only studying the competitive position of one country's technology at the price pattern for tradable goods of the other country (Bureau and Kazlaitzandokanes, 1995).

It is also worthwhile to remember that bilateral coefficients do not refer to the nondistorted situation, as it is supposed for ordinary DRC and EPC; it means, in the case of domestic resources, the 'social' cost of resources in the reference country or in the case of a protection level, to the net of the policy situation. Particularly, direct payments that are not fully decoupled might significantly bias our judgement about the comparative advantage and effective protection levels between questioned countries. Therefore, in light of the note at the beginning of this chapter, DRC(EU) indicates competitiveness rather than comparative advantage.

Relationship between EPC and PSE

The Organisation for Economic Co-operation and Development (OECD) definition of PSE (OECD, 1997) is:

$$PSE_i = MPS_i + DP_i - LV_i + OS_i$$

where MPS is market price support, DP is direct payments, LV is levies on production, and OS is all other budget-financed support. Further,

$$MPS_i = Q_i * (P_i - P_i^b)$$

where Q is volume of production and i equals CR or EU.

According to the OECD methodology, OS includes input support (IS) and general services (GS). Let us omit GS for a moment, assuming that they are not output relative and hence, completely decoupled. Denoting unit PSE by small letters (pse) and taking into account that

$$\frac{IS_i}{Q_i} = \sum_{j=1}^{k}(w_j^b - w_j)a_{ij},$$

we derive

$$pse_i = (P_i - \sum_{j=1}^{k}a_{ij}w_j) - (P_i^b - \sum_{j=1}^{k}a_{ij}w_j^b) + \frac{DP_i - LV_i}{Q_i}.$$

If DP and LV are in some respect output relative, then we can include the last term directly in the domestic price, now denoted P*, and called the incentive price.[1] Thus,

$$pse_i = (P_i^* - \sum_{j=1}^{k} a_{ij} w_j) - (P_i^b - \sum_{j=1}^{k} a_{ij} w_j^b).$$

If pse$_i$ incorporates only tradable inputs, the brackets can be seen as the numerator and denominator of the EPC* defined by the first formula in equation (2):

$$EPC_i^* = \frac{P_i^* - \sum_{j=1}^{k} a_{ij} w_j}{P_i^b - \sum_{j=k+1}^{n} a_{ij} P_j^b}. \quad (5)$$

Some simple algebra yields:

$$EPC_i^* = \frac{P_i^* - \sum_{j=1}^{k} a_{ij} w_j}{P_i^* - \sum_{j=1}^{k} a_{ij} w_j - pse_i}. \quad (6)$$

This illustrates some kind of equivalence between the PSE and EPC methodology. Whenever pse is positive, EPC is larger than 1. The quasi-equivalence between EPC (DRC) and PSE does not hold when the support policy is concentrated on nontradable inputs and factors, such as interest subsidies. However, despite being an important policy instrument, interest subsidies have not increased to such an extent that they significantly bias our judgement about the competitiveness of Czech agricultural products at world prices. If we assume that tradable inputs are traded at world prices and that there is no other support than price support, then (5) simplifies to

$$EPC_i = \frac{P_i - \sum_{j=1}^{k} a_{ij} w_j}{P_i - \sum_{j=1}^{k} a_{ij} w_{j_i} - MPS_i}. \quad (7)$$

Unfortunately, the OECD methodology includes interest subsidies (evidently a constituent of value added) in the input support and hence, (7) can only be considered as a good approximation of the right hand side in equation (2).

Revealed Comparative Advantage (RCA)

Another option used to assess the competitiveness of Czech products with respect to the EU market is to examine bilateral trade. We will concentrate only on a particular concept that comparative advantage should be revealed in relatively high shares of export markets (Balassa, 1977). This idea is incorporated in the following measurement:

$$RCA_i^{r,s} = \frac{X_i^r / X^r}{X_i^s / X^s} \qquad (8)$$

where X_i, X denote export values of the commodity i and total export of manufactured goods. The superscripts differentiate between countries. A comparison of the export share of a particular commodity in the total export of one country to the export share of that commodity in the total export of another country should indicate a value larger than 1 when country r has a comparative advantage in the commodity subsector i with respect to country s. As is discussed later, because of market distortions this concept is closer to the meaning of competitiveness than comparative advantage. Similar to (8), we may define a coefficient that examines only bilateral trade:

$$BT\_RCA_i^{r,s} = \frac{X_i^{r,s} / X^{r,s}}{X_i^{s,r} / X^{s,r}} \qquad (9)$$

where $X_i^{r,s}$, $X^{r,s}$ denotes export values of the commodity i and total export of manufactured goods between both countries. The interpretation is straightforward.

Trade with the EU

Among Czech trading partners the most important is the EU with a share of around 40 per cent of Czech agricultural exports and more than 50 per cent of imports. The commodity structure of exports and imports differ: while the CR tends to export agricultural commodities on which the CAP rests (cereals, beef, dairy products), imports are dominated by Mediterranean products and highly processed food products. This section is included not to give a detailed picture of the trade between the CR and the EU, but rather to illustrate what short term effects the exposure to more liberal conditions for the agricultural trade have had on Czech producers.

Since opening borders to international exchange in 1991, it has been in the interest of both partners to make bilateral trade easy. This effort resulted in the signing of the AA under which tariffs were reduced for a large number of commodities, however, often only for limited volumes. Quotas were defined for the most sensitive commodities such as dairy products, meat, or cereals. For Czech exports, there are about 113 items subjected to quantity restrictions, while there are only 30 EU import items with quota restrictions. More than 40 per cent of agricultural exports and around 37 per cent of imports with the EU belonged to commodities which could be traded under the AA in 1995 and 1996. However, the specific regime could not be applied to total exported volume because of quota restrictions. On the other hand, for certain commodities not all quotas were used.

Unfortunately, there has been little administration and monitoring of trade under the AA. Rough estimates suggest that less than 20 per cent of the value of Czech agricultural exports to the EU actually benefited from the preferential regime. There are two aspects of the relatively small effect of the AA: quotas for commodities of interest to Czech exporters were too low e.g. for malting barley, malt, hops, or skimmed milk powder (SMP); and only 40 per cent of (export) quotas were fully used by Czech exporters in 1995 and 1996.

One has to wonder why there was almost no exports for some products were included in the special regime of the AA. Either these products never had a production base in the CR or information dissemination was unsatisfactory. There are three additional reasons why quotas may not have been exploited: the imposition of additional trade barriers, such as minimum prices, which were not a subject of the AA and complicated administration of the regime in the EU; the low marketing experience of

Czech exporters; and the minimal reduction of tariffs relative to the appreciating Czech currency.

Appreciation of the Czech crown (CZK) also stimulated imports from the EU, which grew significantly in ECU (by 43 per cent) and in volume between 1994 and 1996, while stagnating in real CZK (increase of only 8.5 per cent).

Competitiveness of Czech Agriculture

For our analysis of competitiveness, we use the DRC which represents comparative advantage, and the EPC which incorporates the essence of market distortions. Because the value added at market prices approximates value added at opportunity factor costs, the EPC approximates the DRC. As shown previously, a PSE implies that the EPC is larger than 1, hence, the DRC coefficient is also larger than 1. This implies that the commodity sector is not competitive at the world market price.

In assessing the competitiveness of Czech agriculture, we concentrate on five main commodities (wheat, barley, milk, beef, and pork meat), and on two target markets (competitiveness on the world market and competitiveness on the EU market). Analysis is made under two policy situations: current Czech agricultural policy (AP) with the current CAP in both 1994-1996, and current Czech AP in 1996 with a reformed CAP according to the Agenda 2000 proposal.

Because of the lack of data, some assumptions and some simplifications had to be made. First, since the technical coefficients $a_{i,j}$ are not known, the consumption of inputs was expressed only in values which were gathered from sample farm budget surveys by the Czech agricultural research institute, VÚZE. While prices of outputs are collected using information from the Czech Statistical Office (CSO) and OECD, prices for inputs were accessible only in a limited range. Thus, the identity (equality) of world and domestic prices for tradable inputs (except animal feed) was assumed and justified by the fact that there were no trade restrictions on these inputs and because the CZK was overvalued rather than undervalued. The cost of tradable inputs in animal production at world prices was adjusted according to the cereal price ratio. Although tradable (nonagricultural origin) inputs in the EU were also not subjected to high tariffs, their price level was significantly higher than in the CR in the period examined. This might be because of higher derived demand due to higher output prices and costly marketing. Evaluation of inputs at the EU price level was done using an index which was derived from a comparison of input prices for selected tradable inputs as monitored by the CSO and EUROSTAT.

Denominators of all equation (2)-like coefficients were evaluated in CZK by using an average nominal exchange rate for the year in question. The pse approximation, equation (5), is used for calculating the EPC coefficient at world prices. Otherwise, equation (2) is used with costs adjusted by the appropriate index.

Competitiveness at World Market Prices

The results of the DRC and EPC calculations are interesting in several respects (tables 3.1 and 3.2, figures 3.1 and 3.2).

In general, cereals were competitive at world market prices, while animal products were not in recent years. It indicates that animal production was 'socially' inefficient. The margin that could be earned from selling cereals on the world market was more than sufficient to cover opportunity costs of domestic resources while for animal products, margins were insufficient. Also notice that the policy that stimulated the domestic price for wheat above the world price in 1994 had no justification in comparative disadvantage. On the other hand, domestic producers could not compete with the 'depressed' world price for barley and the Czech market was effectively protected that same year. Because animal production was comparatively disadvantaged, domestic producers were effectively protected. However, the opportunity cost of nontradable inputs and factors was never fully compensated by the domestic price for livestock products.

Cereals and dairy products were competitive at the EU price structure. Beef production lost competitiveness and pig production was truly inefficient between 1994 and 1996. Cattle breeding (dairy and beef production) was highly protected with respect to the world market (EPC>1) but was not protected toward the EU (EPC(EU)<1). It is noticeable that beef production had no 'comparative advantage' with respect to the EU market (DRC(EU)=1.18) in 1996 and was not effectively protected toward the EU (EPC(EU)=0.86).[2] Although the EU output prices for pork were on average 8.4 per cent higher than the domestic price, the price squeeze due to the high cost of inputs (on average 83 per cent more expensive in the EU than in the CR) that would not allow Czech producers to generate sufficient margin to cover the opportunity cost of domestic resources under current technology.

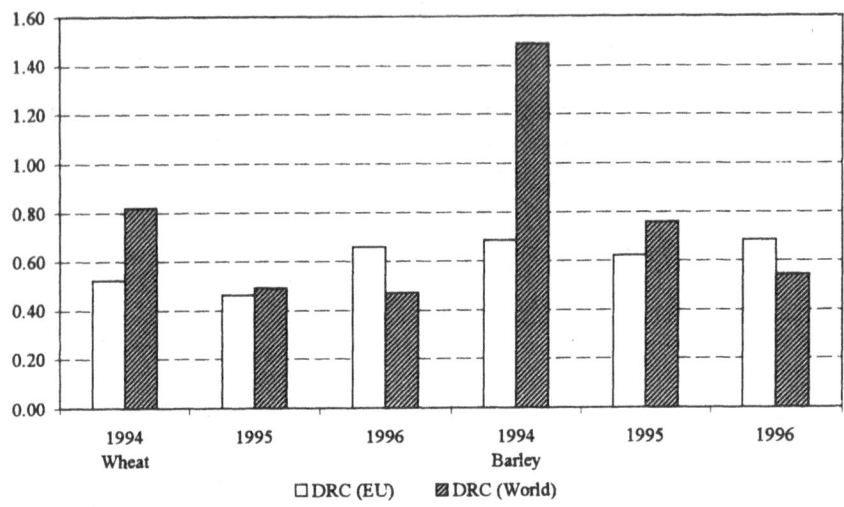

Figure 3.1 Comparative advantage of Czech agricultural production - cereals (OECD prices)

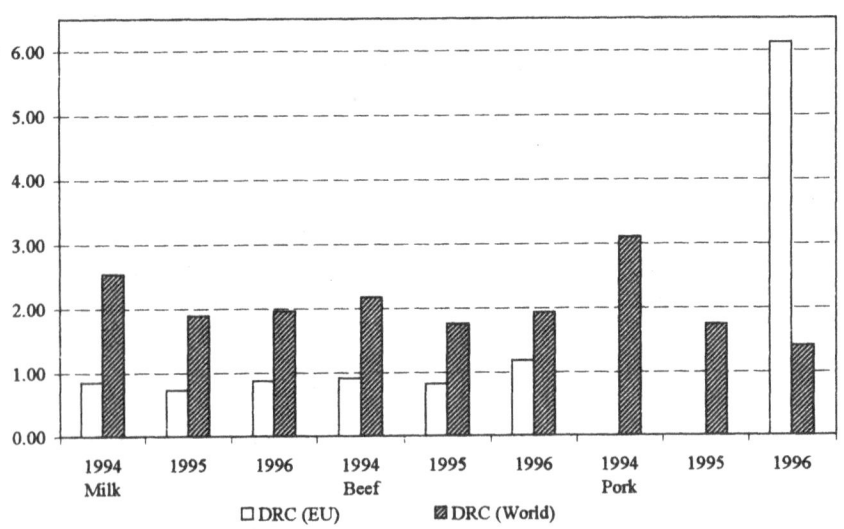

Figure 3.2 Comparative advantage of Czech agricultural production - livestock (OECD prices)

Table 3.1 Comparative advantage and effective protection - cereals, CZK per ton

		Wheat			Barley		
		1994	1995	1996	1994	1995	1996
Cost of tradable		934	965	1 083	982	1 035	1 015
Cost of nontradable		783	666	787	954	814	868
Cost of factors		660	632	805	802	796	867
Domestic Price	OECD	2 648	2 691	3 650	2 393	2 462	3 309
Border Price	OECD – reference price	2 699	3 614	4 478	2 163	3 158	4 208
PSE		16	-1 108	-993	349	-779	-992
EU Price		4 027	4 105	3 877	3 889	3 989	3 905
Input price multiplier	(EU/CR)	1.35	1.35	1.35	1.35	1.35	1.35
Domestic VA (N+F)	non-tradable + factors	1 442	1 298	1 593	1 756	1 610	1 735
Domestic VA	price-tradable	1 713	1 726	2 567	1 412	1 427	2 294
DRC (World)	VA (N+F)	0.82	0.49	0.47	1.49	0.76	0.54
EPR (World)	pse approximation	1.01	0.61	0.72	1.33	0.65	0.70
EU VA	using input price multiplier	2 769	2 805	2 418	2 566	2 595	2 538
DRC (EU)	VA (N+F)	0.52	0.46	0.66	0.68	0.62	0.68
EPC (EU)	VA	0.62	0.62	1.06	0.55	0.55	0.90

Source: Data from Poláčková, 1995, 1996, 1997; Kraus et al. 1997.

Table 3.2 Comparative advantage and effective protection - livestock, CZK per ton

		Milk			Beef			Pork		
		1994	1995	1996	1994	1995	1996	1994	1995	1996
Technical coefficient	LW/DW				1.92	1.92	1.92	1.45	1.45	1.45
Cost of tradable		1 308	1 123	1 404	12 264	10 638	14 252	22 905	24 954	28 130
Cost of nontradable		4 860	4 746	4 852	52 010	49 739	50 636	13 812	10 623	10 665
Cost of factors		2 781	2 284	2 672	17 684	18 641	19 142	7 137	7 700	7 301
Domestic Price	OECD	5 895	6 435	6 847	59 309	64 266	64 956	37 228	40 246	46 205
Border Price	OECD-reference price	4 303	4 934	5 321	44 153	51 634	52 343	29 446	36 654	41 998
PSE		1 890	1 935	2 052	17 974	16 976	17 127	10 774	5 570	6 669
EU Price		10 666	11 101	10 476	96 990	100 948	82 359	38 885	40 472	54 791
Feed price adjustment	World/CR	0.99	1.08	1.06	0.97	1.19	1.14	0.99	1.05	1.04
Input price multiplier	(EU/CR)	1.31	1.31	1.31	1.63	1.63	1.63	1.84	1.84	1.84
Domestic VA (N+F)	non-tradable + factors	7 641	7 030	7 524	69 694	68 380	69 778	20 949	18 323	17 966
Domestic VA	price-tradable	4 587	5 312	5 443	47 045	53 628	50 704	14 323	15 292	18 075
DRC (World)	VA (N+F)	2.54	1.89	1.96	2.16	1.76	1.93	3.10	1.74	1.40
EPR (World)	pse approximation	1.70	1.57	1.61	1.62	1.46	1.51	4.04	1.57	1.58
EU VA	using input price multiplier	8 952	9 629	8 636	77 035	83 638	59 170	-42 213	-5 530	2 934
DRC (EU)	VA (N+F)	0.85	0.73	0.87	0.90	0.82	1.18	'inf	'inf	6.12
EPC (EU)	VA	0.51	0.55	0.63	0.61	0.64	0.86	'inf	'inf	6.16

Source: Data from Poláčková, 1995, 1996, 1997, Kraus et al. 1997.

The revealed comparative advantage methodology was used only for depicting competitiveness between the CR and the EU (table 3.3). The revealed trade pattern confirms the inability of the Czech pig subsector to compete with producers in the EU. The trade data also reveal the competitiveness of the Czech dairy sector with respect to the EU market. This was partly because of the sector's comparative advantage (lower resource cost) but in large extent due to government export support to butter and, consequently, SMP.

Obviously, beef is a much larger share of total EU exports than of Czech exports, but the pattern of bilateral trade is the opposite. This could reflect the effect of relaxing some trade barriers to Czech exporters by the AA. Concerning cereals, trade did not reveal a comparative advantage in wheat production while it did for barley and malt.

Table 3.3 Revealed comparative advantage: EU - CR trade

RCA	Export to the World		Only the CR-EU trade	
Item	1995	1996	1995	1996
Wheat	0.89	0.17	26.33	0.07
Barley & Malt	1 381.02	0.89	219.81	137.31
Dairy products	5.08	5.13	4.53	2.86
Beef	0.35	0.27	1.74	1.56
Pork	0.00	0.02	0.00	0.46

Competitiveness in an Integrated EU Market

After assessing the recent situation, one might raise the question of how Agenda 2000 would affect the competitiveness of Czech agriculture with respect to the EU. Therefore, an extreme scenario supposing a fall in the EU prices to the level of intervention prices proposed by the Agenda was prepared. The scenario includes an assumption that animal feed prices change in the same direction as the change in cereal prices (i.e. they both fall). Other input prices, however, are assumed to remain at 1996 levels. Czech technology and prices are frozen at the level of 1996.

Under this scenario (table 3.4), Czech producers would retain a slight competitive advantage in cereal and milk production. Due to a significant drop in cereal prices in the EU, Czech technology for pig fattening would become competitive. Beef production would deepen its inefficiency.

80 Agriculture and East-West European Integration

Table 3.4 Agenda 2000 Scenario - comparative advantage and effective protection, CZK per ton

		Agenda 2000/ CR 1996					Agenda 2000/ CR with appreciated currency			
		Wheat	Barley	Milk	Beef	Pork	Wheat	Barley	Milk	Beef	Pork
Technical coefficient	LW/DW				1.92	1.45				1.92	1.45
Cost of tradable		1 083	1 015	1 404	14 252	28 130	1 040	975	1 349	13 689	27 019
Cost of nontradable		787	868	4 852	50 636	10 665	837	922	5 155	53 802	11 332
Cost of factors		805	867	2 672	19 142	7 301	727	868	3 933	19 087	6 750
Domestic Price	OECD	3 650	3 309	6 847	64 956	46 205	3 650	3 309	6 847	64 956	46 205
Border Price	OECD-reference price	4 478	4 208	5 321	52 343	41 998	4 301	4 042	5 111	50 276	41 998
PSE		-993	-992	2 052	17 127	6 669					
EU Price		3 286	3 286	9 428	67 197	54 791	3 156	3 156	9 056	64 544	52 628
Input price adjustment	World/CR	1.00	1.00	1.06	1.14	1.04	1.00	1.00	1.02	1.10	1.00
Input price multiplier	(EU/CR)	1.35	1.35	0.93	1.15	1.30	1.29	1.29	0.89	1.10	1.25
Domestic VA (N+F)	non-tradable + factors	1 593	1 735	7 524	69 778	17 966	1 563	1 790	9 088	72 889	18 082
Domestic VA	price-tradable	2 567	2 294	5 443	50 704	18 075	2 610	2 334	5 498	51 267	19 186
DRC (World)	VA (N+F)	0.47	0.54	1.96	1.93	1.40	0.48	0.58	2.43	2.07	1.20
EPR (World)	pse aprox.	0.72	0.70	1.61	1.51	1.58	0.80	0.76	1.46	1.40	1.28
EU VA	using input price muliplier	1 827	1 918	8 129	50 819	18 165	1 811	1 894	7 857	49 433	18 837
DRC (EU)	VA (N+F)	0.87	0.90	0.93	1.37	0.99	0.86	0.94	1.16	1.47	0.96
EPC (EU)	VA	1.40	1.20	0.67	1.00	1.00	1.44	1.23	0.70	1.04	1.02

Source: Vološin, 1997.

If domestic policy kept prices for cereals at the 1996 level, the cereal subsector would experience significant protection. It also indicates that cereal farmers would have net revenue gains from this policy. On the other hand there would be no effective protection of the livestock sector toward the EU market.

Now, we may link our thoughts from the introduction with the concept of comparative advantage and the DRC calculation. Incorporating exchange rates into equation (2) we obtain:

$$DRC_i^{t+1} = \frac{\sum_{j=k+1}^{n} a_{ij} w_j^{t+1}}{e^{t+1}(P_i^{w,t+1} - \sum_{j=1}^{k} a_{ij} w_j^{t+1})} \cong \frac{wx_{(N+F)}}{ex\, PPI_{world}} \frac{\sum_{j=k+1}^{n} a_{ij} w_j^{t}}{e^{t}(P_i^{w,t} - \sum_{j=1}^{k} a_{ij} w_j^{t})}, \quad (10)$$

where world prices are expressed in the foreign currency (e.g. US dollars) and in which e is the exchange rate; ex is the nominal adjustment of the exchange rate; wx is the price index of factors and nontradable inputs; and PPI is the producer price index.

It is obvious that appreciation of the currency (decreasing e) increases the DRC coefficient and, as such, worsens competitiveness. The last part of equation (10) illustrates three processes: a domestic cost increase for nontradables and factors; an increase of prices for tradable goods for the world or other country (the EU); and nominal exchange rate adjustments. If the first fraction is bigger than 1, then the DRC coefficient will increase, which in turn means the subsector is losing its comparative advantage. This exactly illustrates what we are discussing in the following modification of the above scenario.

Judging from the monetary target of the Czech National Bank and the Czech government, the currency should appreciate by 6.5 per cent in real terms by the time of accession (Kraus et al., 1997). It will definitely bring with it a serious change in price patterns. Accordingly the price level of tradable nonagricultural goods (inputs) should decline to 93 per cent of their 1996 base. Prices of nontradable services should increase by 10 per cent and wages by 20 per cent, all in real terms. On the other hand, capital will become cheaper (see first section).

These assumptions are now implemented in the Agenda 2000 scenario (figure 3.3). Evidently, the highly labor intensive cattle breeding sector will be hardest hit by the monetary policy. Also, high protection rates for cereals (leading to higher prices) would contribute to a worsening performance of both the dairy and bull fattening subsectors.

Obviously, cereal producers would be over compensated by prices at 1996 levels. They would not only earn revenue from having a comparative advantage at EU prices, but would also earn substantially more from protective measures.

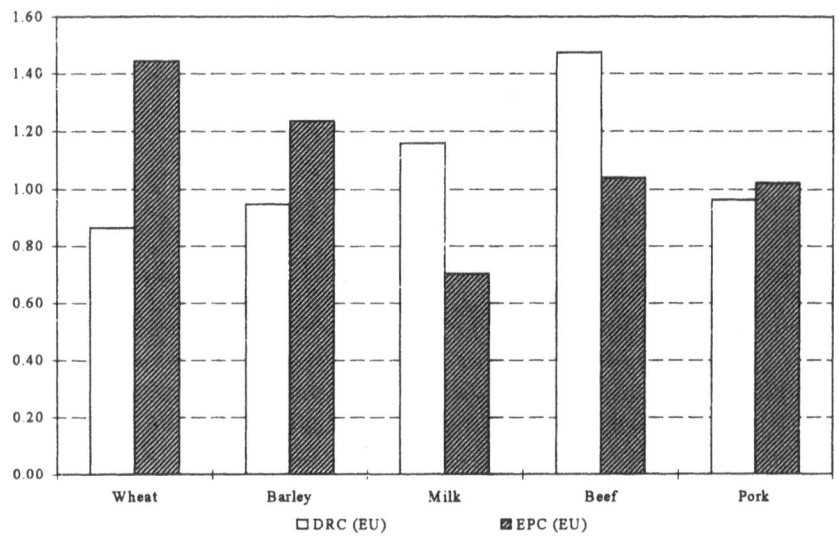

Figure 3.3 Competitiveness of Czech agriculture, the Agenda 2000 Scenario with appreciated national currency

Conclusions

It is largely believed among the agricultural public (as well as the general population) that Czech agriculture has comparative advantage in respect to the EU, mainly because of cheaper resources. However, a simple evaluation of trade under the preferential regime of the AA suggested suspending this belief and investigating the matter more carefully.

This investigation confirmed that the generally large scale Czech farming system has been efficient in the employment of scarce economic resources in cereal production and hence, is competitive at world market prices as well as at current EU prices. On the other hand, the livestock sector has exhibited a comparative disadvantage with respect to the world market. Cattle breeding has already appeared near the threshold of losing competitiveness with respect to producers in the EU and pig production has no chance of survival under the current EU input/output price ratio.

It can be expected that Czech cereal producers will still earn revenue above the compensation of domestic resources if CAP reforms are implemented in the direction proposed by Agenda 2000. This would hold even under progressing national economic reforms and stabilization policies.

Since the cut of cereal prices will relax the input/output squeeze in pig production, Czech breeders will improve their competitive position under Agenda 2000. Surprisingly, it will not help dairy and beef producers. It also can be deduced from our calculations that highly labor-intensive cattle breeding will suffer if the Czech government continues with its current monetary policy.

Except for the pig subsector, current price setting exhibits no effective protection with respect to the EU market. However, this will change under Agenda 2000. Surprisingly, pig producers will get an equivalent margin under Agenda 2000 price setting as under current Czech price policy, while cereal producers would earn less. Given this observation, one may argue that Czech cereal producers would be eligible for compensation payments. However, we should keep in mind that this would result in a net income surplus, since cereals will retain a comparative advantage.

Dairy producers will improve their income when receiving EU price support, even under the Agenda 2000. However, they will face tough competition if the quota system in the EU is abolished.

Notes

1   One can treat general services similarly if they are not considered to be fully decoupled.
2   There might be a problem with the interpretation of effective protection. The common notion is that whenever the value of EPC or RBC is larger than 1, foreign competitors are effectively prevented from penetrating the domestic market, while they would otherwise have access to the market. However, it can happen that the market is effectively protected by a high tariff, but this is not revealed by the coefficients due to the fact that the domestic price is still lower than the price of the other country (or in the extreme case, the world price).

References

Ahner, D. (1997), 'The Future of the CAP, Prospects, Problems, Challenges and First Orientations in Agenda 2000', Working paper, VÚZE, Prague (in Czech).
Balassa, B. (1977), ' "Revealed" Comparative Advantage Revisited: An Analysis of Relative Export Shares of the Industrial Countries, 1953-1971', *Manchester School*, vol. 45, pp. 327-44.
Brent, R.J. (1990), *Project Appraisal for Developing Countries*, Harvester Wheatsheaf, New York.
Buckwell, A., Blom, J., Commins, P., Hervieu, B., Hofreither, M., von Meyer, H., Rabinowicz, E., Sotte, F. and Vina, J.M.S. (1997), 'Towards A Common Agricultural and Rural Policy for Europe', *European Economy*, No. 5, DG for Economic and Financial Affairs, European Commission, 1997.
Bureau, J.C. and Kazlaitzandokanes, N.G. (1995), 'Measuring Effective Protection in European Agriculture', *American Journal of Agricultural Economics*, vol. 77, pp. 279-90.
Corden, W.M. (1974), *Trade Policy and Economic Welfare*, Clarendon Press, Oxford, UK.
European Commission (1995), 'Agricultural Situation and Prospect in the Central and Eastern European Countries: Bulgaria, Czech Republic, Estonia, Hungary, Latvia, Lithuania, Poland, Romania, Slovak Republic, Slovenia, and Summary Report', DG VI, Working document, Brussels.
Freebain, J. (1986), 'Implication of Wages and Industrial Policies on Competitiveness of Agricultural Export Industries', Paper presented at the Australian Agricultural Economic Society Policy Forum, Canberra.
Frohberg, K. and Hartmann, M. (1997), *Comparing measures of competitiveness: Examples for agriculture in the Central European Associates*, OECD, Paris.
Kraus, J. (1997), 'Estimated Impacts of EU Accession for the Czech Republic', Research Report, VÚZE, Prague.
MA CR (1994, 1995, 1996, 1997), *Report on Agriculture*, Ministry of Agriculture of the Czech Republic.
OECD (1997), *Agricultural Policies, Markets and Trade in OECD Countries*, OECD, Paris.
Poláčková (1995), 'Adjusted Results of Cost Survey 1994', Working Paper 25, VÚZE, Prague.
Poláčková (1996), 'Adjusted Results of Cost Survey 1995', Working Paper 38, VÚZE, Prague.
Poláčková (1997), 'Adjusted Results of Cost Survey 1996', Working Paper 46, VÚZE, Prague.
Safin, M. (1995), 'Direct and Indirect Policy Impacts on the Polish Livestock Sector and the Perspective of the Accession to the European Union', Ph.D. thesis, Wye College, University of London.
Vološin, J., Dubovická, Š., Šlaisová, J., Tuček, P. and Vacek, J. (1997), 'Characteristics of Czech Agrarian Trade, Total, with the EU, and in the Frame of European Agreement', Working Paper, VÚZE, Prague (in Czech).

4 The Effect of European Union Accession on Poland's Agricultural Markets and Budgetary Expenditures

WLADYSLAW PISKORZ

Introduction

Knowledge of the scope and nature of the consequences of extending the Common Agricultural Policy (CAP) to Polish agriculture is essential for those who are involved in the negotiation process and for those who would be affected by these changes. More generally, Agenda 2000 and the announcement of the accession negotiations' starting date have increased the interest of the general public in the possible impact of European Union (EU) accession on the Polish agricultural sector.

It is often argued that Poland's accession to the EU could present difficult challenges in the agricultural sector because of the sheer size of Poland's farm population. Expectations of increases in agricultural output in Poland due to increased incentives under the CAP cause fear among farmers of present Member States that there may be market destabilisation and income losses. Farmers in present EU Member States may therefore advocate a long transition period for Polish agriculture. Further, if the budgetary costs of extending the CAP to new Member States will be significant, then current EU taxpayers will pressure for Poland's exclusion from some payments. The extent of possible food price increases after EU accession may also influence support by the general public for integration.

This chapter analyses the effects of Polish accession to the EU for agriculture using simulations with the European Simulation Model (ESIM). Earlier ESIM simulations of the possible effects of EU accession on Poland's agricultural markets focused on the impacts of different levels of nonprice-related yield increases and effects of different dates of accession with differing adjustment periods (SAEPR/FAPA, 1995).

The simulations were based on average data for the years 1991-93, which was, in macroeconomic terms, the most turbulent phase of Poland's transition. Since 1994, major domestic and international economic conditions changed for the agricultural sector: the Polish economy has become more stabilised, up- and downstream markets have become more efficient, and prices on world markets for cereals reached peaks unknown in the last two decades which resulted in an increase of domestic prices. In general terms the market risks of agricultural producers have become more predictable.

Recently, several researchers across Europe have been involved in updating the ESIM. The team from the Agricultural Policy Analysis Unit (SAEPR) was involved in collecting new data sets which allowed a change of the model's base from 1991-93 to 1994-96. Münch and Guba (1997) upgraded and refined the model. The calculations on which this chapter is based were possible thanks to the cooperation of Wolfgang Münch from the University of Göttingen.

Results of the simulations give some understanding of possible implications of present and reformed CAP on agricultural output, farm prices, agricultural net trade, farm revenues, budgetary spending, and consumer food expenditures. The model used for the purpose of this chapter was calibrated with more recent and more accurate data sets. The assumptions concerning exogenous variables were verified by taking into account the nature of the transformation process.

Previous studies which analysed the influence of the CAP on Poland's agriculture were based on the traditional, current CAP which relies on high internal prices and substantial transfers from consumers to farmers. This model of CAP was seen as promising for Poland's farmers due to resultant higher farm prices. For example, Rowinski (1998) argues that the traditional CAP could have a positive, stimulating effect on Polish agriculture and that this policy should be adopted quite quickly.

However, some economists from Western Europe suggested that the higher farm prices would lead to substantial increases of production and contribute to market distortions. It was shown that a substantial part of the costs of extending CAP to Poland's agriculture will be borne by Polish consumers. The basic assumption of this reasoning was that by the time of accession, prices in Poland will be lower than at present in EU. It is often argued that prices paid to farmers in Central and Eastern European countries (CEECs) would increase at the time of EU accession. Consequently farmgate price increases would lead to a strong increase in agricultural production in those countries after they join the EU. This could have a negative impact on EU markets and destabilise farm incomes in the EU and the CEECs. This kind of reasoning should be backed with detailed analytical evidence and price forecasts.

It is expected that the first CEECs to become EU members will do so in 2002-03. It is very difficult to forecast price five to six years in advance. However, it is generally thought that by the time of CEEC accession farm prices may decline, at least in some countries. The price gap between the EU and Poland has already diminished significantly and could disappear or be minimal by the time of accession.

Poland's agriculture is distinguished from EU agriculture in that it is located in a moderate climate zone with much a lower level of production intensity. As a result there are lower yields of grains, sugar beets, and oilseeds and lower productivity by dairy cows. It is understood that the climatic and soil conditions are generally less favourable than in the EU although the agricultural potential is not yet fully utilised. To increase the competitiveness of this sector it is not only necessary to restructure and modernise agriculture but also to increase the intensity of production to a level which is rational in the EU economic environment. Agriculture in Poland may benefit from policy that stimulates growth, but not from policy which leads to stabilisation. Policy measures should not lead to a reduction of production which is currently at a much lower level of intensity compared to the EU.

Research Objectives

This chapter analyses simulation results of two scenarios that extend the CAP to Polish agriculture. Calculations were conducted with the use of ESIM. The model is calibrated to the base period 1994-96 and allows one to make predictions up to the year 2010. It also includes new European Commission proposals included in Agenda 2000 for CAP reform.

The focus of the analysis is the possible effects of policies on Polish agricultural markets. Additional calculations were made to analyse the impact of changes in some exogenous parameters which are needed for simulation (e.g. real exchange rates, technical progress for crop and livestock production, the level of production quotas for sugar and milk).

The core of the analysis consists of three major scenarios:

- Continuation of the current Polish national policies
- Accession without reform of the current CAP
- Accession under a new CAP as outlined in Agenda 2000

Model

Table 4.1 presents macroeconomic assumptions concerning exchange rates, gross domestic product (GDP) growth, population growth, and rates of technical progress for crop and livestock production.

Table 4.1   Nonpolicy scenario assumptions (per cent per annum)

	Base (1994-96) to 1999	2000-02	2002-10
I. Macroeconomic Indicators			
Real exchange rate (USD/PLN)[a]	-0.1	0.8	0.0
Population growth	0.3	0.3	0.3
Income growth	7.0	6.0	5.0
II. Productivity Growth[b] (selected commodities)			
Wheat	1.0	1.0	1.5
Barley	1.0	1.0	1.5
Corn	1.0	1.0	1.5
Other grains (rye, triticale)	1.0	1.0	1.5
Sugar	1.0	1.0	1.5
Rapeseed	1.0	1.0	1.5
Milk	1.0	2.0	2.0
Butter	0.0	0.0	0.0
Cheese	0.0	0.0	0.0
Beef	1.0	1.0	1.0
Pork	1.0	1.0	1.3
Poultry	2.0	3.0	3.0
Eggs	1.0	1.0	1.5

[a] The forecast of exchange rate development is based on results of CGE model simulation made by Martin Banse from University of Göttingen, Germany.
[b] Assumed productivity growth rates are based on historical observations and expert opinions.

ESIM models CAP policies in detail with most of the price and market policy instruments of the current CAP implemented. The ESIM version also attempts to model the headage payments for livestock which are proposed in Agenda 2000 to compensate farmers for decreasing intervention prices.

It was assumed that adjustment to the CAP will take place in one year (2002) and in 2003 Poland would be granted full EU membership. In previous studies it was assumed that adjustment to the CAP will take several years (SAEPR/FAPA, 1995; Münch and Guba, 1997).

As a reference, a scenario without acceding to the EU was calculated. This scenario was calculated with the assumption that the EU will introduce reforms according to proposals in Agenda 2000. Table 4.2 sets out the working assumptions incorporated in the various scenarios.

Scenario Results

Using ESIM, it is possible to predict changes in production, net trade, and market prices for basic agricultural products (grains, oilseeds, milk, beef, pork, poultry meat, and eggs). It is also possible to calculate the level of budgetary expenditures related to export subsidies and direct payments. The results from two accession scenarios are compared with the Nonaccession Scenario.

Production Effects

Table 4.3 presents the main simulation results of the Nonaccession Scenario compared to historic data from the periods 1988-90 and 1994-96. Without EU accession, production of the majority of agricultural commodities increases quite significantly up to the year 2010. The biggest production increases are predicted for rapeseed, milk, and wheat. Beef production will probably not recover to the pretransition level. In the case of sugar, existing quotas will limit output. On average, the projected 2010 agricultural production level in Poland could be close to the pretransition level.

With accession to the EU, the production of grains may not change very much (increasing by not more then 3 per cent) as there will not be large market incentives to boost grain production. On the contrary, EU accession may reduce rapeseed production, especially under the unreformed CAP

Table 4.2 Scenario assumptions for Polish integration

	Nonaccession	Unreformed CAP	Agenda 2000
Real exchange rates (PLN to USD)*	from CGE-Model	from CGE-Model	from CGE-Model
Real income growth	5-7 % p.a.	5-7 % p.a.	5-7 % p.a.
Return to pretransformation production potentials	no	no	no
Technical progress	low rates with slightly higher rates between 2003 to 2010	low rates with slightly higher rates between 2003 to 2010	low rates with slightly higher rates between 2003 to 2010
Polish agricultural policies, 1998-2001	unchanged	unchanged	unchanged
2001-2010	unchanged	changed	changed
Harmonisation of price and trade policy instruments with EU-15, 2002	no	yes	yes
Single Market, 2003	no	yes	yes
Set aside	no	10 %	0 %
Production quotas	sugar quota	sugar and dairy quota	sugar and dairy quota
Compensatory payments	no	compensatory payments for crops and set aside	unified compensatory payments for crops and set aside at 66 ECU/base t
CAP Prices	national Polish prices	as currently defined in EU	administrative prices decrease by: • cereals 20 % • beef 30 % • dairy products 15 %

* calculated by M. Banse.

(by -23 per cent). The oilseeds market in the EU does not enjoy market intervention and prices are close those of the world market. The profitability of sugar production in Poland after EU accession could increase significantly. An increase in production is expected up to the quota assigned to Poland. The level of this quota will be fixed during the accession negotiations. In the calculations, it is assumed that Poland will be granted a quota of 2 million tonnes of white sugar, however the proposed reforms of the CAP do not refer to a sugar regime. In this case, both accession Scenarios are producing the same output of sugar.

Table 4.3   Polish agricultural production in the pretransition period, the base period, and in 2005 (million tonnes)

	1989-90	1994-96	2005 Non-accession	2005 Unreformed CAP	2005 Agenda 2000
Wheat	8.77	8.30	8.91	8.99	9.19
Rye and triticale	14.36	15.95	17.03	17.49	17.51
Rapeseed	1.40	0.86	1.08	0.88	0.98
Sugar	1.85	1.73	1.93	2.00	2.00
Beef	0.78	0.41	0.46	0.50	0.47
Pork	1.87	1.94	2.24	2.33	2.32
Poultry	0.34	0.36	0.45	0.28	0.28
Milk	16.16	11.56	13.49	16.00	16.00
Butter	0.31	0.16	0.19	0.22	0.22

The development of milk production in Poland after EU accession will be crucial for hundreds of thousands of Polish farmers. In Poland there are good natural conditions for milk production. Poland is also a market with a large and relatively stable demand for milk products. Consumers are accustomed to drinking milk and consuming milk products.

In Poland, only 22 dairy cows are held per 100 hectares of agricultural area. This density is 4 times less than in The Netherlands and 50 per cent less than in Germany. The productivity of dairy cows in Poland is very low compared to the EU (3,136 liters per cow per year in Poland; 5,271 liters in the EU). In Poland dairy cows are held in small herds. Around 80 per cent of all dairy farms keep not more than 5 cows and only 2 per cent have more than 20 cows.

In the calculations it was assumed that Poland will be granted a milk quota of 16 million tonnes. EU accession could contribute to significant milk price increases. This will stimulate production which could quickly reach the quota ceiling. With EU accession, milk production in Poland could increase by 18 per cent by 2005 compared with the Nonaccession Scenario.

Beef production in Poland declined rapidly (by more than 50 per cent) during the period 1990-96. Prior to the outbreak of the BSE crisis and before the announcement by the European Commission of proposed beef price cuts, it seemed possible that beef production in Poland would grow quickly after EU accession. However, present calculations do not support this expectation. Accession may not change beef production growth rates very much.

Poland is an important pork producer in Europe. In the EU, only Germany and France are larger producers. Protection of the pork market is less extensive in the EU than for beef or milk. The accession may still give incentives for specialisation when producers in Poland face competition from EU producers. In Poland, pigs are kept in small herds. Traditional farms rely heavily on potatoes as feed. These traditional small farms are not very cost efficient and therefore it is difficult to anticipate that they will successfully compete on EU markets. The calculations show that pig production in Poland may grow quite quickly during coming years which will not change significantly with EU accession. It is expected that the importance of potatoes as feed for pigs will systematically decline.

The demand for pork in Poland is relatively high and is an important component in the diet of consumers (the share of pork reaches 60 per cent of all meat consumed). However, changes in consumer preferences are leading to an increase of poultry meat consumption at the expense of beef and pork.

Poland has good conditions for the development of poultry production as environmental constraints are not a limiting factor. Relatively high and increasing demand for poultry meat (yearly growth rate of poultry meat consumption of 4 to 5 per cent) also provides good prospects for future market development. There are, however, some factors which may limit the growth of this sector: weak vertical integration among producers and processors, underdeveloped standards, and low cost effectiveness. Polish poultry meat and egg producers may face high competitive pressure after EU accession. Since 1994, Polish farmgate prices for poultry meat are higher than in the EU but face very unstable market prices. The feed conversion ratio in poultry production in Poland is 2.2, whereas in the EU it is much lower (2.0), but the scale of broiler production in Poland is relatively low. In most cases, one farm produces 16 to 18 thousand chickens. There is a relatively high labour input and high use of energy for heating and ventilation because buildings are poorly insulated. In the EU this sector is much better vertically integrated than in Poland. In recent years, Poland has made significant progress in terms of the scale of production, quality of feeds utilised, and technological equipment. Without further progress in narrowing the present gap in efficiency between Polish and EU poultry producers, many domestic producers may lose markets after EU accession. Calculations show that poultry meat production may decrease by more than 100 thousand tonnes.

Net Trade Effects

Despite an abundance of land and labour, Poland is forced to import significant amounts of basic agricultural products: grains, oilseeds, poultry meat, etc. The dependence on imports has increased gradually since 1991. Poland ranks fourth among importers of agricultural products from the EU. Consequently, with the exception of sugar, Poland is not applying any export subsidies for agricultural commodities. Poland offered very preferential access for Central European Free Trade Area (CEFTA) agricultural commodities. Thus it is reasonable to expect that in the medium term Poland will remain a small net importer of agricultural products. It is not clear to what extent accession to the EU will change this position.

Regardless of any anticipated agricultural production increase without EU accession, Poland may still be a small net agricultural importer (table 4.4). Food consumption will increase at a rate similar to agricultural output. The results of simulations suggest that EU accession may reduce the amount of wheat imports (by more than 1 million tonnes) and increase exports of rye and triticale (by around 1 million tonnes). Total net trade in grain may not change very much due to EU accession.

Under the Unreformed CAP Scenario, Poland may increase imports of rapeseed. In the case of sugar, a rapid price increase may lower domestic consumption and generate an additional 300 thousand tonnes available for export. This is well above the World Trade Organization (WTO) export subsidy limit for Poland (around 100 thousand tonnes per year).

Table 4.4 Net trade of agricultural products in the pretransition period, the base period, and in 2005 (million tonnes)

	1989-90	Base (1994-96)	2005 Non-accession	2005 Unreformed CAP	2005 Agenda 2000
Wheat	-0.852	-1.085	-2.652	-1.388	-1.461
Rye and triticale	-0.616	-0.538	0.000	0.926	0.954
Rapeseed	0.607	-0.136	0.090	-0.112	-0.012
Sugar	0.058	0.107	0.000	0.310	0.310
Beef	0.006	0.000	0.000	0.099	0.025
Pork	0.027	0.068	0.000	0.033	0.036
Poultry	0.015	-0.042	-0.060	-0.338	-0.327
Milk	-	0.108	0.136	0.167	0.166
Butter	-0.001	0.005	0.011	0.105	0.099

Under the same Scenario, higher domestic beef prices will reduce demand and, despite lower production, exportable surpluses could appear of approximately 99 thousand tonnes. This would also be in excess of WTO limits (of 40 thousand tonnes for all meat). In the Scenario with a reformed CAP, beef export would be much lower.

The net export of pork could gradually increase after EU accession from 33 thousand tonnes in 2005 to 128 thousand tonnes by 2010. Unlike beef and sugar, it is possible to export pork without subsidies.

Under both accession Scenarios, the net export of skimmed milk powder and butter are much higher than under the Nonaccession Scenario. In 2005 the possible net export of skimmed milk powder may exceed WTO commitments by four times. Poland does not have provisions to subsidise butter exports.

Price Effects

Since 1990, agricultural prices have converged between Poland and the EU. The convergence has occurred for all products but with different magnitudes of effect on the price gap. Generally, the price gap has remained substantial for products with higher market protection in the EU (sugar, beef, milk) and has declined substantially for products with more liberal and reformed regimes (grains, oilseeds, pork). Due to differences in marketing margins, the magnitude of agriculture price gaps between Poland and the EU at the farm level may differ slightly from that at the wholesale level.

Price convergence has occurred due to forces acting on both sides. In the case of the EU, the prices of grain and rapeseed have declined due to the implementation of the MacSharry reform. The long term declining trend of beef prices was amplified due to the BSE controversy while, for the same reasons, pork prices have increased. In general, Polish prices have revealed a tendency to increase. In real terms (nominal prices divided by the consumer price index) there have been substantial price increases for grain, white sugar, and rapeseed while animal product prices stabilised or slightly declined. At the same time, all Polish prices have been increasing relative to their trade parity level (proxy for world market prices). The most important factor in the price gap development for 1994-96 is the process of almost constant appreciation of the real exchange rate of the Polish zloty (PLN) to both the US dollar (USD) and the ECU. This macroeconomic effect brought about a significant decrease in the price competitiveness of most Polish agriculture commodities (Münch and Guba, 1997).

Whatever the reasons for the price convergence, the consequences for the integration effects should be significant and should be reflected in the simulation results. A diminishing price gap means that the expected supply response due to the introduction of CAP regimes in Poland will be smaller then estimated in previous (1995) SAEPR simulations.

Table 4.5 presents likely price developments under the various Scenarios. Polish grain producers may expect moderate price increases. The increase may be higher for rye and triticale and smaller for wheat. This would benefit the numerous rye producers in Poland.

Sugar producers will receive very attractive prices after EU accession, but to what extent this price increase will be transferred to sugar beet producers is not yet known.

Polish beef prices may rise by one-third providing that the EU retains its current support level. Accession under a reformed CAP would result in a much less significant beef price increase.

The prices of milk may be very attractive for Polish producers in both accession Scenarios. It is, however not clear to what extent small milk producers will be able to meet high EU quality standards.

By 1994, producer prices for poultry meat in Poland already exceeded EU prices. By time of accession, this gap may remain. This will put domestic producers under tough competitive pressure from EU producers.

In addition, domestic demand for poultry meat will grow faster than domestic production resulting in greater imports.

Table 4.5   Market prices of agricultural products in the pretransition period, the base period, and in 2005 (PLN/tonne)

	1989-90	Base (1994-96)	2005 Non-accession	2005 Unreformed CAP	2005 Agenda 2000
Wheat	86	421	385	439	421
Rye and triticale	64	375	342	414	392
Rapeseed	123	894	968	783	773
Sugar	174	1 556	1 563	2 423	2 423
Beef	1 224	6 189	7 097	9 469	7 475
Pork	1 187	4 777	5 190	4 811	4 781
Poultry meat	1 044	5 291	5 555	3 848	3 830
Milk	63	624	639	1 238	1 104
Butter	1 201	4 858	4 969	13 380	11 949

Revenue Effects

Table 4.6 depicts estimates of Polish farm receipts under different accession Scenarios. Polish farmers may expect higher revenues from milk, beef, sugar, and grains but may also experience a reduction of receipts from rapeseed (mainly due to price reductions), poultry meat, and eggs. Receipts from pork sales may not change significantly. Changes in receipts result from changes in the predicted level of production and market prices. Under Agenda 2000 proposals, Polish beef producers should not expect any significant change in market receipts from EU accession.

Direct payments may be a major part of future revenues of Polish grain, beef, and milk producers. The share of those payments in total financial receipts may vary between 10 and 18 per cent (depending on the type of CAP implemented).

Table 4.6 Estimates of farm receipts under different accession scenarios (million ECU)

	Non-accession	Unreformed CAP	Agenda 2000
Sales receipts			
1. Grains	860	1 338	1 213
2. Oilseeds	275	182	200
3. Sugar	797	1 280	1 280
4. Milk	2 145	5 101	4 537
5. Beef	871	1 249	920
6. Pork	3 068	2 963	2 935
7. Poultry	656	283	281
8. Eggs	385	256	254
Total 1-8	9 056	12 652	11 621
9. Oilseed meal used for feed	-270	-322	-312
Receipts from sales net	8 787	12 330	11 310
Receipts from direct payments	0	1 374	2 544
Total receipts	8 787	13 704	13 854

Budgetary Effects

In ESIM it is possible to calculate only part of the budgetary expenditures for CAP. Budgetary spending is calculated as net budget expenditures; i.e. taking revenues from border measures directly into account. Also explicitly calculated are net export refunds and compensatory payments for area, two costly instruments in the current CAP. In reality, CAP includes additional factors which are not accounted for in ESIM calculations, i.e. storage and administration. Moreover, costly products are not included in ESIM such as fruits and vegetables, wine, and silkworms, to name a prominent few.

Budgetary expenditures represent taxpayer costs for market guarantees, i.e. for all market and price policies. During simulations of the Nonaccession Scenario, market guarantee costs are slightly negative, simply reflecting the fact that Poland is a net importing country for agricultural products (table 4.7). This changes in the simulations of accession: for some products, notably beef, dairy, sugar, and coarse grains, net exports increase and with them subsidies needed to sell these surpluses on world markets. Other costly instruments are introduced in 2003, i.e. compensatory payments for area, headage payments, and a milk premium.

The budgetary spending for Poland's accession, which is calculated by ESIM, would amount to around 1.9 billion ECU in 2005 in the Unreformed CAP Scenario. Compensatory payments amount to nearly two-thirds of total spending. Although market price support is lowered in Agenda 2000, expenditure increases to 3.3 billion ECU in 2005. In this Scenario, around one-third of the budget would be spent on beef and milk premiums.

The total of Poland's Aggregate Measure of Support (AMS) commitments for the year 2000 in WTO are set at 3 329 million USD. For 1996, the realised AMS for Poland was far below the limit at 226.5 million USD. Since ESIM does not cover all commodities included in the calculation of AMS, it is not possible to precisely predict the future level of the AMS. However, accession to the EU will significantly increase the AMS. The biggest increase may be expected in the AMS for sugar, dairy products, and grains. Under the Agenda 2000 Scenario, the prices of pork, poultry, and beef will be at the world market level by the year 2005. Hence, the AMS would equal zero for those products. The estimates, although incomplete, are an indication that Poland may exceed the allowed WTO AMS limit after accession. The extent to which this limit is exceeded depends on the progress of CAP reform.

Table 4.7 Budgetary costs of different accession scenarios

Expenditures for:	1994-96 (Base period)	2005 Non-accession	2005 Unreformed CAP	2005 Agenda 2000
Plant production	-63	-53	1 413	1 679
Animal production	-37	-21	537	1 531
Compensatory payments for crop products	0	0	1 374	1 641
Export subsidies for crop products	-63	-53	39	38
Export subsidies for animal products	-37	-21	537	371
Milk and beef premium	0	0	0	904
Total budgetary spending	-100	-74	1 949	3 210

Overall Evaluation of Simulation Results

Sensitivity Analysis

The simulation results depend to some extend on assumed parameters: productivity growth rates, consumers, income growth rates, exchange rates of PLN to ECU, feed conversion rates, etc. A sensitivity analysis was conducted in order to evaluate to what extent the level of those parameters influences the simulation results. Sensitivity analysis involves changing one parameter while leaving all others unchanged. The results are presented in tables 4.8 and 4.9.

Table 4.8 The impact of a 30 per cent increase in productivity of Polish agriculture on simulation results for the year 2005 (compared to scenario with zero productivity change)

	Production Prices		Farmers' receipts		Budgetary spending (mill. ECU)	Net exports (mill. tonnes)
	Poland (%)	EU (%)	Poland (mill. ECU)	EU (mill. ECU)		
Wheat	23.1	-0.3	399	-40	0	-
Rye and triticale	23.1	-0.2	497	-1	0	2.77
Rapeseed	22.9	-0.4	66	-11	-1	0.03
Milk	13.8	-	730	-	55	0.03
Beef	23.0	-0.4	318	-85	-8	0.13
Pork	22.6	-0.9	970	-273	-	0.62
Poultry	23.5	-0.3	84	-26	-	0.07
Eggs	23.3	-0.3	89	-18	-	-
Total	-	-	3 152	-454	47	-

Poland is seen as a country with great agricultural potential which is not yet fully utilised. Farmers in the EU fear that this potential may be exploited to a greater extent if Polish farmers receive higher prices. It is suggested that this may lead to serious market distortions and reduce incomes of EU farmers. The calculations show that those fears may not be justified. Extension of the CAP to Polish farmers may reduce EU farm revenue by only 70-80 million ECU. In order to estimate the importance of productivity changes in Polish agriculture, a scenario with a 30 per cent

100 *Agriculture and East-West European Integration*

increase of productivity was compared to a scenario with no productivity change. This increase in productivity could contribute to high increases in agricultural output. Results show that a 30 per cent increase of productivity could increase farm receipts by 3.15 billion ECU. Surprisingly, significant increases in productivity and agricultural output may have a very small impact on EU agricultural prices (reduced by not more than 0.9 per cent).

The exchange rate of PLN to the ECU has important impacts on the EU accession Scenario results. A 10 percentage point appreciation of the PLN against the ECU may reduce Polish farm receipts by 454 million ECU. It could also reduce farm prices and budgetary spending.

Table 4.9 **The impact of a 10 per cent PLN appreciation rate on simulation results for the year 2005 (compared to scenario with zero appreciation rate)**

| | Production prices | | Farmers' receipts | | Budgetary spending | Net exports |
	Poland (%)	EU (%)	Poland (mill. ECU)	EU (mill. ECU)	(mill. ECU)	(mill. tonnes)
Wheat	-1.5	0.0	-35	5	-13	-
Rye and triticale	-1.0	0.0	-36	-1	-18	-0.06
Rapeseed	-2.5	0.1	-9	3	-4	-0.01
Milk	-2.9	-	-176	-	-61	-0.01
Beef	-2.7	0.1	-37	16	-7	-0.02
Pork	-4.0	0.2	-134	72	0	-0.16
Poultry	-4.1	0.1	-13	10	-	-0.03
Eggs	-4.1	0.1	-12	5	-	-
Total	-	-	-454	110	-103	-

Effects on Food Demand and Consumer Expenditures

The application of CAP instruments to Polish agriculture may influence the cost of food for consumers. This could lead to a decrease of consumption of those food items which become more expensive. Figure 4.1 displays the scope of probable changes in total consumption of basic foods in Poland in 2005 under different Scenarios. Notice that the introduction of the CAP could significantly reduce consumption of cheese, butter, and beef and increase the consumption of poultry, eggs, and pork. Reform of the CAP according to Agenda 2000 could contribute to the increase of poultry and pork consumption.

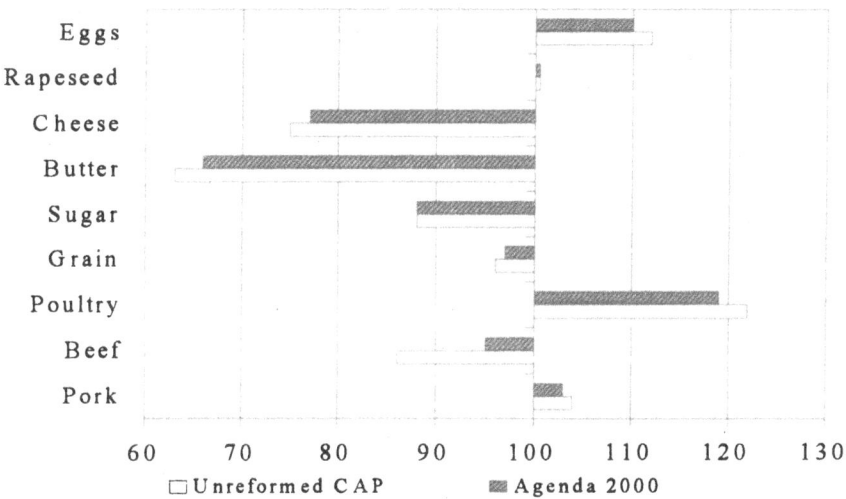

Figure 4.1 Differences in the level of human consumption of agricultural products in 2005 under CAP Scenarios

The model does not include all major food products and does not calculate the prices paid by consumers. Nevertheless it is possible to estimate the scope of changes in consumer expenditures on food by multiplying food demand through respective market prices. Changes in market prices due to the introduction of different policy options would change the quantity consumed of different food products. The model helps to reveal the scope of those changes.

In order to quantify the impact of food price changes on food expenditures, the calculated food prices in all three Scenarios were multiplied by predicted quantities consumed in the Nonaccession Scenario (figure 4.2). In order to keep basic food consumption at the level of the Nonaccession Scenario, Polish consumers will have to spend an additional 827 million ECU under the unreformed CAP. On the other hand, they could potentially save 1,142 million ECU under an Agenda 2000-reformed CAP. The biggest savings would occur in the case of pork, poultry, beef, and grain products.

102 *Agriculture and East-West European Integration*

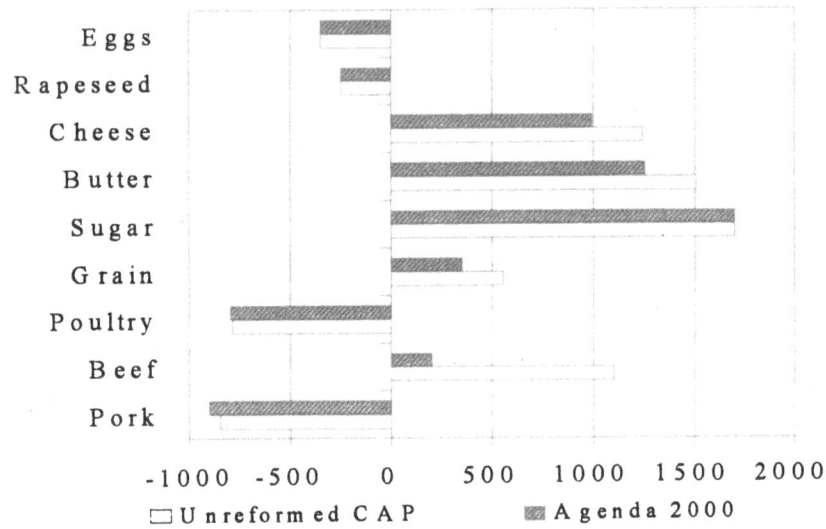

Figure 4.2 Differences in consumer expenditures for agricultural products in 2005 under different CAP Scenarios (compared to Nonaccession Scenario)

Evaluation of Effects of Planned CAP Reform on Poland's Agriculture

Tables 4.10 through 4.12 present comparisons of the simulation results. These figures suggest that CAP reform may be neutral in financial terms for Polish agriculture (provided that they will receive the same treatment as farmers in present EU Member States). The reform could stimulate growth of rapeseed production and reduce production of beef.

Conclusions

Estimates of the impacts of integrating Polish agriculture with the EU are based on specific assumptions concerning the CAP, productivity changes, exchange rates, etc. Changes in one or all of those parameters may substantially change the estimated results. Because of these limitations, this study should be treated as an approach to identify the challenges of integration rather than to precisely quantify the costs and benefits of integration.

The calculations have revealed potentially serious changes in the level of prices for several agricultural products upon integration with the EU. This is a result of the existing considerable price differential between Poland and the EU. Each of the integration Scenarios provides for radical changes in the level of prices for numerous agricultural products (sugar, milk, and butter).

The simulation results do not confirm fears concerning a potentially substantial growth of agricultural output in Poland following the application of CAP mechanisms. However, there will be a certain increase in the output of products which enjoy greatest support under CAP (e.g. milk, sugar).

A marked increase of milk prices will not generate a rapid growth of output because of milk quotas in the EU. The quota arrangements will probably remain in place at the time of Poland's joining the EU.

Table 4.10 Impact on agriculture of Poland's EU accession under an unreformed CAP (compared to Nonaccession Scenario)

	Production in Poland (%)	Prices in Poland (%)	Farmers' receipts Poland (mill. ECU)	Farmers' receipts EU (mill. ECU)	Budgetary spending (mill. ECU)	Net exports (mill. tonnes)
Wheat	1.4	0.1	559	-25	447	-
Rye and triticale	2.7	-2.8	1 334	-79	931	1.21
Rapeseed	-23.1	0.8	4	22	123	0.09
Milk	15.7	-	3 747	-	593	0.08
Beef	6.8	-	473	-7	65	0.10
Pork	5.0	0.0	-96	-67	0	0.06
Poultry	-68.9	0.7	-549	69	23	-0.31
Eggs	-19.9	0.4	-170	17	-	-
Total	-	-	5 302	-71	2 182	-

Table 4.11 Simulated results for year 2005 for Polish agriculture, accession with an Agenda 2000-reformed CAP (compared to Nonaccession Scenario)

	Production in Poland (%)	Prices in Poland (%)	Farmers' receipts Poland (mill. ECU)	Farmers' receipts EU (mill. ECU)	Budgetary spending (mill. ECU)	Net exports (mill. tonnes)
Wheat	3.3	0.1	640	-55	515	-
Rye and triticale	4.2	-0.1	1 469	-14	1 084	1.40
Rapeseed	-11.1	0.7	36	12	127	0.09
Milk	15.2	-	3 692	-	1 251	0.08
Beef	0.7	0.0	405	-31	320	0.03
Pork	4.4	0.1	-113	-74	0	0.06
Poultry	-63.4	0.7	-483	62	36	-0.27
Eggs	-20.6	0.4	-172	15	-	-
Total	-	-	5 474	-85	3 332	35.6

Table 4.12 Simulated results for year 2005 for Polish agriculture, accession with an Agenda 2000-reformed CAP (compared to Unreformed CAP Scenario)

	Production in Poland (%)	Prices in Poland (%)	Farmers' receipts Poland (mill. ECU)	Farmers' receipts EU (mill. ECU)	Budgetary spending (mill. ECU)	Net exports (mill. tonnes)
Wheat	2.0	-1.3	82	1 480	1 057	-
Rye and triticale	1.5	-2.2	131	301	360	0.21
Rapeseed	8.6	-1.5	22	116	60	-0.01
Milk	-0.6	-12.1	-55	1 906	5 629	0.00
Beef	-6.7	-25.2	-73	-1 208	5 068	-0.07
Pork	-0.4	-0.8	-44	117	-	0.00
Poultry	0.1	-0.5	-1	48	-	0.01
Eggs	0.0	-0.5	-2	46	-	-
Total	-	-	61	2 807	12 174	-

References

Münch, W. and Guba W. (1997), 'Poland's Accession to the EU. Market Effects and Budgetary Costs Revisited', December 1997, Institute of Agricultural Economics University of Göttingen, Germany.

Rowinski, J. (1998), 'Proposed changes in Common Agricultural Policy in the years 2000-2006 and their influence on Poland's agri-food sector', Manuscript, Warsaw, (in Polish).

SAEPR/FAPA (1995), 'Scenarios for Integration of Polish Agriculture with European Union', Materials and reports, Warsaw.

5 Slovenia's Accession to the European Union: Implications for the Agricultural Sector

ŠTEFAN BOJNEC AND WOLFGANG MÜNCH

Introduction

The European Commission named and the European Council approved five Central and Eastern European countries (CEECs) for the first round of eastward European Union (EU) accession: the Czech Republic, Estonia, Hungary, Poland, and Slovenia (European Commission, 1997).[1] In April 1998, the first EU accession negotiations began.

Slovenia has a long history of regional trade agreements with the EU as a part of the former Yugoslav republics in the 1970s and the 1980s. With more than two-thirds of the total Slovene trade in goods, the EU is already the most important trading partner of Slovenia. Hence, for economic and other reasons the goal of joining the EU remains of greatest policy importance compared to any other development option (Stanovnik and Svetlicic, 1996).

This chapter evaluates the broader implications of Slovene agricultural accession to the Common Agricultural Policy (CAP) both for the EU budget and Slovene agriculture. The main characteristics and elements of the Slovene agricultural policy vis-à-vis the EU are described to illustrate the similarities and differences. In particular, the chapter focuses on the implications of Slovenian agriculture accession to the EU by using the European Simulation Model (ESIM). The results are presented under different policy scenarios to reflect the ongoing discussion on the shape of the future CAP within the EU countries. Moreover, the paper clarifies and answers the broader questions at the core of policy and public interests such as implications for domestic production, prices, exports, and imports.

The chapter is structured in the following way. The next section analyses agricultural and food market structures and their developments. In the third section, an overview of the agricultural market and trade policies, highlighting implications for agricultural market support, is given.

In the fourth section, the level of agricultural prices and protection in Slovenia is compared with that in the EU and with selected CEECs. In the fifth section, the ESIM model is applied to evaluate implications of Slovenian agricultural price and trade policy adjustment to the CAP of the EU. Finally, section six consists of policy conclusions arguing that Slovene agriculture should be ready not only to join the CAP of the EU, but also be ready to compete in production, processing, and marketing of agricultural and food products on the Single European Market (SEM).

Market Structures and Market Developments

Compared to the CEECs, Slovenia is relatively small with respect to population, size of the agricultural sector, and agricultural area (table 5.1). Also, Slovenia has a high income per capita and a modest share of agriculture's contribution to the gross domestic product (GDP). Agricultural production is mainly located in less favorable areas due to the hilly and mountainous landscape. Slovenia's farm structure traditionally consists of small scale private farms which explains the relatively high share of employment compared to agriculture's contribution to the GDP. Productivity in agriculture is considerably lower than in the rest of the economy. This is caused by the difficult natural conditions, the small size of traditional private farms, and the generally low quality labour engaged in agriculture.

Traditionally, agriculture is viewed as a sensitive sector. Political pressure by the farm lobby to protect domestic production has been strong. Consequently, agricultural markets and policies have never been liberalised to the same extent as in, for example, Poland or Estonia, resulting in Slovenia's farmgate prices being higher than in other CEECs, approaching EU price levels, even, in some cases (e.g. for wheat), exceeding EU levels. Introducing the protective CAP tools during accession is considered an appropriate policy option for the country's integration and hence for future agricultural development in a more open regional environment (e.g. Erjavec et al, 1997).

The small scale farm structure and the unfavorable natural conditions for agricultural production lead to special importance of livestock products with milk as a predominant product. During the 1990s, there were surpluses in milk, poultry, hops, and eggs, while potatoes, fruit, and wine were close to domestic needs (MAFF, 1996b). Except for meat preparations, beverages, and the commodity group of dairy products,

Slovenia is a net importer of food and agricultural products (table 5.2). The regional trade structure shows that about 52 per cent of agricultural and food imports originated from the EU, while only 27 per cent of Slovenia's exports flow to that destination. Prior to Slovene independence in 1991, extensive interrepublican trade relations developed within the former Yugoslavia which still maintain their role in exports (57 per cent).

Prior to transition, domestic markets were characterised by highly vertically integrated systems (i.e. linking private farms, cooperatives, processors, and traders). Farm surpluses were largely traded through the state-organised purchasing system (table 5.3). Private farms sold their agricultural products to local agricultural cooperatives, usually on the basis of contracts. State farms largely sold directly to regional food processing and trade organisations. The agricultural marketing system, processing, and trade were maintained by the state monopolistic organisations.

At the end of the 1980s, restructuring, demonopolisation, and privatisation policies were introduced to contribute to more efficient and competitive market developments. However, a very cautious privatisation and demonopolisation have left important areas of the food processing sector and trade of agricultural products highly concentrated (e.g. sugar, oilseeds, cereals). As a result, new marketing channels, market structures, and economic agents have slowly become involved in the marketing of agricultural and food products.

Although the local peasant markets and the free markets in the cities existed in the past, the quantities traded in these places were relatively small. The importance of free markets in cities did not increase substantially after market and trade liberalisation and their role differs by commodities (i.e. generally vegetables and fruits are more commonly traded on them than are staple foods).

Yet, private companies specialising in trading activities were set up and these compete with the inherited marketing system. Cautiously, this could be interpreted as a sign of the new pattern of the wholesale marketing as it has already occurred in other CEECs.

Transformed and privatised, former procurement chains keep their role in markets which are supported by state policies (e.g. wheat, sugar beet, and milk) or where alternative opportunities for selling were restricted by food quality and food control requirements (e.g. for meats).

110 *Agriculture and East-West European Integration*

Table 5.1 Social, economic and agricultural indicators for CEECs in comparison with EU-15

	Population 1993 (millions)	Territory 1993 (million ha)	Agricultural area 1993 (million ha)	Share of agricultural area 1993 (%)	GDP 1993 (billion ECU)	GDP per capita 1993 (ECU)	Agriculture in GDP 1994 (%)	Agriculture in employment 1994 (%)	Household income spent on food 1994 (%)
EU-15	369.7	323.4	138.1	43	5,905.1	15,972	2.5*	5.7*	22.0*
Total CEEC-10	105.5	107.7	60.6	56	188.3	1,786	7.8*	26.7*	-
Baltic Countries	7.9	17.5	7.4	43	6.0	757	-	-	-
Estonia	1.6	4.5	1.4	31	1.5	938	8.0	8.0	32.0
Latvia	2.6	6.5	2.5	39	2.2	850	8.5	16.9	41.6
Lithuania	3.8	6.5	3.5	54	2.3	627	7.5	23.3	57.3
CEFTA-5	66.4	55.4	32.3	58	151.1	2,277	5.0*	22.1*	-
Czech Republic	10.3	7.9	4.3	54	26.7	2,586	3.1	5.1	31.5
Slovakia	5.3	4.9	2.4	49	8.7	1,643	7.4	8.4	38.0
Hungary	10.3	9.3	6.1	66	32.5	3,150	6.4	6.5	22.3
Poland	38.5	31.3	18.6	59	73.4	1,907	6.0	25.4	33.0
Slovenia	1.9	2.0	0.9	43	9.8	5,018	4.5	10.7	25.2
Bulgaria	8.5	11.1	6.2	55	9.4	1,110	11.0	21.7	39.0
Romania	22.7	23.8	14.7	62	21.8	961	22.0	36.3	60.0

* 1993 data

Source: EU Commission, 1995; OECD, 1996.

Slovenia's Accession to the EU: Implications for the Agricultural Sector   111

Table 5.2 Slovene exports and imports of food and agricultural products, 1995 (million USD)

	Exports					Imports				
	Total Value	Structure (%)				Total Value	Structure (%)			
		EU	CEFTA	Ex-YU*	Other		EU	CEFTA	Ex-YU*	Others
01 Live animals	1.8	75	0.5	24	0.5	25.2	34	66	0	0
02 Meat and edible meat offal	36.9	39	0	59	2	66.5	47	47	3	3
03 Fish and fish products	0.9	38	0	55	7	16.0	48	0	17	35
04 Dairy products, eggs, honey	37.2	19	6	73	2	10.9	55	2	31	12
05 Products of animal origin	0.6	75	4	21	0	5.3	50	2	2	46
06 Trees and other plants	0.6	60	10	29	1	25.8	97	1	1	1
07 Edible vegetables	7.6	69	12	16	3	56.4	70	12	7	11
08 Edible fruits and nuts	9.2	39	7	51	3	60.6	53	3	7	37
09 Coffee, tea, spices	3.5	6	2	83	9	35.5	16	2	3	79
10 Cereals	0.9	29	0	71	0	52.5	9	52	18	21
11 Products of the milling industry	1.6	3	0	96	1	21.1	65	31	2	2
12 Oilseeds and oleaginous fruits	23.0	63	9	16	12	13.4	56	20	12	12
13 Lac, gums, resins, saps, extracts	0.9	64	1	12	23	3.5	88	1	5	6
14 Vegetable materials	0.0	0	0	0	0	0.2	33	0	6	61
15 Animal and vegetable fats and oils	7.4	30	0	65	5	48.8	50	30	8	12
16 Preparations of meat and of fish	46.9	14	2	80	4	18.6	55	6	31	8
17 Sugar and sugar confectionery	18.5	29	4	38	29	41.1	68	3	5	24
18 Cocoa and cocoa preparations	4.1	27	6	53	14	38.7	81	1	13	5
19 Cereals, flour, starch, and other preparations	12.2	5	6	58	31	41.4	59	1	38	2
20 Vegetables, fruit, and nuts preparations	24.1	26	5	51	18	40.4	63	4	14	19
21 Miscellaneous edible preparations	27.3	1	8	85	6	55.8	68	0	27	5
22 Beverages, spirits, and vinegars	42.5	21	4	54	21	40.2	56	2	33	9
23 Waste from the food industry	12.2	39	0	23	38	51.1	39	6	3	52
24 Tobacco	9.5	48	0	40	12	24.8	15	0	17	68
Total	329.4	27	4	57	12	793.8	52	15	13	20

* Former Yugoslav Republics

Source: Statistical Office of the Republic of Slovenia.

112 *Agriculture and East-West European Integration*

Table 5.3 Production and marketing channels of agricultural products

	Production (average per year in thousand tons)			Production procured by state and cooperatives (%)			Share of production marketed on the free markets (%)			Share of other (%)		
	1981-85	1986-90	1991-95	1981-85	1986-90	1991-95	1981-85	1986-90	1991-95	1981-85	1986-90	1991-95
Wheat	154.8	167.3	177.2	33.2	46.4	47.2	0.02	0.03	0.04	66.8	53.6	52.8
Barley	20.1	21.6	33.5	6.0	8.8	8.4	-	-	-	94.0	91.2	91.6
Maize	277.7	312.9	284.5	7.5	13.7	13.0	0.02	0.01	0.02	92.5	86.3	87.0
Hops	3.9	3.7	3.5	79.5	73.0	70.0	-	-	-	20.5	27.0	30.0
Rape oil	2.0	5.2	4.1	61.5	80.8	88.0	-	-	-	38.5	19.2	12.0
Sunflower seed	0.4	0.5	0.2	0.3	0.2	-	-	-	-	99.7	99.8	-
Sugar beet	170.3	158.5	176.4	91.5	99.4	94.2	-	-	-	8.5	0.6	5.8
Potatoes	462.2	400.4	402.0	10.3	9.8	4.3	0.2	0.4	0.3	89.5	89.8	89.9
Apples	80.2	83.6	94.2	49.3	46.9	36.0	2.4	2.4	1.2	48.3	50.7	62.8
Grapes	91.7	100.8	121.3	35.9	26.9	16.5	0.5	0.7	0.2	63.6	72.4	83.3
Wine	48.5	51.3	62.5	30.7	26.9	24.5	-	-	-	69.3	73.1	75.5
Milk[a]	542.4	587.3	573.9	59.1	61.7	63.0	0.1	0.1	0.1	40.8	38.2	36.9
Eggs[b]	376.0	411.8	360.2	36.2	38.4	43.1	1.9	1.5	1.6	61.9	60.1	55.3
Cattle[c]	76.0	81.8	82.0	76.8	60.0	47.0	-	-	-	23.2	40.0	53.0
Pigs[c]	51.4	61.1	76.0	69.3	65.3	53.0	-	-	-	30.7	34.7	47.0
Poultry[c]	84.7	100.1	75.2	92.0	95.1	95.5	0.4	0.4	0.3	7.6	4.5	4.2

[a] Without dairy products
[b] In million pieces
[c] Live weight

Source: Statistical Yearbook of Slovenia, various issues; Statistical Bulletin of Slovenia - Survey of the Results, various issues.

Cereals

Wheat is a key product among cereals in Slovene agriculture in terms of agricultural policy support and state intervention. The directly marketed share of wheat has increased as a consequence of a relatively high wheat price and wheat purchases guaranteed by the state during the harvest season.

Slovenia is a net importer of maize and barley and a large amount is used as a forage for livestock. During the 1990s the price of barley was above world market levels.

Industrial Crops

Sugar beet production was largely introduced in crop production at the end of the 1970s when the country's sole sugar refinery started operation. Initial sugar beet production was imposed on regional producers by political campaigns and pressures from above via production plans. However, political pressures relaxed afterwards as production plans were mostly replaced by the stronger economic incentives of higher sugar beet prices and subsidies for purchased inputs for sugar beet production. As a result of such policies, sugar beet production has expanded substantially due to both larger area and higher yields. This contributed to the higher capacity utilisation of the sugar refinery which was the policy aim. Losses by the state-owned factory were covered by the government budget, which facilitated the two tier price system of high beet prices and relatively low sugar prices. The sugar factory was recently privatised which will likely restrict such cross-subsidies in future.

Sunflower and rapeseed production are relatively low in comparison to the domestic need. Hence, a substantial amount of vegetable oils or oilseeds for processing are imported. In the 1970s, the goal of achieving regional self-sufficiency resulted in duplication of processing facilities. As a consequence, regional large scale oil processing facilities were built based mainly on imports of oilseeds and raw vegetable oils from other parts of the former Yugoslavia for processing into refined vegetable oils for domestic needs. The relatively small amount of domestic rapeseed production in comparison to domestic need was mainly produced by the former large scale 'social' farms. This production was subsidised by a state support mechanism similar to that which was developed for sugar beet production. However, since 1994, the state has not been directly involved in supporting rapeseed production. Hence, domestic rape oil production has declined as a consequence of this government deregulation and as a result of a combination of factors in connection with land restitution and the vegetable oil company privatisation.

It is worth mentioning that the majority of hop production is exported. Hence, hop producers have traditionally been largely integrated into the world markets. Moreover, domestic hop prices are determined by world market prices on the basis of export price taking into consideration additional processing, marketing, export handling, and transport costs to the border.

Potatoes, Vegetables, and Fruits

Production of horticultural products is usually considered to be market driven. Hence, in absence of special government intervention and support, they are often excluded from simulations and calculations of the effects of EU enlargement towards the east (as in this study). This does not mean that these products are not important, but only that their prices are close to world market prices; hence there is no expectation of a significant production response and income redistribution from policy changes after accession. Furthermore, CEEC agriculture is mainly driven by cereals, oilseeds, livestock, and dairy products and hence it is assumed that the major impacts of accession would be seen in these sectors.

Traditionally, except for seed potato production, the majority of potatoes in Slovenia have been produced by small scale private farms. The domestic production has balanced domestic needs, while quantities exported/imported fluctuated as a result of area fluctuations and adverse weather conditions affecting the yields. Moreover, a large part of domestic potato production was used for feed for pigs, thus the traded share from private farms was substantially determined by potato prices which fluctuated cyclically around the border price.

Vegetables are produced both in private household plots and by specialised commercial producers. Domestic vegetable production covers domestic needs during the season, while the substantial need for fresh vegetables over the winter period is covered by imports.

Production of continental fruits (e.g. apples, pears, peaches) covers domestic needs. Moreover, apples may be considered a net export as in most years there has been surplus production.

Grapes and Wine

A major share of grape production in Slovenia consists of grapes for high quality wine production. The area planted with vineyards has remained constant since the midcentury, but there is recent evidence of a slight increase.

The wine industry in Slovenia has developed for both former Yugoslav markets and Western European markets based on provisions stipulated by trade and cooperation agreements. Moreover, the Slovene wine cellars developed production cooperation and joint ventures during the 1970s and 1980s on a 'self-management' basis with grape and wine producers in economically less developed regions of the former Yugoslavia. Slovene wine makers developed skills and capacities for high quality wine making, marketing, export handling, and marketing promotion. Hence, Slovene wine producers and traders were involved in trade and marketing of domestic wine and also for producers from other parts of the former Yugoslavia.

Wine trade between Slovenia and the EU is arranged by a special wine agreement, including mutual preferential trade concessions.

Milk, Dairy, and the Cattle Sector

Milk is the most important agricultural product in Slovenia with significant economic and social dimensions for small scale private farmers. A surplus of milk production continues. In the past, the surplus of milk was mainly processed into cheese and milk powder to be sold in tourist towns during the summer season. The former Yugoslav markets are still important for exports of milk and dairy products. However, their role has deteriorated since independence and efforts have been made towards exports in other markets.

Dairy and cattle sector development have been closely connected. Small scale private farms usually combined milk and cattle production based on home-produced forage consisting of hay, pasture, maize, silage, etc. Young animals and veal have been traditionally exported to the EU under agreed preferential quotas at reduced import duties.

The directly marketed share of milk production is increasing as a consequence of rather stable milk prices, specialisation, and concentration of private farmers in milk production. The Slovene milk and cattle sector are largely concentrated in hilly and mountainous districts using environmentally friendly production technologies. Special government support measures were developed to promote such production, but recently there has been a move to decouple support from promotion of production and shift it towards producers in disadvantaged areas, hence this support could be considered regional assistance (e.g. support per head of cow and no longer on the basis of output or price level). The main development objective of Slovene government supports to breeders located in the areas defined as having difficult production conditions is to maintain the cultivated landscape and to reduce emigration of the farm population from hilly and mountainous areas. Farmers are given incentives and assistance for modernisation and restructuring of farms and for the development of supplementary activities.

Pig Meat and Poultry

Pig and poultry sectors differ according to technology of production and the composition of markets. More than half of pig production and a substantial part of poultry production is by large scale pig and poultry farms which sell directly to slaughterhouses.

Pork is produced on both small scale private farms and on large scale farms originating in the old system. Pig breeding on small scale farms is driven by both market forces and home consumption, while the large scale commercial farms exclusively specialise in production for markets. Mixed feed consisting of cereals (wheat, maize, and barley), potatoes, rape, and household food waste is typical for feeding pigs on small scale farms. In large scale operations, imported maize and feed concentrates represent the main feed used for pigs as well as for poultry production.

The market share of large scale farms is highest for poultry meat production. The surplus of poultry meat production has slightly declined since independence due to a partial erosion of exports on the traditional former Yugoslav markets.

Domestic egg production mainly covers domestic needs. However, Slovenia became a net exporter of eggs in the 1990s. On private farms, there is substantial egg production for home consumption.

A Brief Comparison of Slovene and EU Market and Trade Policies

Due to rather close trade and economic relations of the former Yugoslavia with the EU, the CAP price support mechanisms, structural policies, and other common policies of the EU were extensively analysed in the 1980s (e.g. Vadnal, 1987, Nose and Gliha, 1988, Bojnec, 1988). During the 1990s, adjustment of Slovene agricultural policy to the CAP is ongoing.

The most visible difference between instruments employed in the CAP and Slovenia's agricultural policies results from contrasting the difference of the net trade position of the EU and Slovenia. The EU is a substantial net exporter of agricultural commodities, while Slovenia is a net importer. Therefore, market price support in Slovenia is delivered through import measures and state marketing systems rather than export subsidies. While the CAP covers a large range of products from wheat to silkworms, Slovenia focuses its intensive support on a smaller number of products. Price support policies are applied to wheat and wheat flour, sugar, and milk, while for other products, import measures shield domestic markets.

For efficiency reasons the CAP instruments aim at the first stage of processing or wholesaling, for example intervention prices for cereals are wholesale, not farmgate, prices. Slovenia's price policies, on the other hand, aim additionally at farmgate and, to some extent, consumer prices. These kinds of policies need institutions and regulations other than those found in the CAP. Therefore, substantial differences in instrumental settings and level of market control exist between the EU and Slovenia.

The downstream sector in Slovenia is heavily biased by monopsonistic structures due to two factors. First, the markets are small in size such that often only one enterprise exists for initial stage processing in a protected environment (e.g. sugar and oilseeds). Second, the state storage reserves control a two tier price system in which domestic agricultural producers receive high prices from the state and preferential imports are purchased to maintain prices for consumers at levels lower than the c.i.f. price plus normal duties. To avoid circular trade, most imports are purchased for the state storage reserves by public tender without any import duties. Any operational losses are covered by the government budget. This policy plays a crucial role for wheat, wheat flour, rye, and sugar (OECD, 1996).

For milk, the government sets a basic price, while the producer price for farmers depends on the quality of milk delivered to dairies (e.g. Bojnec, 1994, 1996c). No special government intervention purchases into the state storage reserves were required. However, the government has from time to time provided support for promotional activities for sales of dairy products in both domestic and foreign markets and, therefore as hidden export subsidies. The main instruments of protection for the domestic milk and dairy markets are custom duties consisting of ad valorem and specific tariffs. In contrast the EU delivers support to the dairy sector in four ways: direct constraints on production (quotas), market intervention to withdraw surplus stocks of storable dairy products, export subsidies for a wide range of products, and prohibitive import barriers.

Generally, processing industries in Slovenia are protected by escalating tariffs and tightly controlled foreign trade. In the case of sugar, the sole processing facility in Slovenia imports its raw materials, especially raw sugar, mostly tariff free as long as any implicit quotas are not violated, while white sugar is subject to high tariffs.[2] Moreover, the government compensated the factory for losses caused by the two tier price system. Similar practices were applied for oilseeds, raw vegetable oil, and refined vegetable oils handled by the Slovene oilseed processing facility.

This environment systematically discourages emerging private downstream activities. Consequently, trade flows to the private downstream sector are still not as important as in other transition countries. The European Commission in its judgment of Slovenia's application for membership came to the conclusion that 'State monopolies in the cereals, oilseed and sugar sector will have to be dismantled ...' during accession (European Commission, 1997, p. 79).

A comparison of price and trade policy measures of Slovenia and the EU reveals both similarities and differences (table 5.4). While Slovene agricultural policy is moving closer to the CAP's product market organisations, more in-depth comparisons show that there are still considerable differences in methods and levels of the administration of policies. Price support measures in Slovenia are applied for three groups of commodities: wheat, sugar, and milk and related products. The range of basic commodities covered by price support mechanisms and institutional price setting is much wider in the EU. The price support mechanism in Slovenia is based on direct intervention at different levels of the markets (farm, wholesale/processing, and retail). Compared to the EU, Slovenia's price support system relies more heavily on administrative approaches and ad hoc measures coordinated by the state reserves system's monopolistic position on wheat and sugar markets. Import protection measures in Slovenia are similar to those of the CAP. Both consist of tariffs, often with an adjustable part expressed as specific import tariff rates.

The use of export subsidies in Slovenia is restricted or excluded from implementation by General Agreement on Tariffs and Trade/World Trade Organization (GATT/WTO) commitments, while in the EU they are an important instrument to remove surpluses from domestic markets. However, some temporary ad hoc selling and promotional activities, including those oriented towards foreign markets (e.g. for dairy products where surplus is registered), are applied in Slovenia.

Table 5.4 Comparison of Slovene and EU agricultural policy measures, 1996-97

	Price Support Mechanism / Institutional Price		Tariffs		Adjustable Tariff Component		Export Subsidies		Set Aside / Area and Headage Payments		Production Quotas		Input Subsidies and Related Measures	
	Slovenia	EU	Slovenia	EU	Slovenia	EU	Slovenia	EU	Slovenia	EU	Slovenia	EU	Slovenia	EU
Wheat	Yes	Yes	Yes	Yes	Yes	Yes	No	Yes	No	Yes	No	No	Yes	No
Maize	No	Yes	Yes	Yes	Yes	Yes	No	Yes	No	Yes	No	No	No	No
Barley	No	Yes	Yes	Yes	Yes	Yes	No	Yes	No	Yes	No	No	Yes	No
Sugar beet	Yes[a]	No	Yes[a]	Yes	No	–	No	No	No	No	No	Yes	Yes	No
Sugar	Yes	Yes	Yes	Yes	Yes	Yes	No	Yes[c]	No	Yes	No	No	–	No
Oilseeds	No	No	No	No	No	No	No	No	No	–	No	No	Yes	No
Vegetable oils	Yes[a]	No	Yes	Yes	Yes	No	No	Yes	No	–	No	No	Yes	No
Hops	No	No	Yes	No	No	No	No	No	No	–	No	No	Yes	No
Potatoes	No	No	Yes	No	No	No	No	Yes	No	No	No	No	No	No
Fresh fruit	No	No	Yes	Yes	Yes	Yes	No	Yes	No	No	No	No	No	No
Fresh vegetables	No	No	Yes	Yes	No	Yes	No	Yes	No	No	No	No	Yes	No
Wine	No	No	Yes	Yes	Yes	Yes	No	Yes	No	No	No	–	Yes	No
Milk	Yes	No	Yes	Yes	Yes	Yes	No	Yes	Yes	–	No	Yes	No	No
Butter and cheese	No	Yes	Yes	Yes	Yes	Yes	Yes[b]	Yes	No	No	No	–	Yes	No
Cattle / beef	No	Yes	Yes	Yes	Yes	Yes	No	Yes	Yes	Yes	No	No	No	No
Pigs	No	No	Yes	Yes	Yes	Yes	No	Yes	No	No	No	No	Yes	No
Poultry	No	No	Yes	Yes	Yes	Yes	–[b]	Yes	No	No	No	No	Yes	No
Eggs	No	No	Yes	Yes	Yes	No	No	Yes	No	No	No	No	No	No
Sheep meat	No	No	Yes	Yes	No	Yes	No	Yes	Yes	Yes	No	No	Yes	No

[a] Not always applied
[b] Ad hoc selling promotion for domestic and foreign markets
[c] Cross-subsidy from A and B sugar

Source: Bojnec, 1996b, 1996c, Answers of the Republic of Slovenia on the Questionnaire of the EU (1996).

Changing market policies in Slovenia also indicate an alignment of agricultural support with that of the CAP. In particular, the introduction of direct headage payments for cattle and sheep in mountainous areas, support for suckling calves, and subsidies for a gene bank program for traditional cattle breeds represent a policy switch toward direct payments (OECD, 1997a). At this stage, direct payments are still lower than in the EU, but one could expect that this is the most likely direction of agricultural policy which will be followed during the preenlargement period.[3]

One of the aims of Slovenia's agricultural policies, i.e. basing income support more on direct payments, has been reached for cattle and sheep in mountainous areas (OECD, 1997a). The role of supply-restricting instruments such as dairy and sugar quotas and set asides are nonexistant in a small, net importing country such as Slovenia.

Input subsidies were an important policy instrument under the previous system. These subsidies are still in use for seeds, fruit trees, plants, and breeding animals. However, the Slovene government aims to convert them to direct payments.

In conclusion, agricultural markets in Slovenia are still largely influenced by direct interventions of the government at the micro level through state monopolies and state trading. In the process of adjusting agricultural policies to be more closely aligned with those of the CAP, direct payments become important future policy objectives.

Market Price, Direct Budgetary, and Other Support to Agriculture

To evaluate the level of agricultural and food prices in Slovenia, and to evaluate the level of support to Slovene agriculture, we are using two measures: nominal protection rates (NPRs) and the producer subsidy equivalents (PSEs).

Nominal Protection Rates (NPRs)

NPRs are calculated with data at the farm level and at the wholesale/processor level where the CAP in the EU is applied. The level of agricultural prices at the farm level, as measured by the NPR for nine agricultural products (wheat, maize, barley, rapeseed, sugar beet, milk, beef and veal, pork, and poultry) for Slovenia and the EU are presented in table 5.5.[4] Farmgate prices in Slovenia as well as in the EU are considerably higher than border prices. This indicates that farmers in both

Slovenia and the EU were nominally protected. There are some differences in the level of protection by commodity. Farmgate prices for maize, milk, and beef in Slovenia were lower than in the EU, while considerably higher for wheat, rapeseed, and pigs. However, rapeseed production in Slovenia is not particularly important, even in terms of domestic consumption (domestic production covers about 5 per cent of domestic needs). With the implementation of the 1992 MacSharry CAP reform, the NPR for wheat decreased for the EU. Since 1992, the EU wheat producer price has been lower than in Slovenia. The main instrument keeping the Slovene wheat price above the EU level is the system of guaranteed wheat purchases and a guaranteed price which is high for the prescribed quality of domestic wheat during the harvest season. Farmgate prices for barley and sugar beet in both Slovenia and the EU are far above border prices, while for poultry producers, prices are moving closer to the world market level.

Table 5.5   Nominal protection rates for Slovenia and the EU

	Wheat	Maize	Barley	Rapeseed	Sugar beet	Milk	Beef	Pork	Poultry
Slovenia									
1989	1	30	22	25	158	14	15	40	10
1990	41	89	82	88	123	138	51	75	36
1991	110	75	88	84	125	69	42	63	21
1992	71.	48	88	108	135	73	42	62	28
1993	84	37	129	67	178	69	41	97	14
1994	77	22	126	70	76	84	44	86	14
1995	43	9	32	86	108	77	74	111	23
1996	25	9	41	77	130	56	61	61	11
EU									
1989	25	55	45	0	95	103	95	14	34
1990	53	100	91	0	112	186	90	24	25
1991	131	111	119	0	186	158	86	34	22
1992	63	93	99	0	210	150	99	24	21
1993	55	62	107	0	169	134	113	33	16
1994	50	45	113	0	126	130	130	26	9
1995	15	47	49	0	131	130	120	10	8

Source: OECD, 1997b; Bojnec and Swinnen, 1997.

Figure 5.1 compares the average NPRs for nine commodities at the farm level for the EU, Slovenia, and four members of the Central European Free Trade Agreement—Hungary, Poland, Slovakia, and Czech Republic (CEFTA-4). On average, Slovene farm prices are higher than in the CEFTA-4 countries and only a bit lower than in the EU. Slovene farm prices were lower on average than in the EU due primarily to lower Slovene farm prices for key commodities such as milk and beef. Compared to the EU, Slovene farm prices were higher for the net importing wheat and oilseeds.

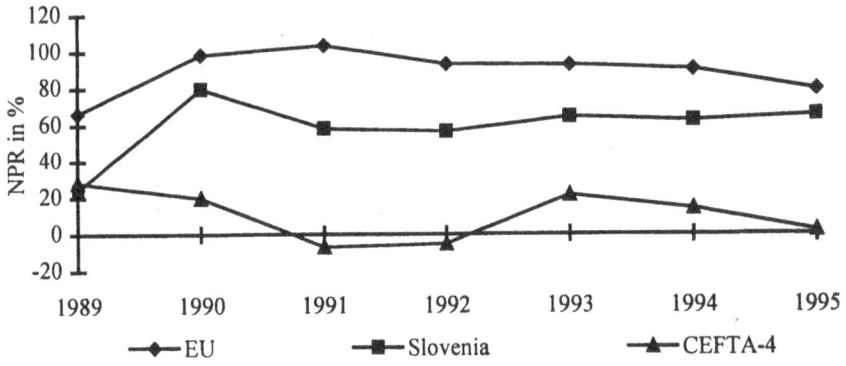

Figure 5.1 Nominal protection rates at the farm level

Source: Bojnec and Swinnen, 1997, OECD, 1997b.

The current levels of farm prices in Slovenia could have broad consequences for agricultural policy design. Slovenia has already concluded an Association Agreement with the EU and has opened negotiations for EU membership while levels of agricultural support differ substantially between CEECs and the EU both overall (figures 5.1 and 5.2, and Bojnec, 1996a) and by commodity (table 5.5, OECD, 1997a, 1997b, Bojnec and Swinnen, 1997). While Slovenia accepted the interim multilateral rules of the CEFTA agricultural agreement, farmers are demanding compensation for income losses due to trade liberalisation. While at the farmgate level, Slovene agricultural protection is on average lower than in the EU, the Slovene average protection rate is higher than in the EU at the wholesale and processing level (figure 5.2). Slovene border protection increases with the degree of product processing. For some raw agricultural products, such as sugar beet and oilseeds, border protection measures are low or are not implemented, while import tariffs increase with the degree of processing as is the case for white sugar and vegetable oil. Furthermore, the CAP and Slovenia's agricultural policies use quite different instruments. The most striking difference is that CAP price policy instruments are not directly aimed at the farm level. Institutional prices are applied to products at the first stage of wholesaling or processing. Therefore, under the CAP the vertical transmission of prices is crucial for the share of support which eventually arrives at the farm. On the other hand, in Slovenia key areas of support are characterised by direct and indirect intervention by the state on several levels of the markets and the existence of state-owned and private monopolies.

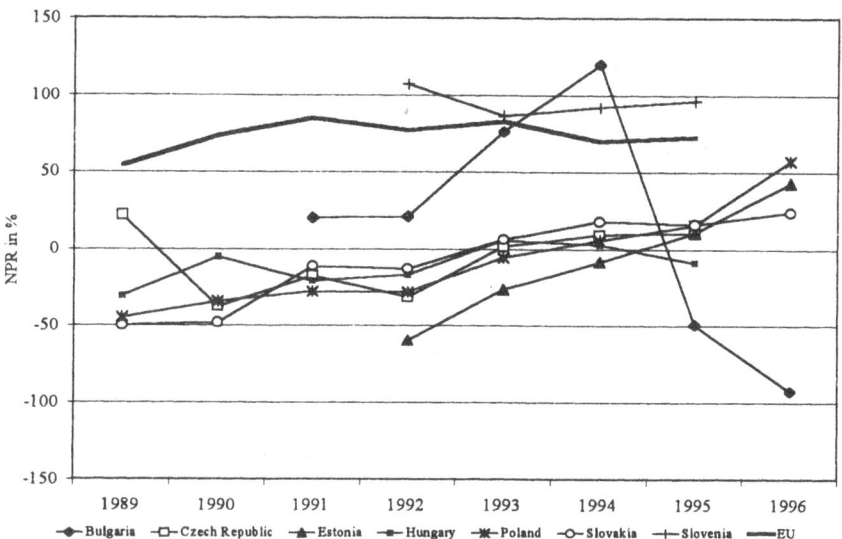

Figure 5.2 Nominal protection rates at the wholesale/processing level
Source: ESIM calculations.

Producer Subsidy Equivalents (PSEs)

The average level of agricultural protection in the EU, as measured by PSEs calculated by the Organisation for Economic Co-operation and Development (OECD), was substantially higher than in CEECs (figure 5.3). Moreover, the average PSE for Estonia was negative in 1994. Between 1994 and 1996, the average PSE declined for the Czech Republic and Hungary as well as for the EU and Slovenia. Although PSEs for Estonia increased, they were still lower than in other CEECs. However, the average PSE increased in Poland and in 1996 approached the average PSE level for Slovenia.

124 *Agriculture and East-West European Integration*

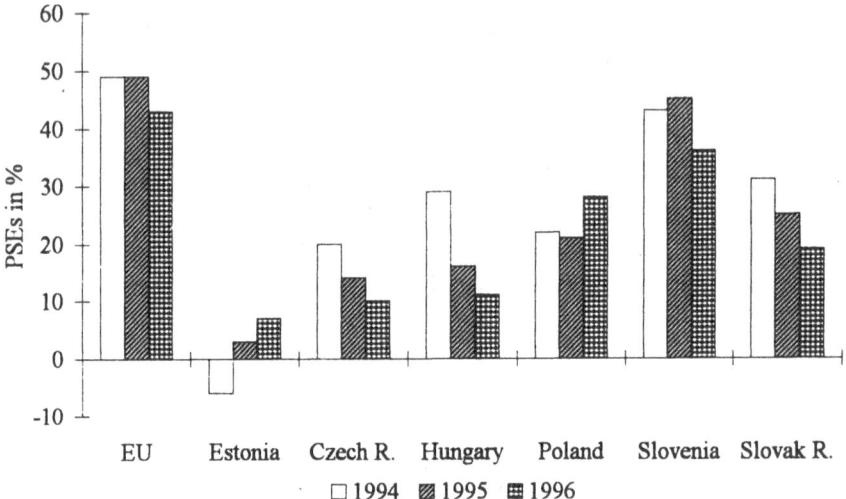

Figure 5.3 Producer subsidy equivalents for the EU and selected CEECs

Source: OECD, 1997a, MAFF, 1997.

As indicated in PSE calculations for CEECs, market price support measures play a dominant role among the total subsidies to agriculture (figure 5.4). However, there is an indication that market price support in the EU is declining, while direct budgetary and other support is increasing (OECD, 1997c).

Market price support measures dominated the total transfers to Slovene agriculture at more than 80 per cent of the gross PSE. This share was rather stable over the 1990s. There is an indication that market price support is likely to decline due to the agricultural part of CEFTA. However, this will probably result in a simultaneous increase of direct budgetary and other support to compensate farmers for income losses resulting from alignment of agricultural policy towards the CAP. Direct payments are likely to be introduced for wheat and sugar beet producers. This will change the structure of PSEs by increasing the importance of direct budgetary and similar supports vis-à-vis the previous market price support.

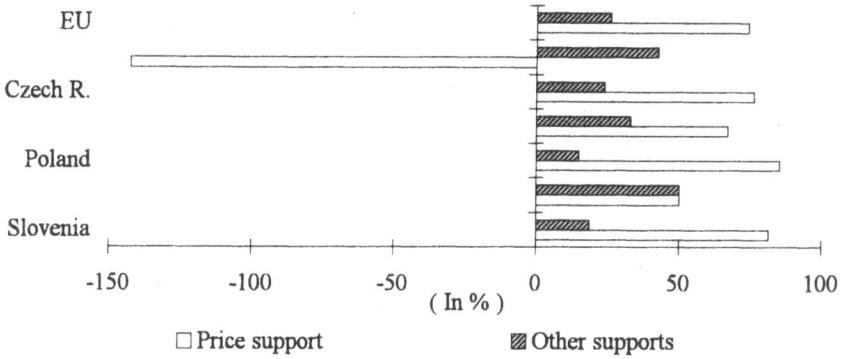

Figure 5.4 Market price support and other supports in the PSE, 1993-95 (per cent)

Source: OECD, 1997c, 1997d; MAFF, 1997.

Effects of EU Accession

A literature of analyses of possible effects of agricultural accession to the EU has developed, but focuses on the effects in those CEECs where protection is expected to rise significantly during accession (e.g. Tangermann and Josling, 1994, SAEPR, 1995, European Commission, 1995, Berkum and Terluin, 1995). In this respect Slovenia is a special case since its levels of protection are close to that of the EU (figures 5.1 and 5.2, table 5.5).

The aim of this analysis is to show the possible effects of adopting the CAP on agricultural markets. To reflect the current discussion in the EU about the future CAP, three accession scenarios are constructed and compared to a Nonaccession scenario. From 2000 to 2002 Slovenia adopts CAP measures prior to EU membership. Accession is assumed to take place in 2003 with full integration into the SEM, i.e. full bilateral liberalisation of trade between the EU and Slovenia.

Three scenarios with variations of the CAP are tested. First, the CAP as currently defined is implemented including set aside and area payments (CAP scenario). The other two scenarios reflect current debate on Agenda 2000 proposals. According to one argument, direct payments are designed to compensate farmers for losses due to reforms, but since prices are expected to increase during accession, no compensation is needed for CEEC farmers. The Agenda scenario implements Agenda 2000 measures but without direct payments are at least partly coupled to production and, more importantly, are neither digressive nor temporary in nature. Therefore, they are an integral part of CAP support. Without them the new members would be excluded from important CAP privileges. Our scenarios analyse both of these positions. The third scenario, Agenda Premium, features an Agenda 2000 which includes all direct payments (for scenario details, refer to table 1.1, chapter 1).

These policy scenarios are calculated in the partial equilibrium model, ESIM, which was developed by the United States Department of Agriculture/Economic Research Service in cooperation with Tangermann and Josling (1994) and extended recently by Münch (1995, 1997). The data base is 1994 and 1995. In an extension of previous analyses, the macroeconomic figures needed as exogenous parameters for simulations, i.e. exchange rates and income, are included in a combined analysis between ESIM, a partial equilibrium model, and a computable general equilibrium model (Banse, 1997).

For the ESIM simulations, wholesale and processing sector price data are used where CAP price and trade policy measures are applied. For example, the intervention price for beef is not a live weight, farmgate price but a carcass weight, wholesaling price. As a rule, the more efficient the downstream sector is estimated to be, the better the transmission of support to farms. To identify the potential pressures during accession, the efficiency of markets has been assumed to be unchanged.

Results

Recent analyses of accession impacts on Slovenia's agriculture by Erjavec et al. (1996) and Rednak and Volk (1996) indicate that the impact of accession to the EU on the level of Slovene farm incomes will largely depend on conditions under which Slovene farmers join the CAP of the EU. If Slovene farmers join with the same status as present members, farm incomes may slightly increase, ceteris paribus. However, it is possible that the agricultural and food sector in Slovenia are among those sectors where negative effects of accession to the EU can be expected (Potocnik and Majcen, 1996). Hence, Erjavec et al. (1997) concluded that Slovene farm incomes would increase in the situation where the EU grants the CAP of 1995-1996 including its market price supports, compensation payments, and structural policies to Slovene farmers. If compensation payments are not a part of the accession package, the overall incomes of Slovene farmers still increase due to price increases and budgetary supports, but decline for those products where producer prices are currently higher than in the EU.

Our analysis focuses on market and budgetary effects. Table 5.6 indicates that effects of accession would be stronger on markets which are intensely protected under the CAP. In the other CEECs these are coarse grains, beef, dairy, and sugar. Because Slovenia already has high processor and wholesale protections for beef, sugar, and some dairy products, the introduction of the unreformed CAP raises prices only for sugar and butter and decreases market prices only slightly for the other products. However, the less protected market regimes are under the CAP, the more significant the decline of real market prices when the policies are applied to Slovenia's markets. These include, for example, cereal-fed livestock production (35 and 23 per cent for pork and poultry respectively), oilseeds, and oilseed products.

Table 5.6 Projected change in Slovene real market prices by 2010 relative to 1994-96 under three scenarios (per cent)

	Nonaccession	CAP	Agenda
Wheat	-13	-31	-35
Barley	-13	-2	-28
Rapeseed	-1	-19	-21
Sugar	0	20	22
Milk	0	1	-7
Butter	0	62	49
Beef	0	-4	-45
Pork	11	-35	-51
Poultry	1	-23	-44

Source: ESIM Scenario Calculations.

In figure 5.5 the development of average processor/wholesale NPRs under different policy scenarios are shown.[5] Under continuing domestic policies, the Nonaccession scenario, the weighted average NPR of 22 agricultural and food products increases from the base level of 75 per cent to almost 90 per cent in 2010. The figure shows CAP implementation in Slovenia between 2000 and 2002 prior to full EU membership. The alignment to CAP prices increases protection, especially in the CAP scenario, by 20 percentage points. This simply means that the current import regulations of the CAP are more protective than those of Slovenia.

With Slovenia's integration into the SEM, imports from the EU enter the markets tariff free in the enlarged customs union. Even under the current CAP, protection falls by 20 percentage points in 2003. This effect is even stronger under the proposed Agenda 2000 reforms with protection falling by almost 60 percentage points. The production structure in Slovenia is especially sensitive to the proposed reform package because key markets crucial to Slovene agriculture are protected at least as much as in the EU. These products are targeted within the Agenda 2000 reform proposal. Other CEECs are less affected because their production structure is more diversified in less protected markets.[6]

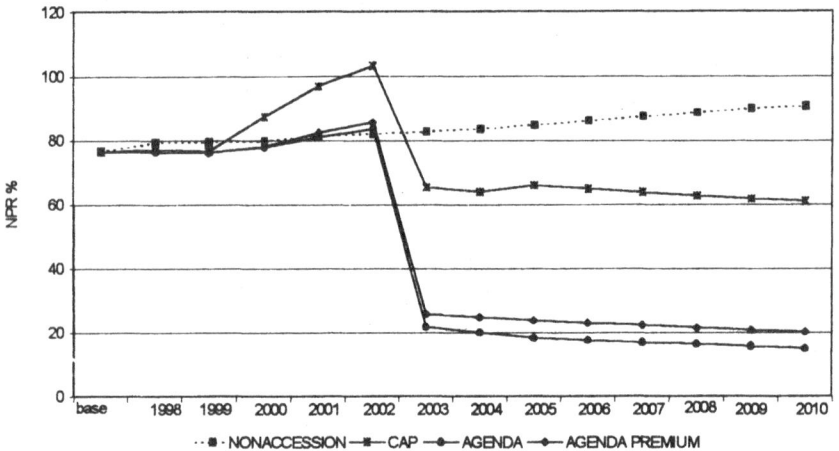

Figure 5.5   Development of agricultural and food protection under four policy scenarios (weighted average NPR, per cent)

Source: ESIM Scenario Calculations.

This decrease of protection is transmitted to the farm level, because the efficiency of the downstream sector is not assumed to increase with accession. Under these assumptions, overall agricultural production will decline under conditions of the SEM. The only commodity where surpluses increase is dairy products (table 5.7), while the current surplus in poultry production will almost disappear under the Agenda and Agenda Premium scenarios. Budgetary expenditure increases, relative to other CEECs, only by relatively small amounts. Net imports of cereals decline under unreformed CAP conditions because prices for coarse grains increase giving an incentive to produce. The set aside requirement in the CAP scenario of an assumed 17.5 per cent (the reference rate) does not have a great effect on production because of the large number of small producers. Therefore, the effective set aside is less than 3 per cent. Agenda 2000 reforms reduce protection for coarse grains, therefore production of cereals decline slightly compared to the unreformed CAP scenario. Oilseed production definitely will lose competitiveness because current high protections will be phased out during accession. This is the case in the unreformed CAP, Agenda, and Agenda Premium scenarios in comparison to the Nonaccession scenario.

Sugar production may increase especially under Agenda and Agenda Premium scenarios. However, Slovenia remains a net importer of sugar.

Beef production increases under the Nonaccession scenario, but decreases under the Agenda scenario without premium payments. However, in the Agenda Premium scenario, beef production slightly increases.

Pork and poultry production are likely to decline in Slovenia under all three accession scenarios caused by price declines to EU levels. The production decline is higher under Agenda 2000 conditions (Agenda and Agenda Premium scenarios). Moreover, with expanding domestic incomes, the domestic demand for pork and poultry meat would increase, acting as an additional factor driving up Slovenia's net imports of pork and poultry meat.

Regarding these market reactions, the projected future Guidance Section of the European Agricultural Guidance and Guarantee Fund (FEOGA) spending for Slovenia is less affected by export subsidies and other operations which are very important in the current CAP for removing surpluses from markets.[7] However, for Slovenia, direct payments are especially important accounting for 70 per cent of the total FEOGA spending for Slovenia (figure 5.6).[8]

The scenario results suggest that introducing the unreformed CAP during accession would not cause large market effects, especially when compared to the other accession candidates. Agenda 2000 reforms would lower protection in Slovenia significantly. Moreover, the scenario results also reveal potential pressures which Slovenia's downstream sector could face as it begins to compete on the SEM.

130 *Agriculture and East-West European Integration*

Table 5.7 Projected Slovene production and net exports under four policy scenarios

Production (in thousand tons)	Base	Nonaccession	2003 CAP	2003 Agenda	2003 Agenda Premium	Nonaccession	2010 CAP	2010 Agenda	2010 Agenda Premium
Cereals	520.00	658.59	687.58	670.14	672.94	658.59	687.58	670.14	672.94
Oilseeds	4.50	5.45	4.37	4.40	4.41	6.01	5.01	5.63	6.33
Sugar	42.81	43.73	58.64	61.87	61.77	44.54	55.36	58.71	58.66
Milk	560.70	648.08	560.00	670.49	719.24	734.20	560.00	727.42	790.95
Butter	1.87	2.26	2.00	2.83	3.24	2.67	1.77	3.17	3.71
Beef	44.97	51.89	52.69	43.87	47.69	58.71	58.18	48.48	52.48
Pork	67.77	82.37	46.39	41.77	41.57	97.60	51.02	46.42	46.29
Poultry	50.10	57.49	48.94	39.61	39.36	65.06	49.58	40.47	40.38

Net exports (in thousand tons)	Base	Nonaccession	2003 CAP	2003 Agenda	2003 Agenda Premium	Nonaccession	2010 CAP	2010 Agenda	2010 Agenda Premium
Cereals	-1002.35	-258.88	-85.93	-286.41	-310.60	-258.88	-85.93	-286.41	-310.60
Oilseeds	-100.52	-77.26	-73.07	-74.76	-74.90	-73.55	-70.51	-70.84	-70.31
Sugar	-42.19	-45.40	-14.07	-10.40	-10.51	-46.70	-14.08	-10.49	-10.53
Milk*	–	–	–	–	–	–	–	–	–
Butter	0.34	0.45	0.76	1.57	2.01	0.64	0.41	1.85	2.45
Beef	-7.97	-14.68	-0.66	-23.20	-19.40	-21.36	-0.91	-26.29	-22.27
Pork	-22.17	-24.07	-66.99	-79.19	-79.36	-23.21	-68.59	-81.89	-81.99
Poultry	19.57	19.33	14.06	2.16	1.92	19.81	10.26	-1.99	-2.08

* A nontradable commodity in ESIM

Source: ESIM Scenario Calculations.

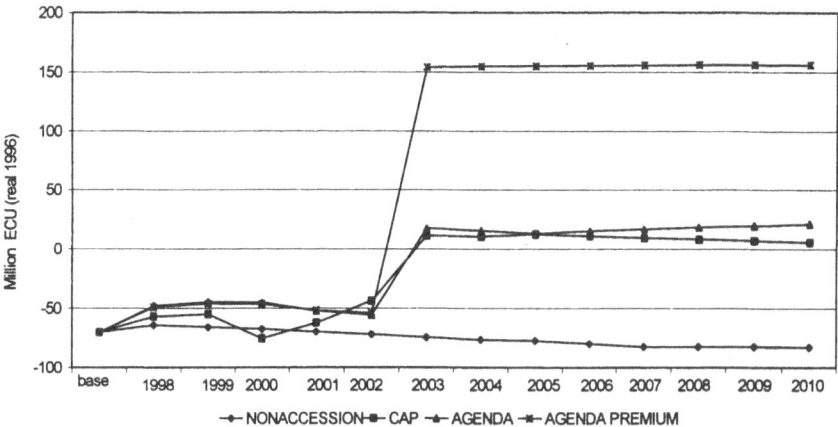

Figure 5.6 Adjusted net budgetary spending for market guarantees under four policy scenarios

Source: ESIM Scenario Calculations.

Conclusions

Price and market support to Slovene agriculture is rather high. Slovene farmgate, wholesale, and processing prices are close to, or even above, EU levels. Slovenia's agricultural price policy depends largely on monopolistic structures such as state reserves. Some food processing branches are highly concentrated (e.g. sugar). Regarding relatively low market efficiency, the downstream sector could well be among those facing strong competitive pressures on the SEM after accession. The positive or negative effects of implementing the EU price policies on farms will largely depend on the ability of the downstream sector to adjust to the competitiveness of the SEM. The scenarios indicate that without adjustment and restructuring of Slovenia's wholesale and processing sector, the farm sector will suffer price declines during accession. In this case direct payments would have a more important role than in the EU and it would be even more difficult to withhold them from Slovenia's farmers.

The estimated costs of the Slovene agricultural sector's accession for the EU budget are smaller than for other CEECs because of the smaller agricultural sector, the small size of the economy, and the net importation of food and agricultural products. The most important spending item would be direct payments. The Slovene adjustment to the CAP would not involve a substantial shock that would either boost price increases or create large production responses as producer prices are already high. Hence, in comparison with other CEECs, the simulation results are less sensitive on the farm price alignment because Slovene farm prices are close to, or even above, EU levels (e.g. wheat).

The simulation results widely depend on assumptions about EU direct payments for area and cattle. The simulation results indicate that the most sensitive issue in the negotiations between Slovenia and the EU in relation to the CAP is expected to be direct payments for new members which were often argued against in the EU debate. However, Slovene agricultural policy adjustment to the CAP is an ongoing process, financed by domestic consumers and taxpayers.

Notes

1   For simplicity, in this chapter, we will use the acronym EU to refer to both to the European Union and to the European Community.
2   For 1998, imports of sugar beet and raw sugar for processing are free of import duties. Imports of other raw sugar are subject to a 17 per cent ad valorem tariff rate, while imports of refined sugar are taxed at a 14.5 per cent ad valorem tariff rate plus an import levy (specific rate tariff).
3   The Central European Free Trade Agreement (CEFTA) will also create pressures for internal trade liberalisation and, hence grant larger budgetary support as demanded by farmers to cover farm income losses following trade liberalisation (Bojnec, 1998).
4   NPR = $[(P^d / P^b) - 1] * 100$ where P^d is the domestic producer (farmgate) price in current USD valued at the official exchange rate, and P^b is the border price (border price of a particular product used as world market price by the OECD [1997b] in estimating PSEs for the EU). Further details in Bojnec and Swinnen (1997).
5   The NPRs are calculated as production-weighted averages of 22 agricultural and food products. The slight differences between 1998 and 2000 are due to changes in exchange rates.
6   E.g. Hungary or Poland (Münch, 1997).
7   ESIM calculates net spending, i.e. export subsidies minus import tariff revenues. To get close to actual FEOGA figures, coefficients have been applied which include measures not captured by the model such as storage and some market regimes.
8   Note that the spending in the NONACCESSION scenario does not reflect current spending, i.e. the operational costs of the state reserves and other subsidised state monopolies in the downstream sector.

References

Anderson, K. and Tyers R. (1993), *Implications of EC Expansion for European Agricultural Policies, Trade and Welfare*, Centre for Economic Policy Research, London.
Banse, M. (1997), 'Macro-economic Implications of EU-Accession', in S. Tangermann, (ed) *Agricultural Implication of CEEC Accession to the EU*, Interim Report, University of Göttingen, Göttingen.
Berkum, S. van and Terluin I. (1995), *Accession of the Four Visegrad Countries to the EU: Costs for the Agricultural Budget*, Agricultural Economics Research Institute, The Hague.
Bojnec, Š. (1988), 'Osnovni principi agrarno-ekonomske politike kod nas, u EEZ i SAD', *Ekonomika*, vol. 24, no. 12, pp. 23-9.
Bojnec, Š. (1994), 'Agricultural Reform in Slovenia', in J.F.M. Swinnen (ed), *Policy and Institutional Reform in Central European Agriculture*, Aldershot: Avebury, pp. 135-68.
Bojnec, Š. (1996a), 'Integration of Central Europe in the Common Agricultural Policy of the European Union', *The World Economy*, vol. 19, pp. 447-63.
Bojnec, Š. (1996b), 'The Cereal and Oilseed Sectors of Slovenia: Recent Policy Development and Main Issues', Report for OECD Group on Cereals, Animal Feeds and Sugar, 14-17 October 1996, Paris.
Bojnec, Š. (1996c), 'The Meat and Dairy Sectors in Slovenia', Report for OECD Group on Meat and Dairy Products, 18-21 November 1996, Paris.
Bojnec, Š. and Swinnen, J. (1997), 'The Pattern of Agricultural Price Distortions in Central and Eastern Europe', *Food Policy*, vol. 22, no. 4, pp. 289-306.
Bojnec, Š. (1998), 'The Central European Free Trade Agreement in Agriculture: The Case of Slovenia', in the Joint Research Project *Agricultural Implications of CEEC Accession to the EU*, Working Paper No. 1/5, University of Göttingen, Göttingen.
Erjavec, E., Rednak, M. and Majcen, B. (1996), 'Slovensko kmetijstvo in evropske integracije: Ucinki vkljucevanja Slovenije v mednarodno integracijo na slovensko kmetijstvo', Ljubljana.
Erjavec, E., Rednak, M. and Volk, T. (1997), 'Slovensko kmetijstvo in Evropska Unija', CZD Kmecki Glas, Ljubljana.
European Commission (1995), *Agricultural Situation and Prospects in the Central and Eastern European Countries: Summary Report*, Directorate General for Agriculture (DG VI), Brussels.
European Commission (1997), *Agenda 2000*, vol. I and II, Brussels.
MAFF (1996a), 'Answers of the Republic of Slovenia on the Questionnaire of the European Union', Chapter 2: Agriculture, mimeo, Ministry of Agriculture Food and Forestry, Ljubljana.
MAFF (1996b), *Porocilo o stanju kmetijstva, živilstva in gozdarstva v letu 1995*, Ministry of Agriculture, Forestry and Food, Ljubljana.
MAFF (1997), *Porocilo o stanju kmetijstva, gozdarstva in živilstva v letu 1996*, Ministry of Agriculture, Forestry and Food, Ljubljana.
Münch, W. (1995), 'Possible Implications of an Accession of the Visegrad Countries to the EU. Can the CAP do without Reform?', Paper presented at the *Agricultural Economic Society One-Day Conference*, December, London.
Münch, W. (1997), Effects of CEC-EU Accession on Agricultural Markets and Government Budgets in the CEC, in S. Tangermann (ed), *Agricultural Implications of CEEC Accession to the EU*, Interim Report, Göttingen, Germany.

Nose, M. and Gliha, S. (1988), 'Zajednicka agrarna politika Evropske Zajednice - karakteristike, rezultati i tendendce', *Privredna izgradnja*, vol. 34, no. 3, pp. 19-34.

OECD (1995), *Agricultural Policies, Markets and Trade in the Central and Eastern European Countries, Selected New Independent States, Mongolia and China: Monitoring and Outlook 1995*, OECD, Paris.

OECD (1996), *Agricultural Policies, Markets, and Trade in Transition Economies: Monitoring and Evaluation 1996*, OECD, Paris.

OECD (1997a), *Agricultural Policies, Markets and Trade in Transition Economies: Monitoring and Evaluation 1997*, OECD, Paris.

OECD (1997b), *Tables of Producer Subsidy Equivalents and Consumer Subsidy Equivalents 1979-1994*, OECD, Paris.

OECD (1997c), *Politiques Agricoles des Pays de L'OCDE: Measure de Soutien et Informations de Base 1997*, OECD, Paris.

OECD (1997d), *Review of Agricultural Policies: Slovak Republic*, OECD, Paris.

Potocnik, J. and Majcen, B. (1996), 'Slovenia and the European Union: Analysis of Possible Consequences of Approaching Europe: CGE Approach', Report for Institute for Economic Research, Ljubljana.

Rednak, M. and Volk, T. (1997), 'Slovene Agriculture and the European Union', in M. Soma (ed) *Agricultural Accession of the Central and Eastern European Countries to the European Union*, Institute for World Economics of the Hungarian Academy of Sciences, Budapest, pp. 105-13.

SAEPR (1995), 'Scenarios for Integration of Polish Agriculture with the European Union', (on the basis of simulations), Materials and Reports, Warsaw.

Stanovnik, P. and Svetlicic, M. (1996), 'Slovenia and the European Union', Paper presented at the experts meeting *The Economic Aspects of Slovenia's Integration into the European Union*, April 1996, Bled.

Tangermann, S. and Josling, T.E. (1994), 'Pre-accession Agricultural Policies for Central Europe and the European Union', Study prepared for DG-I of the EU Commission, Göttingen, Stanford.

Vadnal, K. (1987), 'Kmetijska zunanjetrgovinska politika EGS', *Sodobno kmetijstvo*, vol. 20, no. 12, pp. 505-09.

6 Integration with the European Union and the Competitiveness of the Bulgarian Agro-Food Sector

MATTHEW GORTON AND SOPHIA DAVIDOVA

Background

In the postwar period, economic and political systems have become more internationally integrated. States, by joining global and regional decision making institutions (the European Union and United Nations) and signing agreements such as the General Agreement on Tariffs and Trade (GATT) and the Central European Free Trade Agreement (CEFTA), have tended to endorse and promote economic interdependence. By signing an Association Agreement (AA), Bulgaria has made a commitment to start aligning itself with the European Union (EU) with the ultimate objective of full membership.

Terms like 'integration', 'interdependence', 'harmonisation', and 'unification' are often used interchangeably, but in practice may imply different political and economic arrangements. In order to avoid confusion, it is useful to think in terms of a spectrum of integration which stretches from minimum integration on the extreme left hand side to complete unification between countries on the far right (figure 6.1). An example of minimal integration would be the economic relations between Cuba and the EU which are limited to very small and highly protected trade flows. In contrast the policy of complete unification of the former East and West Germany lies on the extreme right of the spectrum.

Bulgaria is now attempting to move right along this spectrum and become a full member of the EU. In June 1993 the European Council agreed that the associated countries of Central and Eastern Europe (CEEC) that so desire shall become members of the EU with accession occurring 'as soon as an associated country is able to assume the obligations of membership by satisfying the economic and political conditions required'

(European Commission, 1996a). These conditions include a requirement for the existence of a functioning market economy as well as the capacity to implement all EU policies and to cope with competitive pressures and market forces within the Union (European Commission, 1996b).

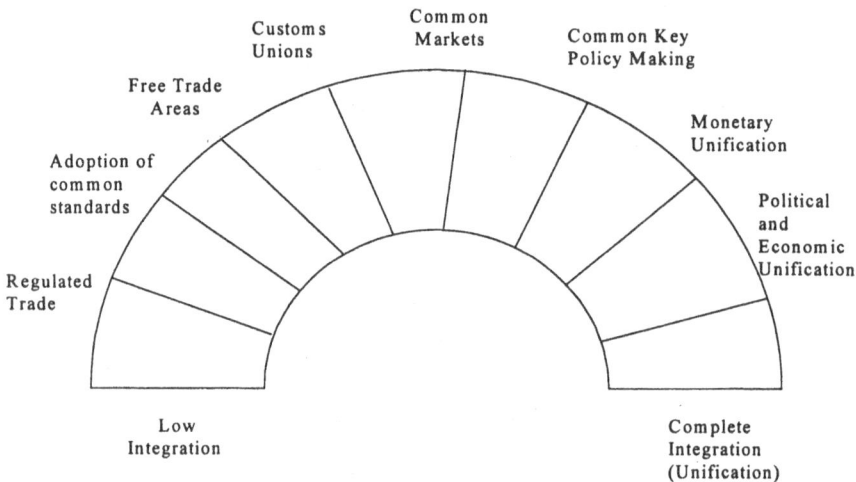

Figure 6.1   Spectrum of international integration

This chapter considers the progress made to date on alignment and competitiveness of the Bulgarian agro-food sector vis-à-vis the EU. It is divided into six sections. The next section presents an overview of policy and institutional developments in Bulgaria. This is developed in the third section, which covers trade integration and discussions of price alignment at the farm level. The following section evaluates the price and quality competitiveness of the downstream Bulgarian agro-food sector. The final section argues that little progress has been made to date with regard to integration with the EU.

Policy and Institutional Alignment

The issue of policy alignment has two dimensions: the instruments used and the level at which they are applied. Both of these dimensions are discussed in this section. The Common Agricultural Policy (CAP) has afforded a high degree of protection to farmers in the Union through the combined effects of market price support measures (such as intervention buying), factor subsidies, trade measures, supply management initiatives (e.g. production quotas), and direct payments to farmers (compensation payments). By 1996 about 39 per cent of CAP budgetary expenditure was channeled to farmers via direct payments (either per hectare of cereals, oilseeds, and protein crops or per head of cattle); 5 per cent on agro-environment, forestry, and early retirement measures; 9 per cent on structural funds; and the remaining 47 per cent on market support measures (Buckwell, 1997). In 1993, direct payments accounted for 20 per cent of total EU producer subsidy equivalents (PSEs) with two-thirds of these direct payments allocated to crops and the rest to livestock (Hertel et al., 1997). Our calculations for a three year average, 1995-97, show that this share increased to 29 per cent, market price support accounted for 57 per cent, and all other types of support to 14 per cent.

Analysis of current government expenditure on support measures to agriculture in Bulgaria indicates that they are insignificant compared to the EU. For 1996, total budgetary expenditure on agriculture amounted to 17.3 billion leva (100 million ECU) of which 13 per cent was used to support minimum purchase prices; 23 per cent for interest rate subsidies channelled through the agricultural fund; and the remainder for government managed services such as agricultural education, veterinary controls, breeding, irrigation, and research and development. The total expenditure of 17.3 billion represented a fall in real support of 15.4 per cent compared to 1995 and throughout the transition period inflation has risen faster than the nominal value of the agricultural budget. Support for indirect services such as veterinary care, irrigation, and breeding have all been cut back or withdrawn.

Agricultural policy in Bulgaria until 1998 has been burdened with substantial social functions, namely providing food to the population at lower-than-market prices. This involved the use of various instruments that are inconsistent with instruments used in the EU. The first one is the contract price system introduced in 1997. This system forces producers to negotiate the retail price at which their product should be sold to consumers. The negotiated prices are compulsory for the retailer until they are renegotiated. The contract price system is an implicit tool to control profit margins within the food chain. It is targeted at consumers at the expense of producers and distributors.

The second specific instrument, export restrictions, is also used with the objective of keeping prices on the domestic market below world market prices. They apply mainly to bread and feed grains and from time to time, live animals. The same measure is used in order to allow food industries to be supplied with agricultural raw materials at prices below world market levels (e.g. sunflower seeds, raw skins, and hides).

Table 6.1 Comparison of policy instruments in the EU and Bulgaria

Policy	EU	Bulgaria
Price support	• target prices • intervention prices	• previously minimum announced prices (wheat) • since 1998 no price intervention
Domestic market interventions	• intervention purchases • quotas	• state procurement in wheat market
Credit subsidies, tax relief	• not applied at EU level	• interest subsidies on loans • tax exemption on income from agricultural activities for family farmers and on profit from farming for corporate farms
Foreign trade measures	• import duties • export refunds	• import duties • previously export bans, taxes, licenses • since 1998 exports liberalised
Compensation payments	• arable • cattle	• none
Structural policy	• ecological direct payments • land retirement scheme • structural programmes (Objective 5a, 5b)	• small subsidy for increasing numbers of animals

Third, the policy response to temporary imbalances on the domestic market takes the form of changes in the export and import regime (e.g. introduction of decreased import duty quotas or zero import duty quotas, export quotas or export bans, and others). Fourth, explicit support to agriculture is provided via interest rate subsidies, mainly on short term loans for working capital. Another measure of support is the exemption of agricultural producers from taxes on profits and income derived from agricultural activities for several years. Direct support measures have not been used and there are no environmental objectives built into agricultural policy. Logically supply control has not been used because of the understanding that policy should aim to stop the contraction of the sector and to increase supply, despite the fact that the instruments that were implemented have not been adequate to achieve this objective.

In 1998, fulfilling World Bank Agricultural Structural Adjustment Loan (ASAL) conditions, Bulgaria streamlined its agricultural policy. Distortive measures aimed at supporting consumers were removed. These included the contract price system and export impediments. The main instruments that remained in place are credit subsidies, tax exemption, and the provision of services to agriculture.

In general the combination of policy instruments implemented in Bulgaria have been inconsistent with the instruments used by the EU (table 6.1). Agenda 2000 decisions on further CAP reform are in the direction of less market price support and toward policies that are more decoupled from product markets such as direct payments. Such CAP reforms will necessitate deep adjustments in Bulgaria because of the requirement to introduce several new policy instruments and institutions for which there is a lack of knowledge and experience.

Trade Integration

Overview

Bulgaria has always been a net agricultural exporter although as a small country has never been a major player in world trade. In the prereform years, the country had a substantial role as an agricultural supplier to the Council for Mutual Economic Assistance (CMEA) market. The postreform period has been marked by a diversification of the geographical structure of the agro-food trade.

Simple analysis of trade flows between Bulgaria and the EU is, however, not an easy task because of substantial differences in reported mutual trade between Bulgaria and the EU. In this chapter, only Bulgarian data are used to show the overall importance of the EU in the Bulgarian agro-food trade. For the analysis of trade with the EU and the measures of competitiveness, EUROSTAT data are used. In order to give some idea of data discrepancies, the differences in results based on different data sets are shown on a few occasions.

The EU share in Bulgarian exports of primary agricultural products gradually increased from 31 per cent in 1992 to 58 per cent in 1997 (table 6.2).[1] For several product groups the EU market currently absorbs more than half of Bulgarian exports (meat, fruit and vegetables, and oilseeds). However, for processed products the share of exports going to the EU market is stagnating. Between 1992 and 1997 the EU market accounted for about one-fifth of Bulgarian exports. The most important exportables are wines and some dairy products, including Bulgarian white cheese in brine. Therefore, as far as Bulgarian agro-food exports are concerned, development of closer relations with the EU have only been observed for raw agricultural products.

On the import side, the importance of the EU has slightly decreased in relative terms reaching 29 per cent in 1997. The share of the EU in the imports of primary agricultural products increased from 25 per cent in 1992 to 33 per cent in 1997, but imports of processed products contracted from 36 per cent to 27 per cent (table 6.3). There have thus been few clear signs of intensification of trade relations between Bulgaria and the EU in 1990s.

Looking at the value of Bulgaria's agro-food trade with the EU, the clearest finding is that it has been unstable. This was mostly due to the instability of the Bulgarian economy and the deep recession in 1996. Exports to the EU increased between 1993 and 1995, and particularly in 1995 when the macroeconomy was more stable and there was positive, export-led growth (figure 6.2). Once the 1996 recession started, exports contracted and in 1997 were nearly at 1994 levels. Due to the contraction of import demand in Bulgaria, the decrease in agro-food imports from the EU was even sharper (figure 6.3). During the first recession year, 1996, this decrease was due to a cut in both primary and processed products imports. In 1997 the imports of raw agricultural products recovered, whilst that of processed products stagnated. As a result total imports increased again. These developments towards an increase in imports of primary agricultural products and a cut in processed products in 1990s (with the exception of the recovery year, 1995) have been consistent with the economic and agricultural situation in Bulgaria. The supply side has been disrupted by slow and inconsistent reforms, whilst the demand for higher value added products has been constrained by a dramatic fall in real incomes.

The problem of inconsistent statistics is illustrated by differences in the reported balance of agro-food trade. The Bulgarian data, for the period 1992-97 indicate that Bulgaria's agro-food trade balance with the EU was positive. Data from EUROSTAT, however, reports that the balance was negative until 1995. It switched to positive in 1996 due to the drastic fall in import demand and stayed positive in 1997 at 71 and 75 million ECU respectively (European Commission DGVI, 1998).

Competitiveness of the Bulgarian Agro-Food Sector 141

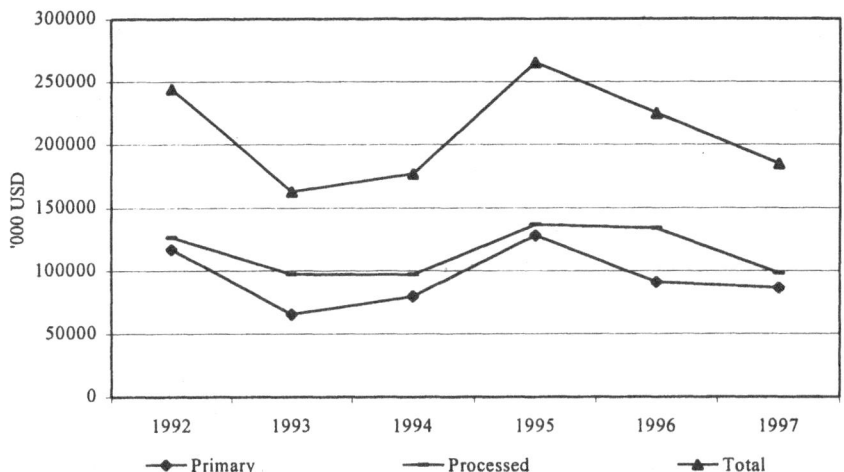

Figure 6.2 Bulgarian agro-food exports to the EU, 1992-97

Source: Bulgarian Foreign Trade database, electronic version; World Bank calculations.

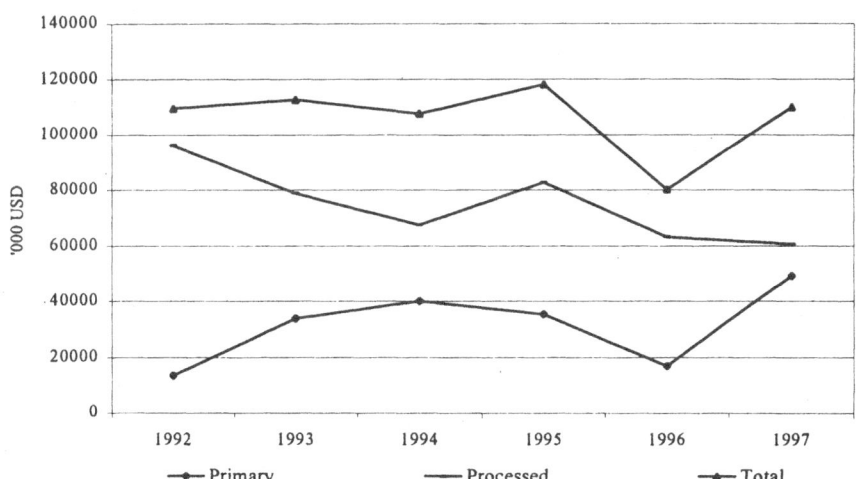

Figure 6.3 Bulgarian agro-food imports from the EU, 1992-97

Source: Bulgarian Foreign Trade database, electronic version; World Bank calculations.

Table 6.2 Bulgarian exports of agricultural products, 1992-97 ('000 USD)

Harmonised System Code	1992 Total	%*	1993 Total	%*	1994 Total	%*	1995 Total	%*	1996 Total	%*	1997 Total	%*
Primary agricultural products												
01 Live animals	103 757	14	43 469	20	45 113	24	22 898	63	17 868	10	2 258	35
02 Meat and edible meat offal	70 678	39	34 783	69	33 122	69	38 033	77	54 483	51	49 754	61
07 Edible vegetables	51 318	50	22 679	29	39 397	40	39 677	62	32 252	57	22 996	67
08 Edible fruit and nuts	19 228	56	20 089	43	68 529	18	35 962	33	25 992	53	21 739	58
10 Cereals	79 661	17	13 482	1	4 932	1	123 676	14	4 215	16	14 092	4
12 Oilseed, oleagi fruits	53 200	44	33 227	54	30 387	61	56 102	86	39 305	71	37 848	73
14 Vegetable plaiting material	562	44	328	51	265	35	952	26	837	14	294	22
Total primary	378 404	31	168 057	39	221 745	36	279 267	46	174 952	52	148 981	58
Processed agricultural products												
04 Dairy prod; birds' eggs	63 789	25	43 897	39	49 062	28	39 199	27	31 560	35	31 156	22
11 Prod milling industry; malt	13 255	1	4 101	3	2 590	0	26 357	2	1 697	0	2 144	0
15 Animal/vegetable fats & oils	15 025	19	31 592	10	19 811	15	48 308	17	17 942	2	21 944	8
16 Prep of meat, fish	12 800	10	16 335	3	8 032	2	13 483	1	11 399	3	10 379	4
17 Sugars and sugar confectionery	18 654	2	22 536	2	21 990	1	53 130	6	55 537	7	24 876	9
18 Cocoa and cocoa preparation	5 377	7	4 206	2	2 866	2	4 779	3	7 426	9	11 714	0
19 Prep of cereal, flour	2 282	1	3 449	4	3 106	2	11 391	1	11 750	1	12 203	1
20 Prep of vegetable, fruit	55 235	29	60 745	15	52 556	13	56 212	17	70 355	14	67 364	16
22 Beverages, spirits	101 980	40	120 159	37	152 057	26	194 909	31	177 609	37	145 415	44
24 Tobacco and manufactured	316 042	7	233 173	7	221 253	7	905 991	7	249 059	11	164 661	7
Total processed	604 439	21	540 193	18	539 103	18	761 146	18	638 433	21	491 856	20

* to the EU

Source: Data from World Bank; Bulgarian Customs Statistics for 1997, electronic data base.

Competitiveness of the Bulgarian Agro-Food Sector 143

Table 6.3 Bulgarian imports of agricultural products, 1992-97 ('000 USD)

Harmonised System Code	1992 Total	%*	1993 Total	%*	1994 Total	%*	1995 Total	%*	1996 Total	%*	1997 Total	%*
Primary agricultural products												
01 Live animals	4 386	79	5 326	81	3 980	84	4 025	54	1 703	57	4 417	78
02 Meat and edible meat offal	2 344	34	19 476	47	30 539	39	31 907	31	12 648	27	40 041	35
07 Edible vegetables	3 690	17	8 181	12	9 755	19	7 018	19	3 305	20	9 457	17
08 Edible fruit and nuts	18 631	42	33 661	41	48 693	42	38 394	47	17 100	56	12 246	65
10 Cereals	8 198	0	29 739	14	4 631	5	6 079	16	55 630	1	79 201	27
12 Oilseed, oleagi fruits	16 931	6	3 309	41	5 207	43	5 669	53	3 851	45	3 322	31
14 Vegetable plaiting material	2	0	10	60	27	26	77	48	79	81	41	30
Total primary	54 182	25	99 702	34	102 832	39	93 169	38	94 316	18	148 726	33
Processed agricultural products												
04 Dairy prod., birds' eggs	6 934	51	18 114	33	21 087	21	17 109	58	8 169	47	11 396	64
11 Prod milling industry, malt	579	58	2 532	31	25 563	27	1 089	78	5 467	37	7 377	38
15 Animal/vegetable fats & oils	10 203	61	21 332	41	20 835	52	21 477	76	20 186	52	17 689	71
16 Prep of meat, fish	2 896	53	2 324	71	2 474	50	3 129	84	1 362	77	2 600	93
17 Sugars and sugar confectionery	104 437	18	74 824	11	110 546	2	140 244	3	92 230	2	107 283	5
18 Cocoa and cocoa preparation	19 506	33	19 055	47	16 191	47	16 844	49	13 832	53	12 235	33
19 Prep of cereal, flour	4 520	63	5 919	72	5 579	59	7 638	76	5 327	69	5 227	81
20 Prep of vegetable, fruit	7 832	37	11 280	50	9 328	46	11 061	66	8 166	72	15 828	50
22 Beverages, spirit	33 147	58	24 549	57	30 078	50	37 359	53	22 979	41	13 275	31
24 Tobacco and manufactured	76 494	44	101 610	20	51 974	19	29 487	26	40 274	42	33 568	31
Total processed	266 548	36	281 539	28	293 655	23	285 437	29	217 992	29	226 479	27

* from the EU

Source: Data from World Bank; Bulgarian Customs Statistics for 1997, electronic data base.

These developments have to be interpreted carefully. They do not show some long term tendency, but are due to the sharp decrease in imports, which stemmed from the economic recession in Bulgaria. Once growth in real incomes reappears, which started in 1998, coupled with the stabilisation of the exchange rate brought about by the currency board introduced in 1997, a switch toward a negative trade balance might occur.

Another feature of the agro-food trade between Bulgaria and the EU is that it has taken place in both directions, generally with lower unit values than average for extra-EU trade (table 6.4). Because the trade flows have been analysed at a four digit level of aggregation it is difficult to identify the factors which have caused this tendency. However, it seems that differences in quality are important. For example, it is known that Bulgaria imports low value cuts of beef which are used in the processing industry. Therefore it is not surprising that the unit value of beef exported by the EU to Bulgaria is lower than the average unit value of the extra-EU exports. The case of tobacco is identical. From the point of view of EU imports from Bulgaria, a similar example is wine. EU imports from Bulgaria are mainly table wines which are not of top quality. As a result, the unit value of these imports is lower than the average for extra-EU imports.

In summary, the integration between Bulgaria and the EU through trade in the agro-food sector has not been strongly developed. From this point of view there has not been high pressure for equalisation of product and factor prices through trade.

Tariff Protection in Bulgaria and the Role of the AA

The part of the AA concerning agro-food trade provides for lower than most favoured nation (MFN) tariffs within or without tariff quotas. Applying the logic from the theoretical framework, it could be expected that, everything else being equal, lower tariffs in mutual trade should result in trade creation. However, the brief analysis of the trade flows between Bulgaria and the EU shows neither trade creation nor trade diversion to the rest of the world. The main question is why this has happened. In order to answer this question, first the MFN rate of protection and then the preferential treatment provided by the AA will be analysed. Both pieces of analysis are undertaken from the point of view of EU imports to Bulgaria.

There are several ways to measure tariff protection (OECD, 1997). In this analysis the import weighted average and the production weighted average are shown. Two ways of determining import weights are applied: by total imports and by net imports (imports minus exports) with tariff lines for which Bulgaria is a net exporter having a weight of zero.[2] The results show separately the protection of primary agricultural products, processed products, and noncompeting agricultural imports.[3]

Table 6.5 shows that the tariff protection of competing processed products is higher than for primary products. The import weighted average for the processed products is 36 per cent; net import weighted 34 per cent; and production weighted 37 per cent. The respective rates for primary agriculture are 24 per cent, 25 per cent, and 27 per cent. Overall, for all agro-food imports, the import weighted protection rate is 31 per cent and the net import weighted 27 per cent. In general about one-third of tariff lines in primary and processed agriculture have tariff protection at 40 per cent (table 6.6). Some tariff lines have protection above 70 per cent (5 per cent of tariff lines in processed products, mainly beverages, and 4 per cent of primary agriculture). Thus the MFN protection of the Bulgarian agro-food sector is relatively high.

The AA provides for preferential access of EU products to the Bulgarian market at reduced tariffs. However, the substantial cuts in the tariffs have been accompanied by quantity limits or the tariffs have remained relatively high despite the cuts (especially at the beginning of the period for which the AA was renegotiated) (Ivanova et al., 1996). In table 6.7, two of the annexes to the AA are analysed in which the preferential duties are granted without quantitative limits. The first one applies to processed products and provides gradual annual tariff cuts over the period 1997-2002. It includes 38 tariff items with ad valorem duty and one with a combined duty including, ad valorem and specific elements (beer). The second annex includes fixed tariff rates for the whole period. It comprises 75 tariff items with ad valorem tariffs and 11 with combined duties. Only the items with ad valorem tariffs in this annex are analysed.

Table 6.7 shows that for items with duties which will be gradually cut, at the beginning of the period the largest portion ranges from 25 and 40 per cent. In 2002 the situation will definitely change, but currently the protection remains relatively high. It is even higher for items with fixed duties. In addition, Bulgaria has included a list of 8 tariff items for which the tariffs might be increased to 52 per cent in 7 of the 8 cases. Thus, tariff liberalisation has been very modest not only with regard to Bulgarian imports to the EU, which is well known and has been widely discussed, but also in respect to EU exports to Bulgaria. The AA has not been effective in terms of encouraging trade creation. Other factors, particularly the state of the Bulgarian economy, have been more powerful in shaping trade flows with the EU than the partial preferential access provided by the AA.

Table 6.4 Unit values of EU trade with third countries and Bulgaria for selected groups of agricultural products (ECU/tonne)*

Imports to the EU

Code	Label	1994 Extra-EU	1994 BUL	1995 Extra-EU	1995 BUL	1996 Extra-EU	1996 BUL	1997 Extra-EU	1997 BUL
0102	Live bovine animals	1 500	1 071	1 525	1 027	1 622	1 191	1 578	1 233
0104	Live sheep and goats	1 943	2 072	1 963	1 843	2 287	2 029	2 505	3 212
0202	Meat of bovine animals, frozen	3 141	7 113	3 095	-	2 837	2 472	2 954	-
0204	Meat of sheep or goats: fresh, chilled, frozen	2 794	3 336	2 551	3 256	2 967	3 232	3 443	3 952
0405	Butter and other dairy fats ands oils	2 086	-	2 253	-	1 788	-	2 029	-
0406	Cheese and curd	4 586	2 860	4 732	2 732	4 262	2 507	3 370	2 170
0809	Apricots, cherries, peaches inc. nectarines	855	322	1 072	589	1 084	753	1 114	757
1512	Sunflower seed, safflower, or cottonseed oil	540	438	547	471	543	451	616	378
1806	Chocolate and cocoa based products	3 753	2 177	3 563	5 300	3 354	-	3 260	-
2007	Jams, fruit jellies, and marmalades	982	603	1 011	806	1 124	841	1 198	709
2009	Fruit juices (nonalcoholic)	777	486	859	1 353	947	884	838	894
2105	Ice cream and edible ices	3 536	-	1 910	-	2 431	-	2 133	-
2203	Beer made from malt	555	429	538	420	560	401	632	388
2204	Wine of fresh grapes	1 485	904	1 124	917	1 238	860	1 748	965
2401	Nonmanufactured tobacco and tobacco refuse	3 480	3 107	3 253	3 031	3 354	2 646	3 846	2 979

Competitiveness of the Bulgarian Agro-Food Sector 147

Table 6.4 Continued

		\multicolumn{8}{c	}{Exports from the EU}
		1994		1995		1996		1997	
Code	Label	Extra EU	BUL	Extra EU	BUL	Extra EU	BUL	Extra EU	BUL
0102	Live bovine animals	916	-	998	-	1 097	-	1 185	1 687
0104	Live sheep and goats	1 737	-	1 969	-	2 322	-	1 788	-
0202	Meat of bovine animals, frozen	1 195	832	1 242	1 014	1 188	1 062	1 299	1 471
0204	Meat of sheep or goats: fresh, chilled, frozen	3 857	-	3 632	-	4 026	-	5 246	-
0405	Butter and other dairy fats ands oils	1 826	1 576	1 783	1 734	1 822	1 909	1 809	1 699
0406	Cheese and curd	2 790	1 822	2 760	1 438	3 020	2 157	3 230	1 474
0809	Apricots, cherries, peaches inc. nectarines	666	276	865	454	637	406	843	602
1512	Sunflower seed, safflower or cottonseed oil	748	979	673	724	600	675	572	1 024
1806	Chocolate and cocoa based products	2 987	2 479	3 030	2 606	3 030	2 377	3 115	2 772
2007	Jams, fruit jellies and marmalades	1 699	427	1 574	646	1 713	994	1 764	956
2009	Fruit juices (nonalcoholic)	811	469	812	650	926	686	1 012	820
2105	Ice cream and edible ices	2 772	3 507	2 691	3 034	2 532	2 063	2 508	3 126
2203	Beer made from malt	756	563	751	665	754	660	765	762
2204	Wine of fresh grapes	1 936	2 612	2 142	2 112	2 344	2 246	2 523	8 825
2401	Nonmanufactured tobacco and tobacco refuse	1 794	1 563	1 177	1 123	1 797	1 012	2 379	868

* Dash (-) indicates that no trade was recorded

Source: Data from EUROSTAT-COMEXT.

Table 6.5 Bulgarian tariff protection in the agro-food sector (per cent)

2-digit level	Import weighted	Net import weighted	Production weighted
Primary agriculture			
01 Live animals	9	9	-
02 Meat	22	15	36
07 Vegetables	37	28	25
08 Fruits and nuts	21	16	61
10 Cereals	26	27	24
12 Oilseeds	10	11	24
14 Vegetable plaiting mat.	40	40	-
Total	24	24	34
Processed agriculture			
04 Dairy	54	58	42
07 Vegetables	40	0	-
11 Prod. milling	20	20	20
15 Fats and oils	13	13	12
16 Meat/fish preparations	33	30	-
17 Sugar	48	46	50
18 Cocoa	25	9	-
19 Flour	52	27	55
20 Vegetable preparations	30	0	-
22 Beverages	20	6	49
24 Tobacco	28	5	38
Total	36	34	37
Noncompeting agriculture and misc.			
09 Coffee, tea, spices	14	16	
13 Gums, resins	10	10	
21 Misc.	32	31	
Total	22	19	
Not included above			
03 Fish	15	15	
05 Animal prod. residues	39	39	
06 Live and cut plants	18	22	
23 Residue from food, fodder	16	17	
Total	17	19	
Grand Total	31	27	

Source: Data from World Bank, 1997.

Table 6.6 Distribution of tariff rates in Bulgaria for agricultural products (8-digit)

Tariff rates	Processed	Primary
>70 %	5 %	4 %
40-70 %	12 %	5 %
40 %	34 %	30 %
25-40 %	7 %	4 %
25 %	18 %	28 %
10-25 %	12 %	11 %
0-10 %	12 %	18 %

Source: Data from World Bank, 1997.

Table 6.7 Distribution of the preferential tariff rates granted by Bulgaria to the EU without quantitative limits

Tariff rates	Items with decreasing duties		Items with fixed duties
	1997	2002	
25-40 %	41	5	71
25 %	3	18	7
10-25 %	36	28	19
0-10 %	21	49	4

Source: Data from World Bank, 1997.

Trade Relations Between Bulgaria and the EU: Measures of Market Share

Balassa (1977) claims that a comparative advantage is revealed by relatively high shares of export markets and a comparative disadvantage by low shares of export markets. The revealed comparative advantage (RCA) of a country for any particular good is the share of the international market for that good divided by its share of the international markets for all goods. This fraction is multiplied by 100 for ease of presentation and figures above 100 indicate a revealed comparative advantage and vice versa. The formula can be expressed as:

$$RCA = (X_i/X_{iw}/X_m/X_{mw}) \cdot 100$$

where X_i is the value of exports of commodity i from the country in question, X_{iw} the value of exports of commodity i from all countries, X_m

the value of exports of all manufactured goods from the country in question, and X_{mw} the value of exports of all manufactured goods from all countries.

The RCA measure is therefore taken to identify sectors for which an individual country has a comparative advantage and a comparative disadvantage (Pitts et al., 1995). To derive a more focused set of measures for analysis, the RCA has been adjusted here to derive a commodity weighting index and an EU share index. The commodity weighting index compares Bulgaria's share of imports to the EU for a given commodity against Bulgaria's share of total EU agro-food imports from nonmember countries. For example, if Bulgaria accounts for 5 per cent of EU live animal imports but only 3 per cent of total agricultural imports to the EU, one can say that that there is a revealed comparative advantage for Bulgaria compared against other non-EU members for this commodity. The commodity weighting index compares the share of Bulgarian exports of a particular commodity going to the EU against the share of total Bulgarian agro-food exports that go to the EU market.

Table 6.8 details the highest scoring products in the commodity weighting index. The highest scores were achieved by jams, fruit jellies, marmalades, fruit or nut purees, wine, cucumbers and gherkins, and meat and edible offal from fowls, ducks, geese, turkeys, guinea fowls (in that order). Sunflower seeds, assorted vegetables, and sheep and goat meat also show a RCA.

Table 6.8   Commodity weighting index for Bulgaria

Product	Index
Jams, fruit jellies, marmalades, fruit or nut purees	2 560
Wine of fresh grapes	2 178
Cucumbers and gherkins, fresh or chilled	1 050
Meat and edible offal from fowls, ducks, geese, turkeys, guinea fowls: fresh, chilled, frozen	620
Fresh or chilled vegetables	550
Natural honey	532
Birds' eggs (not in shell) and egg yolks: fresh, dried, cooked	482
Vegetables: cooked or uncooked	455
Sunflower seeds	448
Meat of sheep or goats: fresh, chilled, frozen	437
Live bovine animals	150

Source: Data from EUROSTAT-COMEXT, 1997.

The lowest index scores were derived for tropical fruits and nuts, which Bulgaria does not produce. However, Bulgaria also achieved below 100 scores for the main commodities of milk and dairy sectors (except cheese), wheat and barley, and pork. Therefore Bulgaria has revealed comparative disadvantage for some of its main tradable agro-food products.

Table 6.9 analyses the EU share of Bulgarian agro-food exports. There is a high degree of correlation with the commodity weighting index. The highest indexes are again for meat of sheep and goats; jams, fruit jellies, and marmalades; and meat and edible offal from fowls, ducks, geese and turkeys. Likewise, Bulgaria performs poorly for milk and dairy products (except cheese); wheat and barley; and pork. Bulgaria's main advantage would, thus, appear to rest with a specific range of niche products (wine, apricots, sunflower seeds, etc.) rather than staple commodities.

Table 6.9   EU share of Bulgarian exports index, 1996

Product	Index
High index scores	
Meat and edible offal from fowls, ducks, geese, turkeys, guinea fowls: fresh, chilled, frozen	147
Meat of sheep or goats: fresh, chilled, frozen	140
Sunflower seeds	132
Apricots, cherries, peaches: fresh	128
Jams, fruit jellies, marmalades, fruit or nut purees	124
Birds' eggs (not in shell) and egg yolks: fresh, dried, cooked	108
Natural honey	101
Wine of fresh grapes	99
Live bovine animals	89
Scores for other agro-food products	
Live sheep and goats	28
Fish fillets and other fish meat, fresh, chilled, frozen	1
Milk and cream (fresh)	0
Wheat and meslin	30
Maize	3
Wheat flour and meslin flour	54
Olive oil	0

Source: Data from EUROSTAT-COMEXT, 1997.

However, such trade indexes should be treated with caution for Bulgaria, where the link between exporting and competitiveness may be weak due to the use of domestic export impediments, including bans, especially for grains and live cattle. These impediments were finally removed in 1998, but trade data from that year were not available. Another reason why market shares may not be a good proxy for international competitiveness are the tariff and quality restrictions of foreign customs unions such as the EU, which strongly affect Bulgarian agro-food exports. Export market shares should thus be seen only as a limited proxy for measuring comparative advantage of Bulgarian agro-food production.

CEFTA: an Intermediary Step Facilitating Adjustment to the EU?

Trade flows with CEFTA countries Bulgaria joined CEFTA in January 1999. The path to CEFTA was cleared by accession to the World Trade Organization (WTO) in October 1996 and priority was put on CEFTA membership by the new Bulgarian government which came into office in May 1997.

However, Bulgaria's trade with CEFTA members in the postreform period has been rather slender. Trade flows in the agro-food sector have been neither substantial nor stable. CEFTA has a low share of Bulgarian agro-food trade and in 1997 it accounted for only 3.3 per cent of exports and 12.2 per cent of imports (table 6.10). The importance of CEFTA varies according to the chapters of the Harmonised Nomenclature (HN). It is difficult to detect more stable tendencies because the annual fluctuations are very large. CEFTA is important as an export market for Bulgarian fresh vegetables and live animals and has an increasing role for exports of food industry residues. For traditional Bulgarian exports of beverages (especially wine), CEFTA is not a substantial partner. It absorbs only between 3 and 5 per cent of Bulgarian exports. For the other traditional Bulgarian agricultural exports, tobacco and tobacco products, the role of the CEFTA market is decreasing. It absorbed 10 per cent at the beginning of 1990s and only 2 per cent by the end of the decade. On the import side, CEFTA is a substantial supplier of livestock products including live animals, and vegetables.

The relative importance of individual CEFTA member countries has varied over the years. The main trade partners have been Romania and Poland (table 6.11). In 1995 and 1997 only, Hungary had a substantial share, mainly due to a large import of live animals into Bulgaria. Slovakia and Slovenia are insignificant trade partners.

Table 6.10 Bulgarian agricultural trade, 1993-97 (million USD)*

	1993	1994	1995	1996	1997
Total agri exports	758.2	905.6	1 114.5	882.3	701.7
Total agr imports	410.7	451.2	389.5	371.5	428.3
CEFTA exports	49.40	39.86	34.81	29.58	22.8
CEFTA imports	19.07	35.60	8.51	26.81	52.1
Share of CEFTA exp. (%)	6.5	4.4	3.1	3.4	3.3
Share of CEFTA imp. (%)	4.6	7.9	2.2	7.2	12.2

* Trade publications by the Bulgarian National Statistical Institute do not provide data on agricultural trade with CEFTA. Each entry is a transaction registered by a separate customs declaration. For this reason data about total agricultural exports and imports may differ from those published.

Source: Data from Bulgarian Customs Statistics, electronic database.

Table 6.11 Share of Bulgarian agricultural trade with individual CEFTA countries, 1993-97 (per cent)

	Exports				
	1993	1994	1995	1996	1997
Czech Rep.	4.9	7.3	12.2	16.9	11.1
Slovakia	0.7	2.1	3.6	2.1	1.5
Hungary	4.1	7.8	6.6	12.7	13.4
Poland	22.6	15.9	21.1	37.7	46.7
Romania	65.7	64.0	53.3	27.3	22.2
Slovenia	2.0	2.8	3.3	3.3	5.1

	Imports				
	1993	1994	1995	1996	1997
Czech Rep.	15.3	4.5	7.8	4.2	4.4
Slovakia	1.7	1.1	4.8	1.1	2.7
Hungary	11.9	9.1	40.9	14.2	39.5
Poland	35.5	49.9	14.3	4.5	41.2
Romania	28.6	31.5	29.2	75.2	11.6
Slovenia	7.0	4.0	2.9	0.8	0.6

Source: Data from Bulgarian Customs Statistics, electronic database.

Overall, Bulgarian agricultural exports to CEFTA have tended to decrease, while import flows have changed from year to year depending on domestic market balances (figure 6.4). The erratic changes have been due to the import of a few products (e.g. the increase in 1994 was mainly due to the import of flour and in 1996 of grains).

The review of trade flows between Bulgaria and CEFTA allows a conclusion to be drawn that there is still a lack of a more stable trade pattern, particularly in imports from CEFTA. The big fluctuations in the mid-1990s were brought about mainly by internal factors, particularly the badly functioning grain market and the existence of effective shortages of grain and flour. Trade flows during the period when Bulgaria was not a CEFTA member seem to have very little relation to the fundamental comparative advantage of the trade partners. The liberalisation of agricultural trade expected under CEFTA is supposed to allow more competitive imports and may bring about a change in the commodity structure of imports from CEFTA. These imports are expected to be less dependent on the temporary imbalances on domestic markets and be based on more stable economic grounds.

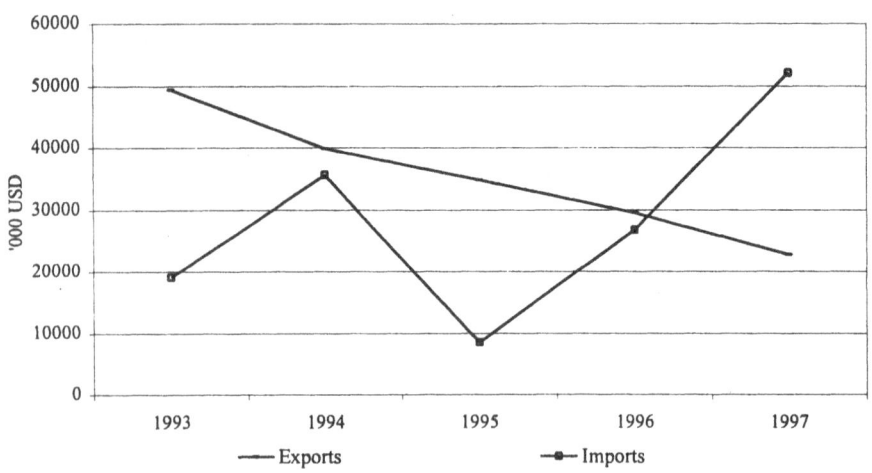

Figure 6.4 Bulgarian agro-food trade with CEFTA countries, 1993-97

Source: Bulgarian Customs Statistics, electronic data base.

Preferential trade access Bulgaria concluded negotiations for accession to CEFTA in 1998 and the agreed preferential arrangements entered into force in 1999. Given that little time has elapsed, it is not possible to analyse the effects of the implementation of the agreement here. The following analysis tries to define to what extent the multilaterally agreed schedules for agricultural liberalisation require cuts in the Bulgarian import tariffs for CEFTA countries and to identify the scope to which the Bulgarian agro-food imports from CEFTA are affected by the liberalisation. Therefore, only the potential effects of the multilateral lists with zero duties and with a set level of duties are studied. Bilateral concessions for 'sensitive' agricultural products are not included in the analysis as they are generally within quotas and the quota quantities are small. As a result, their contribution to trade liberalisation is insignificant.

In Bulgaria the arithmetic average of the tariffs for which a zero duty applies due to accession to CEFTA is 22 per cent.[4] Bulgaria has zero duty on only seven tariff items included in this list. This means that the compliance with the CEFTA schedule will induce a substantial reduction in import tariffs. Measured by the past structure of agricultural imports from CEFTA, about 39 per cent are subject to zero duty. This means that not only is the tariff reduction substantial, but also that it covers more than one-third of Bulgarian imports from CEFTA.

The alignment to the multilaterally set level of tariffs also induces a substantial tariff cut, from 32 per cent to 13.8 per cent arithmetic average. On a historical basis, 37 per cent of Bulgarian agricultural imports from CEFTA were of these tariff items. Thus, only two multilateral schemes cover about three-quarters of Bulgarian agro-food imports from CEFTA countries. As a result, it is likely that imports will increase.

What is the expected effect of joining CEFTA on Bulgarian integration with the EU? The Bulgarian agro-food sector will have to adjust to operate on a wider market with lower tariff barriers. Although within CEFTA the liberalisation of trade with 'sensitive' agricultural products is insignificant and subject to the same philosophy as the AAs, the two multilaterally agreed schedules for liberalisation of 'nonsensitive' products could boost competitive imports. This can potentially induce stronger pressure for restructuring the Bulgarian agro-food chain in order to be internationally competitive and as a result might facilitate its integration with the EU. However, the role of accession to CEFTA for the integration with Western Europe should not be overestimated. It is only one of numerous processes which will push Bulgarian producers to adjust to international competition and standard regulations.

Price and Policy Alignment

The issue of price alignment has been very prominent in discussions about the agricultural aspects of CEEC accession to the EU (Tangermann and Josling, 1995; van Berkum and Terluin, 1995). In this section the main question is whether prices in Bulgaria have started aligning with EU prices and to what extent this is due to policy alignment.

Price Developments in Bulgaria and Divergence from the EU

Bulgarian farm prices in ECU terms roughly doubled during the period 1991-97 (table 6.12).[5] The highest increases were registered for beef, lamb, and pork (threefold and above). However, the prices of some core crop products like maize, sugar beets, and potatoes increased from 50 per cent to 80 per cent, while some prices (apples) even decreased in real terms. The decisive factor for these observed price changes was domestic demand and, in some cases, import competition (e.g. sugar and apples). Before 1997, government policies had a stronger effect on relative prices. The increase in farmers' prices from 1991 to 1997 was by and large in line with the increase in retail prices (table 6.13).

The increase in farmers' prices (in ECU terms) in 1997 decreased the gap with EU institutional prices (figure 6.5). The price of wheat reached 86 per cent of the EU price. However, this was an exceptional situation. Following a grain and bread shortage in 1996, the Bulgarian government announced a quite high minimum price for wheat in 1997. As this policy only led to increasing stocks (export subsidies were not available) it was discontinued in 1998. As a result, the alignment of the wheat price to the EU level cannot be treated as sustainable. Better examples of price alignment are sunflower, pork, and milk. The smaller gap in 1997 was mainly due to the decrease in government intervention through the ending of export restrictions, which previously tried to suppress domestic prices in order to support consumers. However, it is difficult to draw conclusions from the observed pattern. First, farm prices in Bulgaria show a great annual volatility, and second, it is difficult to see Bulgarian prices consistently aligning to the EU even for products which in the EU receive 'light' support. For example the price of mutton 1997 was only 23 per cent of the EU level, whilst the price of pork was 86 per cent. The latter was due to the higher demand for pork in Bulgaria and record low prices in the EU. Thus, it is difficult to conclude that there is price alignment in Bulgarian product prices with the EU. If there was some decrease in the price gap in 1997, it was mainly due to the decrease in government intervention aimed at consumer support and to the overall market situation in Bulgaria and not to closer integration with the EU per se.

Table 6.12 Bulgarian farm prices, 1991-97 (ECU/tonne)

	1991	1992	1993	1994	1995	1996	1997	Ratio 1997/91
Crop products								
Wheat	57	50	81	51	52	101	129	2.3
Barley	54	44	72	48	44	96	116	2.2
Maize	67	58	97	66	68	95	103	1.5
Sugar beets	11	10	12	13	14	14	20	1.8
Tomatoes	49	43	68	39	36	55	111	2.3
Potatoes	124	85	142	114	151	112	209	1.7
Apples	73	47	54	81	85	44	60	0.8
Grapes	85	77	90	126	151	136	-	1.6[a]
Wine grapes	84	78	88	128	151	134	199	2.4
Animal Products								
Cattle[b]	246	307	461	436	728	378	744	3.0
Calves[b]	422	468	589	517	838	547	807	1.9
Sheep[b]	194	221	314	412	508	398	533	2.7
Lamb[b]	400	529	839	548	979	520	1388	3.5
Pigs[b]	396	476	692	595	783	487	1217	3.1
Chicken[b]	431	442	608	546	585	464	872	2.0
Cow milk[c]	75	90	152	130	149	103	157	2.1
Sheep milk[d]	130	137	274	198	288	129	249	1.9

[a] 1996/1991
[b] Live weight
[c] 3.6 % fat content and per 1 000 litres
[d] 6.5 % fat content

Source: Data from NSI, Price Department, unpublished data.

158 *Agriculture and East-West European Integration*

Table 6.13 Bulgarian retail prices, 1991-97 (ECU/kg)

	1991	1992	1993	1994	1995	1996	1997	Ratio 1997/91
White bread	0.11	0.15	0.23	0.18	0.20	0.26	0.28	2.52
Pork with bones	0.90	1.09	2.05	2.14	2.52	1.71	2.36	2.62
Veal with bones	0.93	1.12	1.57	1.60	2.06	1.28	2.03	2.19
Lamb	1.05	1.37	1.15	1.10	2.54	1.33	2.41	2.30
Chicken	0.85	0.97	1.40	1.31	1.34	1.34	1.70	2.01
Butter (0.125 kg)	0.20	0.26	0.33	0.28	0.37	0.31	0.34	1.69
Eggs (each)	0.03	0.05	0.05	0.05	0.05	0.06	0.06	1.71
Fresh pasteurised milk	0.10	0.13	0.25	0.20	0.28	0.20	0.17	1.71
Yoghurt (0.500 kg)	0.07	0.09	0.15	0.13	0.19	0.14	0.14	1.99
White sheep cheese	0.91	1.13	1.99	1.84	2.42	1.56	1.93	2.12
White cow cheese	0.75	0.93	1.61	1.44	1.72	1.26	1.33	1.78
Yellow cow cheese	0.98	1.43	2.34	2.28	2.86	2.02	2.10	2.14
Yellow sheep cheese	1.13	1.63	2.70	2.65	3.71	2.31	2.77	2.45

Source: Data from NSI, 1996, 1997.

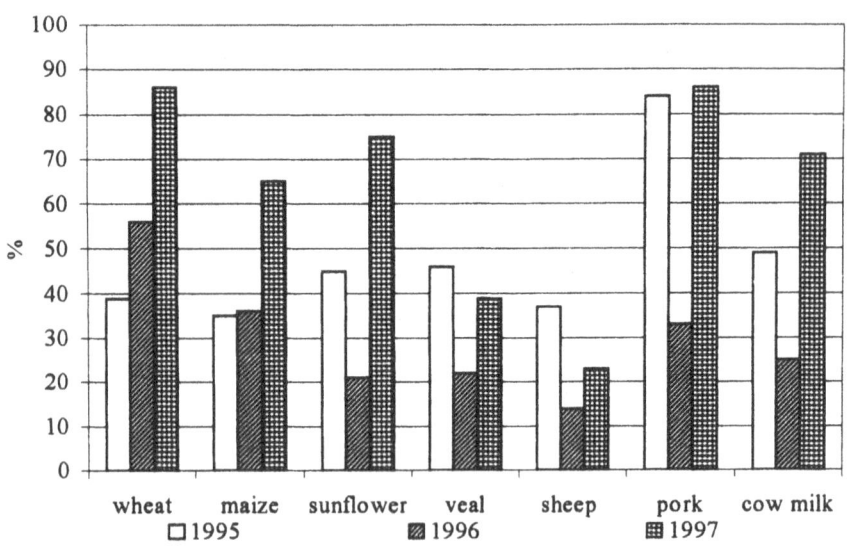

Figure 6.5 Bulgarian farm prices in relation to EU institutional prices, 1995-97

Source: Data from European Commission, Directorate for Agriculture (DGVI), 1998.

Table 6.14 shows nominal protection coefficients (NPCs) for certain dates in July, August, and September 1997 in Bulgaria. The majority of NPCs for these three months were still less than one (indicating an explicit tax). However, the NPCs have increased compared to previous years and in September the NPCs for pigs (1.01), veal (1.08), cheese derived from cows' milk (1.25) and wheat (1.14) were all above 1 (indicating an explicit subsidy). The main reasons for these increases in NPCs were a shortage of cheese on the domestic market; existing duties for cheese and veal; a shortage of fattened pigs for slaughtering as a result of the crisis in the heavily indebted, large breeding units; and rises in feed prices (World Bank, 1997).

Table 6.14 **Nominal protection coefficients for selected farm products in Bulgaria, 1997**

	30 July	20 August	3 September
Live chicken	0.74	0.79	0.79
Frozen chicken	0.81	0.84	0.85
Live pigs	0.78	0.94	1.01
Pork	0.66	0.81	0.87
Calves	0.79	0.87	0.88
Veal	0.98	1.00	1.08
Cow milk	0.44	0.61	0.71
Cow milk*	0.54	0.76	0.88
Cheese from cow milk	0.84	1.15	1.25
Sunflower oil	0.62	0.65	0.65
Maize	0.88	0.84	0.82
Wheat (export parity)	1.39	1.38	1.38
Wheat (import parity)	1.16	1.15	1.14
Flour	0.84	0.83	0.83

* Using New Zealand reference price

Source: Data from World Bank (1997).

Combined Price and Policy Alignment Assessment

The overall effect of agricultural and trade policies in Bulgaria and the EU can be compared by calculating PSEs for the main commodities. PSEs for Bulgaria have been estimated here for the years 1994 to 1996. A previous study (Ivanova et al., 1995) made similar calculations for the years 1990 to 1993 so by comparing the findings of these two complimentary studies, a view of most of the transition period in Bulgaria is permitted. The PSE calculations at farm level are summarised in table 6.15. Total, unit, and percentage PSEs are shown.

The negative PSEs for Bulgaria indicate that farmers, with the exception of milk producers (and maize and veal producers in 1990), have been consistently taxed throughout the era of transition. For milk the New Zealand farmgate price was used as the reference price for this commodity (due to the absence of international trade) as in Organisation for Economic Co-operation and Development (OECD) studies.

The 1996 results must be treated with extreme caution as the year was characterised by a macroeconomic crisis with high inflation, collapse of the Bulgarian lev, and negative growth. Such a large depreciation combined with rapid inflation had an enormous effect on the transfer estimations due to the large exchange rate shift.

It can be seen that the extent of the taxation of the farmers of the seven analysed products rose dramatically in nominal terms from 1.6 billion leva in 1990 to over 7 billion leva in 1991 (the year of price liberalisation). It dropped in 1993, but then grew rapidly each succeeding year, especially in 1996, to 79 billion leva. It is conjectured that the majority of this added taxation of farmers was not purposive agricultural policy, but simply the effect of the depreciation of the currency because of uncontrolled domestic inflation. Throughout the transition period, the wheat sector has been taxed. Veal, pork, and chicken were heavily taxed in the early years of transition. This fell somewhat in 1995, but increased dramatically in 1996. It is a well known feature of PSEs that relatively small changes in domestic or foreign prices or in the exchange rate can have a much larger effect on the per cent PSEs. This is certainly seen in table 6.15, especially for barley. However, generally wheat and barley were more heavily taxed than maize, and meats were sometimes heavily taxed and sometimes not. Only for milk (given the reference price used), was there generally positive support. This highly unstable and seemingly irrational pattern of policy has resulted from the frequent changes in the government price policy and the trade regime but most importantly from the erratic performance of the Bulgarian currency. In the makeup of the PSE, the largest component was consistently the market price element. Government support via the budget has been on a rapid downward trajectory. For example, in 1994, for wheat the net total PSE was minus 8 638 million leva; from this total, minus 8 840 million leva was attributable to the market component. The relatively small direct and indirect transfers had very little effect. The changes in the market price effect were consistently more important to the size of the overall PSE during the transition period.

The size of the price gap can be indicated by the ratio of domestic to world prices; for wheat this ratio rose from 0.62 in 1990 to 0.89 in 1995. Comparing these figures with the commodities for which PSEs are smaller, the main factor for the smaller overall magnitude is the lower price gap between domestic and world market prices. For example in the case of maize (comparatively small PSEs) the ratios of domestic to world prices for the years 1990 to 1994 ranged between 0.72 and 1.00.

Competitiveness in the Downstream Sector

Price Competitiveness

Table 6.16 details the estimations of transfers at the processing level. These were calculated as at the farm level subject to an input adjustment and an appropriate technical conversion coefficient (see Gorton et al., 1997). The transfer analysis reveals that processors have neither been consistent losers (as were farmers) or constant beneficiaries (as were retailers). Covering the period 1990 to 1996, in 15 cases processors were effectively taxed and in 18 cases they were effectively subsidised (in one case net transfers were zero). For the period 1990 to 1996, in no chain were processors either always effectively taxed or always effectively subsidised.

These transfer estimations lend weight to the argument that the processing industries in these food chains are reasonably competitive. While processors have benefited from buying inputs at prices below world market prices they have also tended to sell their output at prices below world market prices. They have not been able to expropriate the rents generated in the food supply chains from farm prices being below world market levels to the same extent as have retailers. This notion of the processing sector being reasonably competitive is supported by information on the market structure of the industry. Table 6.17 details the four-firm concentration ratios at the processing level in Bulgaria and compares them against the figures for other European countries.[6]

Table 6.15 Economic transfers in Bulgarian food supply chains at the farm level[a]

		1990	1991	1992	1993	1994	1995	1996
Wheat	Total PSE	-791.3	-1 072.2	-2 269.9	-3 025.7	-8 637.8	-14 417.7	-28 572.4
	Unit PSE	-149.5	-238.2	-660.1	-831.7	-2 217.1	-4 197.0	-15 995.9
	% PSE	-32.4	-17.1	-39.1	-32.8	-73.4	-92.5	-67.7
Barley	Total PSE	-479.9	-228.2	-383.6	64.6	-829.7	-1 781.5	-3 360.3
	Unit PSE	-345.9	-152.0	-56.1	67.5	-695.5	-1 519.2	-7 368.4
	% PSE	-117.6	-12.4	-28.9	2.9	-26.9	-39.4	-34.3
Maize	Total PSE	19.8	-1 496.5	-517.9	66.2	-96.6	-1 286.9	-6 655.3
	Unit PSE	16.2	-539.2	279.4	63.8	-56.5	-708.2	-6 439.5
	% PSE	2.4	-35.8	-16.6	2.0	-2.8	-12.4	-29.9
Veal	Total PSE	25.2	-1 257.3	-1 813.8	-805.3	-471.1	-45.6	-16 192.6
	Unit PSE	105.2	-5 722.9	-6 131.9	-3 351.6	-2 542.8	-341.5	-105 759.5
	% PSE	1.6	-63.1	-43.9	-17.5	-7.6	-0.5	-110.2
Pork	Total PSE	-600.9	-2 192.7	-1 046.8	-2 201.3	-2 284.0	-2 390.3	-8 805.4
	Unit PSE	-990.7	-4 074.3	-2 204.1	-5 531.8	-7 168.5	-6 124.5	-21 774.0
	% PSE	-22.5	-44.9	-16.1	-24.2	-19.8	-9.0	-20.2
Chicken	Total PSE	-309.6	-662.3	-1 151.9	-797.5	-882.7	-865.1	-15 568.5
	Unit PSE	-1 226.3	-4 755.6	-9 328.2	-6 136.4	-8 636.8	-6 408.8	-121 208.6
	% PSE	-35.0	-48.6	-66.6	-30.5	-26.1	-12.7	-125.2
Milk	Total PSE	464.6	-350.5	-679.3	1 406.4	808.8	3 019.8	-
	Unit PSE	203.1	-181.8	-394.3	1 794.4	696.1	2 675.6	-
	% PSE	20.2	-9.8	-13.9	33.7	14.1	19.5	-
7 product total PSE		-1 672.1	-7 259.2	-7 863.2	-5 295.6	-12 393.1	-17 767.3	-79 154.5[b]

[a] Total PSE in million leva at current prices; unit PSEs in current leva per tonne
[b] 6 products only (excludes milk)

Source: Gorton et al., 1997.

Competitiveness of the Bulgarian Agro-Food Sector 163

Table 6.16 PSEs at the processing level in Bulgarian food supply chains*

		1990	1991	1992	1993	1994	1995	1996
Flour	Total PSE	-405.4	-178.6	516.5	-206.5	1 319.3	3 006.2	8 483.4
	Unit PSE	-324.5	-152.6	544.3	-228.3	1 658.3	3 597.8	11 261.6
	% PSE	-50.8	-6.8	12.1	-4.3	17.5	23.6	19.4
Bread	Total PSE	-68.7	-33.5	-172.6	64.1	350.1	658.0	-10.2
	Unit PSE	-94.8	-49.4	-402.5	206.5	1 297.3	2 296.9	-29.4
	% PSE	-9.2	-1.8	-9.5	3.0	12.2	14.2	0.0
Veal	Total PSE	-369.9	-908.4	309.1	-446.6	595.8	-13 194.2	-3 569.3
	Unit PSE	-3 155.3	-8 785.2	3 029.8	-3 854.8	6 161.1	-191 881.8	-45 034.2
	% PSE	-44.5	-62.8	11.9	-10.1	10.2	-134.5	-20.9
Pork	Total PSE	847.6	-194.2	-4 587.1	1 005.0	1 640.3	-16 280.1	10 222.9
	Unit PSE	2 077.7	-536.2	-14 362.0	3 752.5	1 649.5	-63 234.0	38 302.9
	% PSE	35.8	-3.5	-61.9	10.2	11.5	-57.8	18.3
Chicken	Total PSE	319.6	457.2	507.4	-767.2	-240.8	1 442.4	10 566.6
	Unit PSE	1 758.4	4 559.6	5 706.0	-8 198.6	-3 272.1	14 840.3	114 259.3
	% PSE	34.3	25.9	24.0	-23.3	-5.2	17.4	65.8

* Total PSE in million leva at current prices; unit PSEs in current leva per tonne

Source: Gorton et al., 1997.

Table 6.17 Four-firm concentration ratios in Bulgarian and European food processing industries[a]

	Bread	Milk	Processed Meat	Flour
France	4.5	-	23.0	29.0
Germany	7.0	-	22.0	38.0
Italy	4.0	-	11.0	6.7
UK	58.0	-	-	78.0
Romania	9.1	31.2	11.6	8.5
Bulgaria	6.9	35.2[b]	15.1 (pork products) 20.8 (beef products)	47.6

[a] Figures for Western European countries for 1990; for CEECs, 1996
[b] 1995 data

Source: Data from Sutton, 1991; Gorton et al., 1997.

Production in Bulgaria is no more concentrated for the products studied than in Western Europe and in general four-firm concentration ratios are lower. The 1996 four-firm concentration ratio for flour milling does appear high (47.6 per cent), but this reflects the severe grain shortage in 1996 when grain distribution was state directed to the larger, mainly state owned, mills for processing. In 1994 and 1995 the corresponding figures were 36.2 per cent and 33.9 per cent and provide a more accurate guide. At the bakery level the concentration ratio has been historically lower due to the pattern of smaller, localised production of bread. These figures (6 per cent in 1994 and 6.9 per cent in 1995) are lower than for Romania (9.1 per cent), but are roughly in line with the picture for France, Germany, and Italy in 1990, and far below the 58 per cent recorded for the UK (Sutton, 1991). With regard to meat processing, the private sector has grown substantially and concentration ratios have fallen. The four-firm concentration ratio for processed beef products was 23.1 per cent and 20.8 per cent in 1994 and 1995 respectively. For processed pork products the comparative figures were 16.5 per cent in 1994 and 15.1 per cent in 1995. The concentration ratios are higher than those recorded for Romania (11.6 per cent in 1996), but similar to several Western European countries. In 1990 the four-firm concentration ratios for processed meat products in France, Germany, and Italy were 23 per cent, 22 per cent, and 11 per cent respectively. Interviews conducted by Gorton et al. (1997) also reported that excessive concentration is not an issue in the grain, dairy, and meat chains at the processing level. In part this is due to the development of these industries under communism where plants were developed on a 'one per okrug' principle (there were 28 okrugs, or regions, under the former territorial administrative system). In some okrugs, while there was only one meat processing or milling enterprise, these firms consisted of more than one plant. In a number of cases, when the old system was dissolved these plants became independent and began directly competing with each other. These findings on concentration at the processing level appear consistent with the transfer estimations, which at this stage of the food chain were modest, with these firms either small sources or destinations of transfers.

Quality Competitiveness

Throughout Eastern Europe there is a huge gulf between the food control system inherited from the communist era and EU legislation. Bridging this gap has, and will continue, to require substantial investments both by the Bulgarian government and food firms in Bulgaria. At present only a handful of Bulgarian food firms have EU export licences. The vast majority are, therefore, effectively excluded from the EU market and are not competitive in terms of quality.

The European Commission, in its Agenda 2000 document on Bulgaria's application to join the EU, noted that harmonisation of food industry legislation in Bulgaria with stage one of the *acquis communautaire* is only at an initial point (European Commission, 1997). Bulgarian veterinary legislation does not meet EU requirements. While Bulgaria does have an ambitious timetable to align most legislation to EU requirements by the end of 1998, effective enforcement will require substantial upgrading of inspection and monitoring facilities. This has been hindered by structural changes in veterinary services, together with the fragmentation of livestock units, making disease control difficult. The Commission noted that because of its geographical situation and weak border controls, Bulgaria runs a high risk of animal diseases entering from its eastern borders. Border inspection posts, testing, and diagnostic facilities are still inadequate for EU standards. Additionally, membership will necessitate the end of vaccination against classical swine fever (European Commission, 1997).

Quality inefficiencies in the meat and dairy food chains tend to be passed from farmers to processors weakening the competitive position of the latter. For example, in the dairy chain the average herd size in 1996 was 1.8 cows with production mainly for own consumption. These small scale producers are often unable to store milk appropriately (they do not have cooling facilities), do not register their cows, or have proper health certificates (Davidova, 1997b). Collection points are not always in appropriate buildings with satisfactory hygienic conditions. These collection points, according to government regulations, should check the milk they receive for fat content, impurities, density, and cooling temperature. However, this monitoring is often not enforced. Thus the quality of milk received by processors is variable (but usually poor) in terms of quality, which in some cases means that it is only suitable for the production of cheese.

In the pig industry Bulgaria uses a vaccination against classical swine fever, which is banned in the EU and impedes the export of pork to the Union. The Bulgarian national veterinary service has committed itself to removing (localising) the use of the this vaccination as part of the process of harmonisation with the EU. However, this has been met with resistance in Bulgaria and the risk of the disease spreading, if uncontrolled, is relatively high. Currently there are between ten and twenty epizootic outbreaks per year in Bulgaria (Davidova, 1997b). Similar problems pervade in the neighbouring countries of Macedonia, Romania, and Serbia. Bulgaria thus faces two potential sources of the disease: largely unregistered domestic pigs kept in backyard and fed on kitchen residues, and neighbouring countries, especially via the semiwild East Balkan swine which move freely on pastures and come into contact with other animals.

Low quality competitiveness has severely restricted exports to the EU. Due to unsatisfactory sanitary conditions only a small number of meat enterprises are licensed for exports to the EU. In 1997, 4 slaughterhouses and 8 poultry slaughterhouses (including for geese and ducks) were licensed together with 2 enterprises that process poultry. Due to the low hygienic conditions in dairy processing, the EU banned imports of dairy products from Bulgaria in 1997. Thus, the current low quality competitiveness of the processing industries is impeding the development of Bulgarian exports to the EU. If there are not substantial improvements in future, it could impede closer integration with the Union.

Competitive Advantage

Competitive advantage can be divided into two main forms: a price based strategy (cost advantage) or a differentiation strategy (added value) (Porter, 1980). A price based strategy is commensurate with comparatively healthy profits in the long run only if the organisation has a lower cost structure (usually stemming from economies of scale and scope). If the latter is not in place and price is still the key factor in purchasing decisions, a lower rate of profit has to be accepted.

A differentiation strategy encompasses several options such as technological superiority, reduced risks, after sales care, and effective branding. In the food industry, these strategies are most appropriate for multinationals, having resources for research and development and for support of marketing campaigns required to underpin effective branding. This is not to say new entrants and small firms are excluded, but rather that existing large western European food processors will, overall, be better placed to operationalise such initiatives. Bulgaria's competitive advantage would appear to rest with price based as opposed to differential strategies. Food manufacturers do not have recognised brand names, resources for advertising, or technological advantages to compete on a differentiation basis in the Single European Market. Price based advantages exist for a number of niche products such as wine, apricots, and sunflower seeds rather than for the staple products of pork, milk, and wheat. Within the niches where Bulgaria does have an advantage, its competitive position can be best exploited on price grounds (for example in the wine market by undercutting the prices of other world producers).

Conclusions

Bulgaria, by signing the AA, has made a commitment to start aligning itself with the EU and take on the obligations of membership in readiness for accession. In the agro-food sector the degree of alignment so far has been slow. There have not been clear signs of intensification in trade relations between Bulgaria and the EU in 1990s. Bulgaria's agro-food trade with the EU has been unstable during the transition period. This has in part been due to the instability of the Bulgarian economy, especially the deep recession in 1996. Poor macroeconomic performance has slowed and in some cases reversed the alignment process.

At the farm level, prices and government policies differ substantially between the EU and Bulgaria. For the period 1990 to 1996, farmers in the EU were effectively subsidised to a high degree, while in Bulgaria producers were effectively taxed. Agricultural policy supports in Bulgaria amount to only a tiny fraction of the support afforded by the CAP. Many elements of the CAP such as the supply management mechanisms and structural funds have no comparable equivalent in Bulgaria. In 1997 farm prices in Bulgaria did rise to close to or just above world market levels (as measured by NPCs), but they were below institutional EU prices.

Up to 1997 Bulgarian food processors benefited from purchasing some raw agricultural products at prices below world market levels, but they also tended to sell their output at below world market prices; they were not able to expropriate the rents generated from farmers. The processing sector is reasonably competitive. Many processors in this sector would be able to compete on the basis of price in an enlarged EU, but not in terms of quality. The latter remains a major barrier to trade with the EU. Only a handful of meat processors and no dairies possessed EU export licenses by 1997.

Bulgaria's competitive advantage would appear to rest with price based as opposed to differential strategies in a select number of niches such as wine, apricots, jams, and some live animals. This would not appear to hold for the main staple products of pork, milk, and wheat. In exploiting these niches Bulgarian producers will have to be able to compete largely on the basis of price as Bulgarian food manufacturers do not have well known brand names, resources for advertising, or technological advantages to support premium products in EU markets.

Notes

1. In the following analysis, chapters 1, 2, 7, 8, 10, 12 and 14 of the Harmonised System (HS) are included in the primary agricultural products and chapters 4, 11, 15, 16, 17, 18, 19, 20, 22 and 24 in the processed products. As a result, when trade is broken down into primary and processed products the total does not include chapters 3, 5, 6, 9, 13, 21 and 23.
2. The calculations were undertaken for the World Bank by J. Nash with the support of N. Ivanova and P. Kostov from the Policy Analysis Unit at the Ministry of Agriculture in Bulgaria (World Bank, 1997).
3. Calculations based on 1997 tariff rates.
4. Analysis of tariff cuts resulting from accession to CEFTA is based on the 1997 Bulgarian Customs Tariff.
5. Prices in Bulgaria were liberalised in February 1991. However, the government intervened in the setting of prices for main agricultural products until 1998. Most of the time intervention was through export restrictions and the introduction of low tariff or zero tariff import quotas.
6. The four-firm concentration ratio is the share of industry sales accounted for by the four largest firms.

References

Balassa, B. (1977), ' "Revealed" comparative advantage revisited: an analysis of relative export shares of the industrial countries, 1953-1971', *Manchester School*, vol. 45, pp. 327-44.
Buckwell, A.E. (1997), 'If ... Agricultural economics in brave liberal world', *European Review of Agricultural Economics*, vol. 23, no. 3, pp. 339-58.
Davidova, S. (1997b), 'Bulgaria, Livestock Chain', Report submitted to the World Bank, unpublished mimeo.
European Commission (1996a), *The Agricultural Situation in the European Union 1995 Report*, Office for Official Publications of the European Communities, Luxembourg.
European Commission (1996b), *Pre-Accession Strategy - Relations with the Countries of Central Europe*, DG IA, Brussels.
European Commission (1997), *Commission Opinion on Bulgaria's Application for Membership of the European Union*, DOC/DGVI/08/97/11, 15 July 1997, Brussels.
European Commission, Directorate for Agriculture (DGVI) (1998), *Agricultural Situation and Prospects in the Central and Eastern European Countries, Bulgaria*, Working document, Office for Official Publications of the European Communities, Luxembourg.
Gorton, M., Buckwell, A. and Davidova, S. (1997), *Impediments to Efficiency in the Agro-food Chain: Bulgaria*, Report to the Organisation for Economic Co-operation and Development (OECD), September, Paris.
Hertel, T.W., Brockmeier, M. and Swaminathan, P.V. (1997), 'Sectoral and economy wide analysis of integrating Central and Eastern European countries into the EU: implications of alternative strategies', *European Review of Agricultural Economics*, vol. 23, no. 3, pp. 359-86.
Ivanova, N., Lingard, J., Buckwell, A. and Burrell, A. (1995), 'Impact of changes in agricultural policy on the agro-food chain in Bulgaria', *European Review of Agricultural Economics*, vol. 22, no. 3, pp. 354-71.
Ivanova, N., Trifonova, R. and Kostov, P. (1996), 'Effects of Agricultural Policies on Production, Utilization, Net Trade and Budget Expenditures', Policy discussion paper, MAFI PAU, Sofia, Bulgaria.
NSI (1996; 1997), 'Average Prices of Purchased Food and Non-Food Products by Households', Price and Inflation Indexes, Monthly Bulletin, Sofia, Bulgaria.
OECD (1997), 'Indicators of Tariff and Non-tariff Barriers', update, OECD, Paris.
Pitts, E., Viane, J., Traill, B. and Gellynk, X. (1995), 'Measuring Food Industry Competitiveness', Discussion paper No. 7, EU FAIR Programme *Structural Change in the European Food Industries*.
Porter, M.E. (1980), *The Competitive Advantage of Nations*, Free Press, New York.
Sutton, J. (1991), *Sunk Costs and Market Structure*, MIT Press, Cambridge.
Tangermann, S. and Josling, T. (1995), 'Pre-Accession Agricultural Policies for Central Europe and the European Union', Final report on the study commissioned by DGI of the European Commission, Brussels.
van Berkum, S. and Terluin, I. (1995), *Accession of the Four Visegrad Countries to the EU: Costs for the Agricultural Budget*, Mededeling No. 545, Agricultural Economics Research Institute, The Hague.
World Bank (1997), 'Bulgaria Agriculture Sector Review: Agricultural Competitiveness and Incentives', Report presented to the World Bank, Washington DC.

7 Agriculture and Integration: Trade Liberalisation Versus Migration

ALEXANDER H. SARRIS

Introduction

Transition from communism to capitalism in the countries of Central and Eastern Europe (CEECs) has prompted moves toward more integration with the countries of the European Union (EU). This integration has initially taken the form of the Europe Agreements between the EU and CEECs, that aim at liberalising trade between Eastern and Western Europe. Agriculture has been one of the least liberalised sectors, because of fears that cheap CEEC products would compete with highly protected agricultural products in the EU. Agriculture is also featuring prominently in the current accession negotiations between the EU and several CEECs.

Apart from agriculture, one of the major issues confronting the EU and all other Western European countries in the aftermath of transition in the CEECs is the massive labour migration that has occurred. This migration has raised nationalistic feelings and considerable social tensions during a period of already high unemployment in Europe. The problem is exacerbated by the fact that a large part of this migration is illegal; hence it is largely uncontrolled. Agriculture is one of the sectors in Western Europe that has witnessed massive inflows of illegal labourers willing to work for lower wages than domestic workers. The reasons that agriculture is one of the favoured sectors of employment of illegal immigrants include the difficulty of detection and the relatively modest supply of domestic workers.

Migration of labour is also one of the major issues confronting the EU in the context of further integration of CEECs. Fears range from the possibility of immigrants putting downward pressure on domestic wages to the possibility of social and racist feelings being fueled by the presence and different cultural traits of immigrants. On the other hand, immigration from CEECs of workers who are willing to work for lower wages might maintain the output and competitiveness of EU agriculture via reducing production costs in a period that is witnessing increasing pressures for overall agricultural trade liberalisation. This suggests that there is a link between agricultural trade liberalisation and immigration. One might hypothesise that the larger the influx of immigrants from CEECs to the EU, the easier it would be to liberalise agriculture in the EU, as the cost of production would be lowered, thus bringing lower prices which are easily tolerated. Furthermore, immigration from the CEECs to the EU tends to lower the supply of labour in CEECs, thereby decreasing agricultural production and exportable surplus and easing pressure in the EU for agricultural trade liberalisation toward the CEECs. It, therefore, appears that further integration of CEECs with the EU, and attendant agricultural trade liberalisation between them, might be easier if immigration is made easier rather than more difficult as some have advocated.

This chapter discusses the issues relevant to agricultural trade liberalisation and labour immigration from the CEECs to the EU. The discussion will outline the key determinants and variables that are relevant for the debate, and will utilise simple and stylised graphic models for illustrative purposes. The discussion will also pave the way for more empirically oriented applied work.

The motivation for this analysis is provided by the case of a small CEEC country that is characterised by a relatively large agricultural sector and exportation of considerable amounts of labour to neighbouring EU countries. Albania (and possibly Bulgaria) provides such a case. Albania is a country with a very large share of its GDP from agriculture (more than 50 per cent), a large share of the labour force that has emigrated (about one-third), and a large share of the remaining labour force in agriculture (about 45 per cent). Most of the Albanian emigrants have gone to Greece and Italy, two countries with substantial agricultural sectors. Albania has a very weak export base with a substantial current account deficit financed largely by remittances from emigrants. Of total exports, about 12 per cent are agricultural products, with the rest being inedible crude materials and some low-technology manufactures. Trade is mostly with EU countries, Italy and Greece being the largest trade partners.

The following section reviews some literature on immigration and integration as well as trade liberalisation. Then a simple, stylised, graphic model of two economies with important agricultural sectors that interact via both trade and immigration is presented. The subsequent section discusses the ways in which immigration and agriculture can interact under three different assumptions concerning agricultural trade policies in Western Europe. The final section summarises the results and offers some suggestions for further work.

Immigration and Trade Liberalisation

There are five strands of literature relevant for the discussion of the problem at hand. The first concerns the impact of legal and illegal immigration on the host country. The second relates to the motives of immigrants. The third concerns the impact on the sending country. The fourth examines the relation between trade and factor mobility, while the fifth relates specifically to integration and immigration.

There has been considerable theoretical and empirical research on the impact of immigration on a host country. Most of the early literature concentrated on the case of the United States (US), a country that has been a large recipient of legal and illegal immigrants for many years (Greenwood and McDowell, 1986). The major issues that have been analysed, being of considerable practical and political importance, is whether immigration has a negative impact on the wages of local labour and whether immigration leads to displacement of domestic workers. The basic initial theoretical result that can be obtained with relatively simple two-factor (labour and capital) models is that an influx of immigrant workers who are perfectly substitutable for domestic workers has a negative impact on the wages of local labour and an increase in the overall income of the economy. The more inelastic the demand and supply relationships, the greater will be the reduction of domestic wages; the displacement effect will be larger the more elastic the domestic labour supply and the less elastic the labour demand.

The basic extension of this simple model, relevant for our purposes, has been to assume two major types of labour, namely skilled and unskilled, and to assume that immigrants are mostly unskilled. Chiswick (1982, 1995) uses such a three-factor model, assuming a constant elasticity of substitution production function, and shows that an inflow of low-skilled labour in an economy will increase the marginal products of capital and skilled labour in the short run, while it will decrease the marginal product of similar domestic unskilled labour. Thus it will widen the wage differential between the two types of labour. It will also reduce the aggregate income of domestic unskilled workers, while it will increase the aggregate income of the economy, as well as that of skilled workers and owners of capital. Hence if the ownership of capital and skilled labour is concentrated, immigration will worsen income distribution.

These conclusions, however, depend on both the types of substitutability and complementarity between the various factors, as well as the type of openness assumed for the economy. For instance, Kuhn and Wooton (1991) show that the presence of a nontraded good can result in both labour types losing from immigration. The outcome for labour also depends on the presence or lack of unions (Schmidt, Stilz, and Zimmermann, 1994; see also the models of Altonji and Card, 1991; and the recent surveys by Borjas, 1994, 1995; Friedberg and Hunt, 1995; Zimmermann, 1995a).

Empirical analysis of the impacts of immigration on local labour markets has been done mostly in the US, using cross-section data from metropolitan areas. These studies generally find small, negative elasticities of domestic wages to increases in immigrant labour supply (see the surveys of Borjas, 1994, 1995; Greenwood and McDowell, 1986; Friedberg and Hunt, 1995; Tapinos and de Rugy, 1994). Friedberg and Hunt (1995) concluded that

> Despite the popular belief that immigrants have a large adverse impact on the wages and employment opportunities of the native born population, the literature on this question does not provide much support for this conclusion.

Chiswick (1995) has strongly criticised these types of empirical analyses because they do not disaggregate skill classes and because they implicitly assume that the units of analysis are closed economies; hence they neglect the adjustments of the labour market between regions in response to labour market shocks. Furthermore, such analyses fail to take into account the indirect effects of immigration that operate through good and factor markets. The recent survey by Borjas (1994) concluded that

> A fair appraisal of the literature thus suggests that we still do not fully understand how immigrants affect the employment opportunities of natives in local labour markets; nor do we understand the dynamic process through which natives respond to these supply shocks and reestablish labour market equilibrium.

Empirical analyses in European contexts, however, seem to produce much larger effects, possibly because of the different structure of the European labour markets (Zimmermann, 1995b).

The literature on illegal immigration is much less extensive. The reason is that information on illegal immigrants is much more difficult to obtain; hence one does not know the extent of skill composition of illegals, the wages paid to them relative to those of legals, or the sectors in which they are employed. Jahn and Straubhaar (1995) in their survey point out that most empirical analyses are of the simulation type, precisely because of this lack of data. Theoretically, the economic impact of an influx of illegal immigrants should not be different from that of legal immigrants after accounting for the wage differences due to illegality. Specific issues relevant to illegal immigrants include the impact of stronger regulation and enforcement (Ethier, 1986; Bond and Chen, 1987; Djajic, 1987), and the expansion of sectors that tend to employ immigrants (typically those operating in the informal or underground economy) at the expense of the formal sectors (Loayza, 1994; Djajic, 1995). The theoretical effects of illegal immigration on the host country depend on the skill composition of sectoral employment, on which there is little empirical information.

Chiswick (1988) has surveyed the various policies toward illegal immigration followed by the US over the years, and Zimmermann (1995b) has done the same for Europe. Chiswick describes the 'dilemma' of US immigration policy, whereby low-skilled foreign immigrants can bring benefits to the local economy while potentially creating social problems by staying long, bringing families and different social values, and exploiting domestic social services. Guest worker programs tend to create 'second-class citizens' with adverse social consequences, as the experiences of both the US and Europe amply manifest. Emphasis on deterrence at the border, or domestic policing and employer sanctions do not seem to have produced results.

The impact of illegal immigration on wages and employment of nationals has received little attention. In the US, empirical studies such as that of Bean et al. (1987) find that illegal Mexican immigrants have only a small impact on the wages of other workers. As Tapinos and de Rugy (1994) point out, the reason for the slight effects may be that illegals do not generally compete much with nationals, as they take up jobs in inferior, and therefore complementary, labour markets.

On the motives of immigrants there is also substantial literature. The basic static model of Harris and Todaro (1970), which suggested that migration is a function of expected wage differentials between the origin and destination countries, has been considerably elaborated to include issues of risk, dynamics, labour market duality, and other effects (for reviews see Stark, 1991; Straubhaar, 1988). Nevertheless, the basic idea of the Harris-Todaro model, albeit modified and refined, has remarkably withstood the test of time.

The literature on the impact of migration on the sending country has concentrated on the issue of brain drain (for a review see Wong, 1995, ch. 14). The conclusion is that the sending country loses welfare, as in addition to the labour it sends abroad it also loses human capital. It is also clear that the sending country loses production capacity. Given, however, that immigrants send back a portion of their income as remittances that might be invested in the country, the dynamic consequences of migration might be different than the short run ones. Also the fact that brain drain type of migration is possible might induce increased acquisition of human capital in the sending country in anticipation of later possible migration, and hence larger growth in the sending country. In fact Mountford (1997) has recently shown that through this mechanism, immigration might lead to a higher overall growth rate for the sending country.

Trade liberalisation in goods may change factor prices and the incentives for factor mobility. Venables (1997), in a recent overview of the literature, suggests that trade liberalisation might decrease or increase the incentive to migrate depending on the type of model utilised. In other words trade might be either a substitute for, or a complement to, factor movements.

Finally there has been some recent literature concerning the impact from preferential agreements on migration and agriculture, especially in the context of the North American Free Trade Agreement (NAFTA). The work of Burfisher et al. (1994), Markusen and Zahniser (1997), and Faini et. al. (1997) are typical of this literature. The main result of this literature is that the impact of integration on immigration can have positive overall impacts on the richer of the two integrating countries.

A Model of Two Economies with Agriculture and Immigration

The model utilised in this section has its origins in the specific factors model of Markusen, (1983) and Neary (1995). Consider two economies which we refer to as 'Eastern Europe' and 'Western Europe'. Suppose that the economy in Eastern Europe produces two products: an agricultural one A, and a nonagricultural composite N. Each of the two products uses a specific factor. One can think of land in the case of agriculture and nonland capital in the other sector. Labour is homogeneous and can be used in both agriculture and nonagriculture, or it can migrate to Western Europe. Assume that initially there is no immigration because of restrictions in the movement of labour (this simulates the case of the pretransition, communist phase).

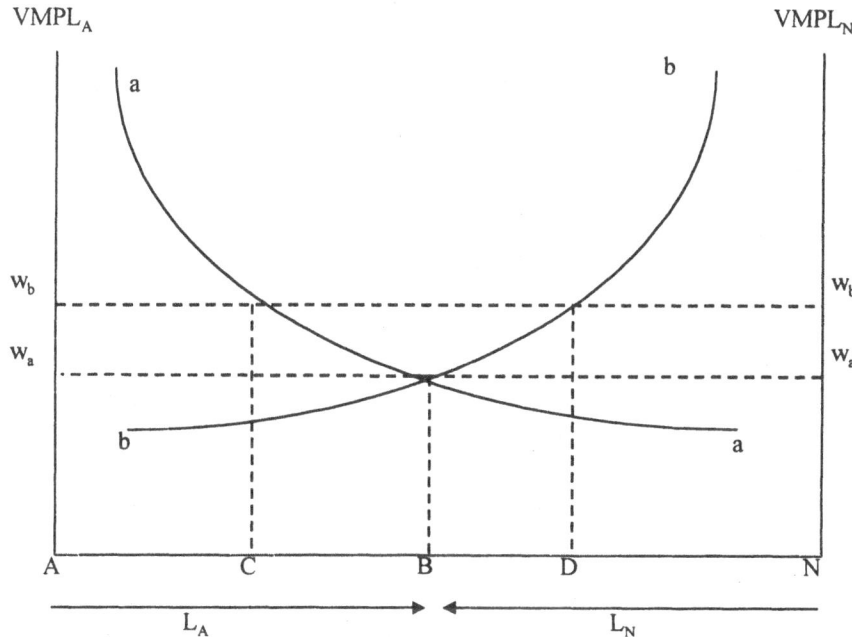

Figure 7.1 Economy of an Eastern European country before and after opening to Western Europe

Figure 7.1 gives the familiar diagram of labour allocation to the two sectors, by graphing the value of marginal product of labour (VMPL) curves for agriculture and nonagriculture. The length of the horizontal line AN is the amount of labour that is employed in Eastern Europe. The initial wage in Eastern Europe is w_a, and the initial allocation of labour to agriculture is AB, with BN labour employed in the nonagricultural sector.

Figure 7.2 depicts the corresponding situation in Western Europe, with the initial allocation of labour being AK to agriculture and KN to nonagriculture. The initial wage in Western Europe is W_1. Both countries are assumed to be small; hence they cannot influence international prices for their products. The agricultural price in Western Europe is a fixed domestic price set by the CAP procedures; the price in Eastern Europe is assumed to be the international one. These assumptions are made only in order to simulate some trade issues and are of no importance to the arguments.

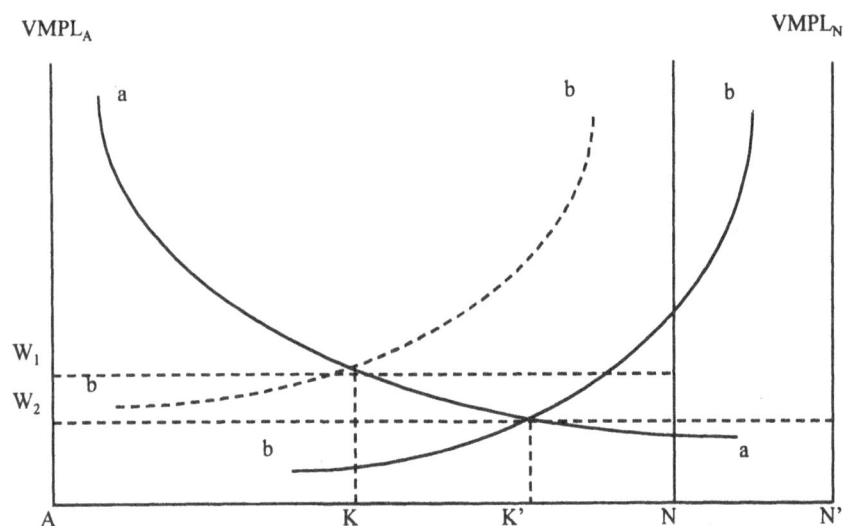

Figure 7.2 Economy of a Western European country before and after opening to Eastern Europe

Opening of the Eastern European economy to Western Europe after the fall of communism has led to substantial immigration from Eastern to Western Europe. In figure 7.1 the amount of labour CD has migrated to Western Europe, and this has diminished labour supply to both the agricultural sector from AB to AC, as well as to the nonagricultural sector from BN to DN. The amount of labour that has migrated can be taken as related to the Eastern/Western wage differentials as in the Harris-Todaro model. The production in both sectors declines (the value of production in one sector is measured by the area under the respective VMPL curve). In Western Europe, on the other hand, the amount of labour has expanded by NN', which is equal to a fraction of CD. The reason for assuming that only a fraction of the labour migrating from Eastern Europe is employed in Western Europe is that most of the Eastern European workers have migrated to Western Europe as illegal immigrants which does not guarantee them full time employment. In fact one also expects the wage received by illegals to be lower than the wage received by legal domestic workers because of both discrimination and the risk premium paid by employers for hiring illegals. These issues are not reflected in the diagram that depicts all labour employed in Western Europe to be receiving the same wage.

The consequences of this initial immigration to Western Europe is to expand production in both sectors and to lower wages of comparable or competing domestic (Western European) workers. Production of both sectors expands because of the lower overall cost of labour to both sectors. These effects can be substantial in Western Europe. Simulations, for instance, of the impact on the Greek economy of the immigration of illegals after transition has suggested that the influx of illegal alien labour effectively expanded the domestic labour force by 3.5 per cent, led to an increase in GDP of about 1.5 per cent, and an expansion of agricultural production of about 1.4 per cent (Sarris and Zografakis, 1997). Clearly then the conclusion, as far as agriculture is concerned, is that the opening of Eastern European countries has led to contraction of their agricultural output and expansion of agricultural output of the Western European countries due to labour migration.

Agricultural Trade Liberalisation and Immigration

The issues surrounding the trade and immigration debate in this context have to do with whether trade liberalisation will induce more or less immigration from Eastern to Western Europe. In terms of the more specific issues of agriculture, one might examine three different options. The first has to do with Western Europe granting agricultural trade preferences to Eastern European countries. The second has to do with the EU lowering overall prices and domestic protection for agriculture, while the third has to do with investment and transfers from Western Europe to Eastern Europe. We will examine each one of these possibilities in turn.

180 *Agriculture and East-West European Integration*

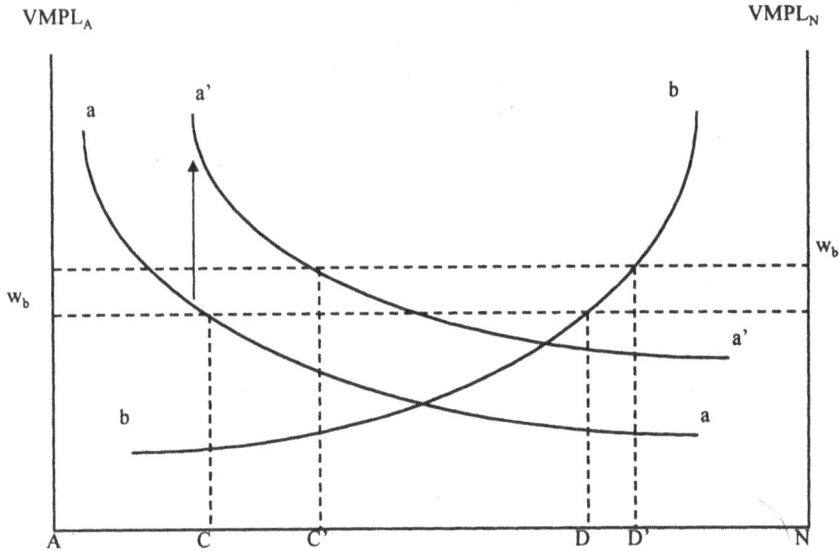

Figure 7.3 Impact of Western European trade preferences on the economy of an Eastern European country

Consider trade preferences for agriculture granted by Western Europe to Eastern Europe. This, in the context of the CAP, implies that Eastern Europe can trade with Western Europe at prices higher than international ones. Hence, it can be depicted in our model by an upward shift of the VMPL curve in agriculture in Eastern Europe. Figure 7.3 depicts the situation. The impact effect of trade preferences is to increase wages in Eastern Europe and hence stem immigration to Western Europe via the 'push effect'. As immigration to Western Europe is lowered, wages there will rise and this will moderate the decline in immigration ('pull effect'). The overall effect, however, will be a rise in the real wage in Eastern Europe from w_b to w_b'. Production of agriculture in Eastern Europe will increase as labour input to agriculture will expand there. However, labour into nonagriculture will decline with an attendant fall in nonagricultural production. The overall immigration to Western Europe will decline to C'D' from the initial prepreference value of CD. Hence in this case agricultural trade preferences to Eastern Europe act to stem immigration and raise agricultural production there, while leading to declines in agricultural production in Western Europe via the decline in immigration and available labour.

Consider the effect of lowering agricultural prices in Western Europe. This simulates the prospect of a CAP with diminished support. The impact effect will be a downward shift of the VMPL in agriculture curve for Western Europe as depicted in figure 7.4. The impact will be a decrease in the equilibrium wage in Western Europe from W_2 to W_2' and a decline of agricultural production. If nothing else happens, then the decrease of wages in Western Europe will stem the migration flows from Eastern Europe because of the reduced wage differential. The decrease in migration from Eastern Europe will increase the supply of labour there; hence decreasing wages and increasing agricultural and nonagricultural production. Thus the likely impact of CAP liberalisation will be a reduction in immigration from Eastern Europe and an increase in agricultural production there.

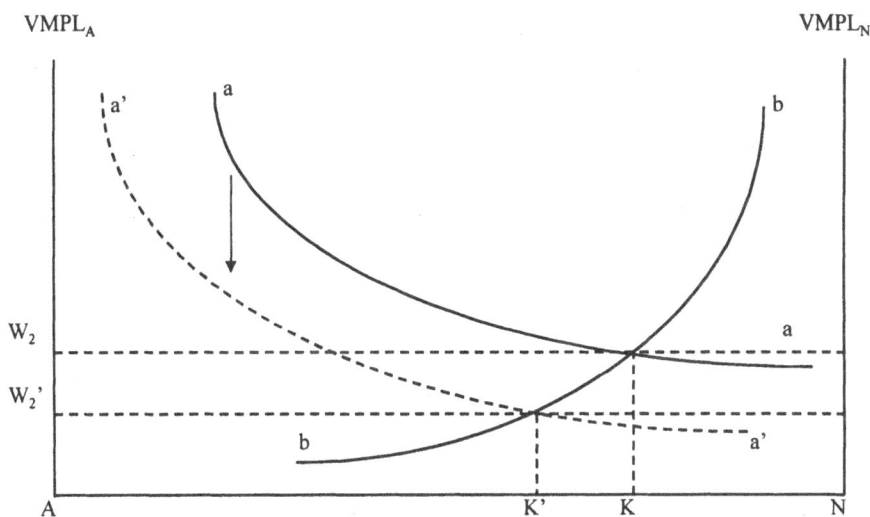

Figure 7.4 The economy of a Western European country after a decline in CAP support

182 *Agriculture and East-West European Integration*

The interesting thing, however, concerns the likely response of Western European agricultural producers to the decline in prices. If there is strong substitution of domestic labour by legal or illegal immigrants from Eastern Europe, then the decline in agricultural prices in Western Europe will lead to an increase in the demand for cheaper workers from Eastern Europe. This will tend to counteract the decline in immigration due to the decrease in relative wage differentials. The overall impact might be an increase in immigration rather than a decline as predicted by the standard model. In this case the effects will be opposite to what was earlier predicted. In other words the decline in CAP prices will tend to lead to increased immigration, an increase (or at least a much smaller decrease) in Western European agricultural production, and a decline in agricultural production in Eastern Europe. In this case 'trade liberalisation' within the CAP leads, via the immigration channel, to opposite effects of what is predicted by a nonmigration model.

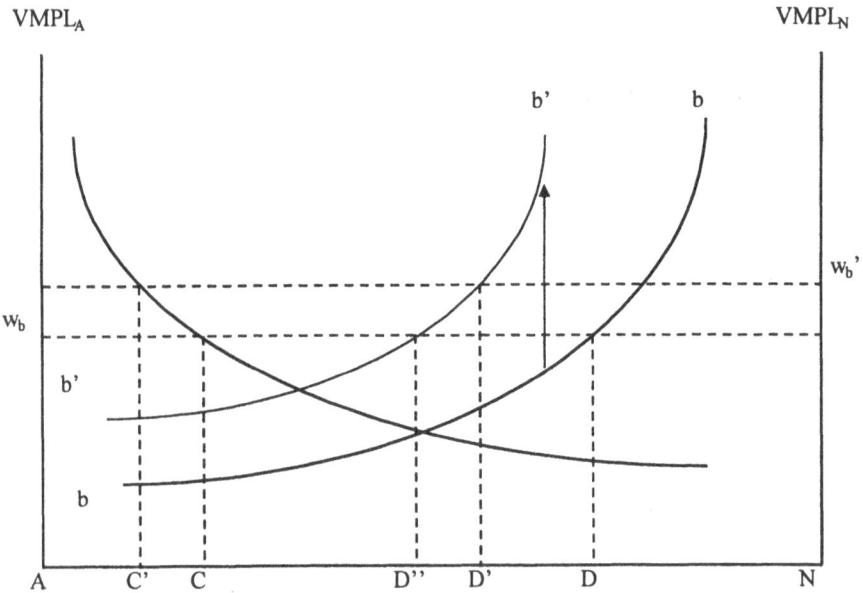

Figure 7.5 **The impact of investments in the nonagricultural sector of an Eastern European country**

Consider finally the impact of increased aid and/or investments by Western Europe in Eastern Europe. Suppose that aid is in the form of investments in nonagriculture so as to raise productivity of labour in nonagriculture in Eastern Europe. This will raise the VMPL curve in nonagriculture in Eastern Europe. Figure 7.5 depicts this scenario. The VMPL in nonagriculture will shift upwards. If the wage in Western Europe does not change neither will the wage in Eastern Europe, and the only impact will be a decline of immigration to Western Europe to CD''. However, this decline of immigration to Western Europe will lead to a rise in wages there. Hence this second round effect will tend to moderate the overall first round decline in immigration. The final impact will, nevertheless, be a decline of immigration to C'D', and a rise in wages in both Eastern and Western Europe. The impact on agriculture will be negative in both Eastern and Western Europe. Clearly this is a strategy that creates the smallest pressures on agriculture in Western Europe.

Summary and Conclusions

The basic thrust of this paper is that immigration interacts with trade liberalisation in ways that might produce effects on agriculture other than those that would be predicted by liberalisation in the absence of immigration. Immigration from Eastern Europe to Western Europe has substantially increased the agricultural labour supply in Western Europe and has boosted agricultural production there. At the same time it has contributed to declines in agricultural labour supply and production in Eastern Europe.

Western European agricultural policies were shown to have an impact via the immigration channel on both Western and Eastern European agricultural and nonagricultural production. It was shown that CAP liberalisation might lead, via the immigration channel, to increases rather than declines in Western European agricultural production, depending on the degree to which domestic labour is substitutable with Eastern European labour. Of course this conclusion might hold only for some of the Western European countries that have large and labour-intensive agricultural sectors. Italy and Greece are candidates for such a possibility.

Western European investment in the nonagricultural sector of Eastern Europe was seen to imply reductions in agricultural production in both regions as well as reduction in immigration and at the same time, increases in nonagricultural incomes in the Eastern Europe. Therefore this policy might serve several Western European objectives at once, and it seems preferable to agricultural trade preferences.

The graphic analysis of this paper could be formalised in a computable general equilibrium model (CGE) of the two regions. Such exercises regarding the NAFTA countries (see Burfisher et. al., 1994), as well as more general archetypal economies (e.g. Faini, 1997) can produce more detailed quantitative results of the above effects. Given, however, the weakness of the currently available databases for the countries of Eastern Europe, this is an exercise that is suggested for future research.

References

Bean, F.D., Telles, E.E. and Lowell. B.L. (1987), 'Undocumented migration to the United States perceptions and evidence', *Population and Development Review*, vol. 13, no. 4, pp. 671-90.

Bond, E.W. and Chen, T. (1987), 'The welfare impact of illegal immigration', *Journal of International Economics*, vol. 23, pp. 315-28.

Borjas, G.J. (1994), 'The economics of immigration', *Journal of Economic Literature*, vol. XXXII, no. 4, pp. 1667-1717.

Borjas, G.J. (1995), 'The economic benefits from immigration', *Journal of Economic Perspectives*, vol. 9, no. 2, pp. 3-23.

Burfisher, M.E., Robinson, S. and Thierfelder, K.E. (1994), 'Wage changes in a US Mexico free trade area: migration versus Stolper-Samuelson Effects', in J.F. Francois and C.R. Shiells (eds), *Modeling Trade Policy: Applied General Equilibrium Assessments of North American Free Trade*, Cambridge University Press, Cambridge, pp. 195-222.

Chiswick, B.R. (1982), 'The impact of immigration on the level and distribution of economic well-being' in B.R. Chiswick (ed), *The Gateway: US Immigration Issues and Policies*, American Enterprise Institute, Washington D.C., pp. 289-313.

Chiswick, B.R. (1988), 'Illegal immigration and immigration control', *Journal of Economic Perspectives*, vol. 2, no. 3, pp. 101-15.

Chiswick, B.R. (1995), 'The economic consequences of immigration: application to the United States and Japan', Paper presented at *The Political Economy of Illegal Immigration*, CEPR workshop, 14-16 September 1995, Halkidiki, Greece.

Djajic, S. (1987), 'Illegal aliens, unemployment, and immigration policy', *Journal of Development Economics*, vol. 25, no. 1, pp. 235-50.

Djajic. S. (1995), 'Illegal immigration and resource allocation', Paper presented at *The Political Economy of Illegal Immigration*, CEPR workshop, 14-16 September 1995, Halkidiki, Greece.

Ethier, W. (1986), 'Illegal immigration: the host country problem', *American Economic Review*, vol. 76, no. 1, 56-71.

Faini, R., Grether, J-M and deMelo, J. (1997), 'Globalisation and migratory pressures from developing countries: a simulation analysis', Development Studies Working

Paper No. 104, University of Oxford, Queen Elizabeth House, Centro Studi Luca d'Agliano.

Friedberg, R.M. and Hunt, J. (1995), 'The impact of immigrants on host country wages, employment and growth', *Journal of Economic Perspectives*, vol. 9, no. 2, pp. 23-44.

Greenwood, M.J and McDowell, J.M. (1986), 'The factor market consequences of US immigration', *Journal of Economic Literature*, vol. XXIV, no. 4, pp. 1738-72.

Harris, J. and Todaro, M. (1970), 'Migration, unemployment, and development: a two sector analysis', *American Economic Review*, vol. 60, no. 1, pp. 126-42.

Jahn, A. and Straubhaar, T. (1995), 'On the political economy of illegal immigration', Paper presented at *The Political Economy of Illegal Immigration*, CEPR workshop, 14-16 September 1995, Halkidiki, Greece.

Kuhn, P. and Wooton, I. (1991), 'Immigration, international trade, and the wages of native workers', in J.M. Abowd, and R.B. Freeman (eds), *Immigration, Trade and the Labor Market*, The University of Chicago Press for the National Bureau of Economic Research, Chicago, pp. 285-304.

Markusen, J.R. (1983), 'Factor movements and commodity trade as complements', *Journal of International Economics*, vol. 13, no. 2, pp. 341-56.

Markusen, J. and Zahniser, S. (1997), 'Liberalization and incentives for labor migration: theory with applications to NAFTA', Development Studies Working Paper No. 107, University of Oxford, Queen Elizabeth House, Centro Studi Luca d'Agliano.

Mountford, A. (1997), 'Can a brain drain be good for growth in the source economy?', *Journal of Development Economics*, vol. 53, no. 2, 287-304.

Neary, J.P. (1995), 'Factor mobility and international trade', *Canadian Journal of Economics*, 28, S4-S23.

Sarris, A.H., and Zografakis, S. (1997), 'A Computable General Equilibrium Assessment of the Impact of Illegal Immigration on the Greek Economy', Paper presented at *The Political Economy of Illegal Immigration*, CEPR workshop, 14-15 February 1997, Athens, Greece, forthcoming in the *Journal of Population Economics*.

Schmidt, C.M., Stilz, A. and Zimmermann, K.F. (1994), 'Mass migration, unions, and government intervention', *Journal of Public Economics*, vol. 55, no. 1, pp. 185-201.

Stark. O. (1991), *The Migration of Labour*, Basil Blackwell, Oxford.

Straubhaar, T. (1988), *On the Economics of International Labour Migration*, Haupt, Bern and Stuttgart.

Tapinos, G. and de Rugy, A. (1994), 'The macroeconomic impact of immigration : review of the literature published since the mid-1970s', in *Organisation for Economic Co-operation and Development, Trends in International Migration*, SOPEMI Annual Report 1993, Paris.

Venables, A.J. (1997), 'Trade liberalization and factor mobility: an overview', Development Studies Working Paper No. 103, University of Oxford, Queen Elizabeth House, Centro Studi Luca d'Agliano.

Wong, K-Y. (1995), *International Trade in Goods and Factor Mobility*, MIT Press. Cambridge, Massachusetts.

Zimmermann, K.F. (1995a), 'European migration: push and pull', in *Proceedings of the World Bank Annual Conference on Development Economics 1994*, Supplement to the World Bank Economic Review and the World Bank Research Observer, pp. 313-60.

Zimmermann, K.F. (1995b), 'Tackling the European migration problem', *Journal of Economic Perspectives*, vol. 9, no. 2, pp. 45-62.

8 From Central Planning to the Common Agricultural Policy: Analysis and Political Economy Aspects of Agricultural Policy in Central and Eastern Europe

JASON G. HARTELL AND JOHAN F.M. SWINNEN

Introduction

Agricultural price and trade policy in Central and Eastern European countries (CEECs) has undergone dramatic changes since the economic and political liberalization that began in 1989. Now, with the prospect of political and economic integration with the European Union (EU), poignant questions are being asked about how the development of CEEC agricultural policy is likely to contribute to the costs of accession for both parties.

Accession costs will depend heavily on the degree of policy alignment both among CEECs and with the EU in advance of membership. Alignment of both the instruments of agricultural policy and the level of their application is a concern. Several factors are important in assessing the potential for policy alignment. Political and economic forces resulting from a combination of liberalization within the general economy and their income distributional effects will largely determine the direction of policies. However, preintegration and international agreements may constrain government response to political pressure for agricultural protection and facilitate agricultural policy coordination.

To focus more closely on the problem, we first analyze actual agricultural trade and price policy developments in the CEECs and investigate their impact on agricultural producers income. A political economy framework is used to help explain these observations and, in conjunction with hypothesized effects of economic structure, institutional constraints, and income distributional effects resulting from policy reform and trade liberalization, elaborate implications for future agricultural policy developments in the CEECs.

Observations on Agricultural Policy

Agricultural Protection Levels

Figure 8.1 shows how average price distortions, measured by nominal protection rates (NPRs), in seven CEECs declined significantly between 1991 and 1992 as a result of price and trade liberalization.[1] In 1993, the level of protection increased again as many CEECs introduced protectionist price and trade policy measures. In 1994 and 1995, the average level of protection in the region first stabilized and then aligned more closely with world market prices.

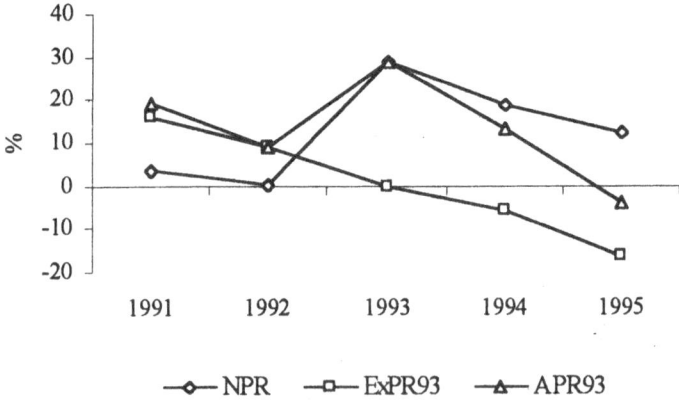

Figure 8.1 Average protection rates for CEEC agriculture, 1991-95*

* The adjusted exchange rate is assumed to equal the nominal exchange rate in 1993.

Source: Bojnec and Swinnen, 1997.

Exchange rate adjustments have in general not followed inflation rate differences between countries. It is unclear to what extent this development is policy-induced but the resulting impact on farm incomes acts as a tax on agriculture, reflected in declining exchange rate adjusted protection rates (APR) in figure 8.1 (Bojnec et al., 1997). The ExPR measures the difference between APR and NPR, reflecting the impact of divergence between domestic and international inflation and exchange rate adjustments on nominal protection. This tax effect is similar to those observed by Krueger et al., (1992) in developing countries.

Agricultural protection levels for individual CEECs and the EU are shown graphically in figure 8.2 using commodity aggregate per cent producer support estimates (PSE). The PSE, as calculated by the OECD, is the annual farmgate value of gross transfers made to agricultural producers from both implicit and explicit policy measures. The per cent PSE is the share of these transfers in the total value of agricultural production.[2]

Agricultural protection for the CEECs as a group has fallen below that of the EU since 1991 and have tended to converge over time. Two exceptions are Bulgaria which has consistently taxed its agricultural producers while Slovenia has maintained a robust and stable protection level. Extreme drops in measured protection for the Baltic countries and, earlier, for Poland reflect the impact of currency devaluation temporarily overwhelming market price transfers and other support mechanisms.

A closer examination reveals the substantial differences between the CEECs' agricultural protection and their more recent modest convergence. Figure 8.3 shows how agricultural protection of the Visegrad-4, the Baltic countries, Bulgaria, and Slovenia were easily distinguishable from each other in 1994. PSEs of the Visegrad-4 were between 20 per cent and 32 per cent, considerably higher than both the Baltics and Bulgaria but considerably lower than support found in Slovenia and the EU. Since 1994 the difference between the Baltics and the Visegrad-4 reduced, except for Poland where overall protection has increased. Bulgaria is distinguished by its heavy producer taxation in 1996. Slovenia's protection rate declined but was still considerably higher than the other CEECs.

Within CEECs there are noteworthy differences in protection levels between commodities. Commodity specific PSE data for the periods 1991-93 and 1996-98 for Estonia, the Czech Republic, Hungary, Poland and the EU is shown in figure 8.4. In contrast to the aggregate figures alone, there is often sizeable changes in protection levels over time and significant variability in the level of protection between commodities.

190 *Agriculture and East-West European Integration*

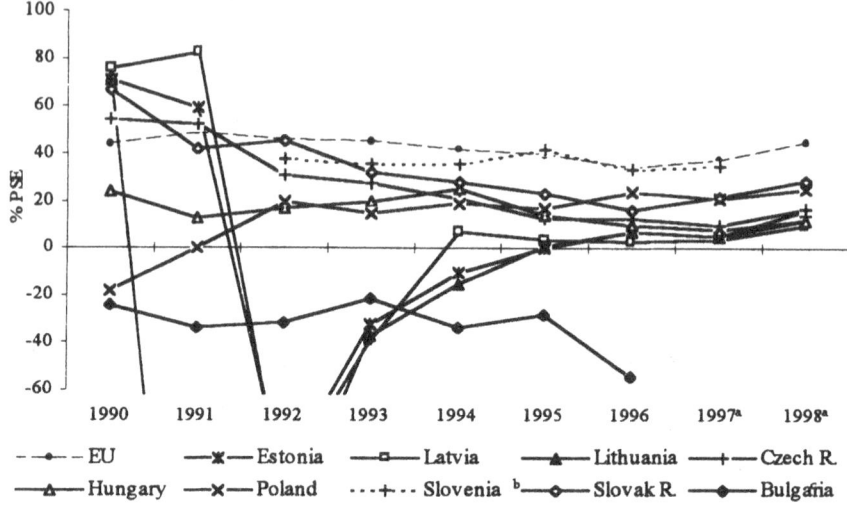

Figure 8.2 Aggregate per cent PSE, 1990-98

[a] 1997 values are provisional; 1998 values are estimates
[b] Producer subsidy equivalents
[c] Calculated as the weighted average of six individual commodity per cent producer subsidy equivalents. Weights are relative (value) production shares.

Source: Data from OECD, PSE/CSE database; MAFF, 1997; Gorton et al., 1997.

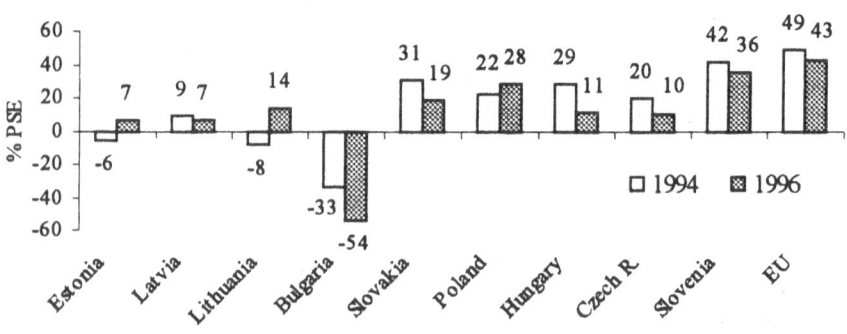

Figure 8.3 Per cent PSEs, selected CEECs and the EU, 1994 and 1996*

* Producer subsidy equivalent; Bulgarian values calculated as in figure 8.2.

Source: Data from OECD, PSE/CSE database; MAFF, 1997; Gorton et al., 1997.

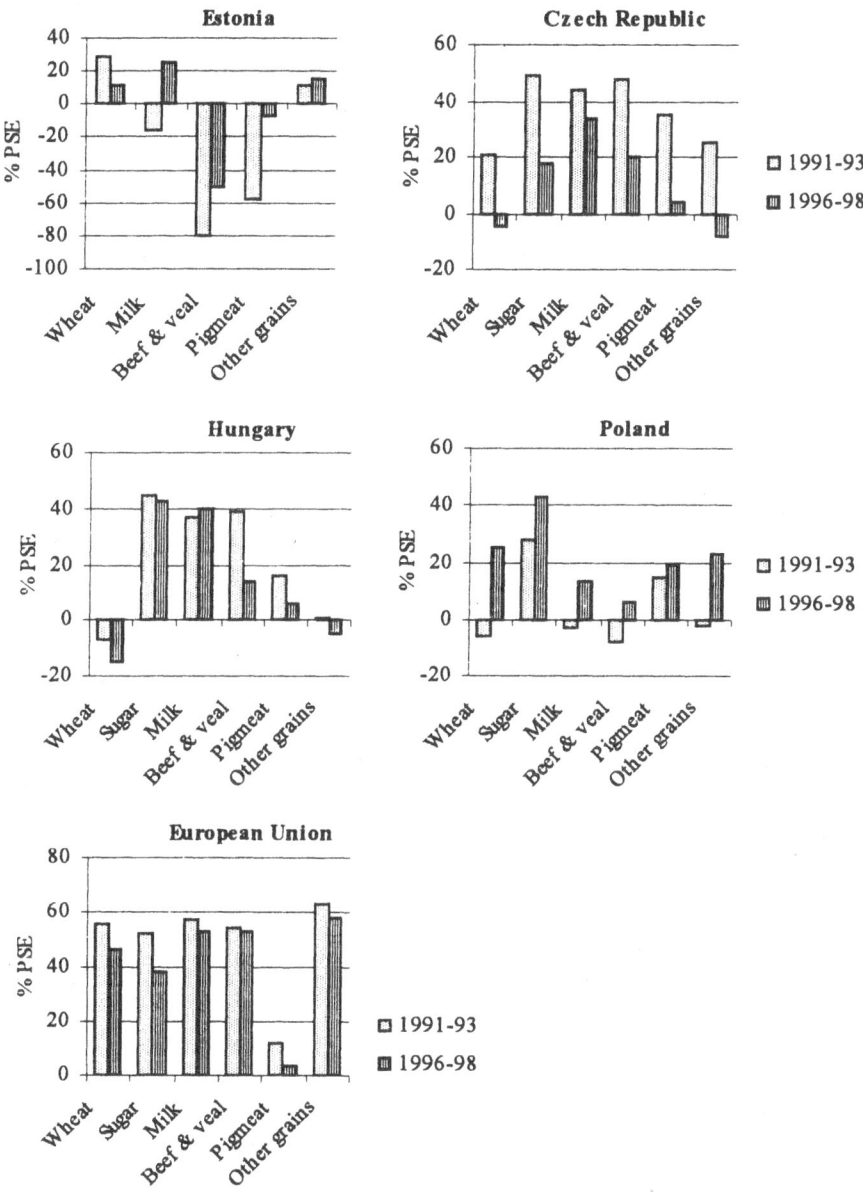

Figure 8.4 Commodity level protection, 1991-93 and 1996-98
Source: Data from OECD, PSE/CSE database.

Protection declined quite sharply in the Czech Republic between 1991-93 and 1996-98 for all commodities while in Hungary the decline was modest except for beef and veal while milk registered a marginal increase. Estonian commodities, except wheat, all recorded an improvement in producer support, particularly for milk which became positive in the second period, and for pigmeat where the level of taxation declined significantly. Protection in Poland increased for all commodities and predominantly so for wheat, milk, beef and veal, and other grains where taxation was replaced with protection ranging between 25 and 6 per cent. Commodity protection in the EU declined marginally in the second period except for sugar and pigmeat which registered slightly larger reductions.

Combining figure 8.4 with table 8.1, giving 1998 commodity PSEs, also shows that within countries, protection between individual commodities varies substantially. A pattern can be distinguished, however, where measure protection for milk and sugar are consistently among the most highly protected commodities. Commodities such as wheat, pigmeat, and other grains have received lower protection or have even suffered from taxation. Exceptions include Poland where milk is not highly protected relative to the others, and the Czech Republic where sugar has received less support since 1994.[3]

In contrast, PSE data for the EU show strong convergence across commodity sectors, with the exception of pork, at between 50 and 60 per cent during the period 1991-93 and at somewhat lower levels during 1996-98.

Table 8.1   PSEs for selected commodities, 1998*

	Estonia	Czech R.	Hungary	Poland	EU
Wheat	19	17	-32	29	56
Sugar	-	13	40	49	43
Milk	36	44	53	22	57
Beef & veal	-46	16	15	-2	62
Pigmeat	5	-9	10	15	8
Other grains	20	17	-18	24	68

* 1998 values are provisional.

Source: OECD PSE/CSE database.

The overall pattern of protection between the CEECs and the EU is further differentiated by the commodity level ranking of protection which can be seen most easily in table 8.1. While there is generally higher protection for sugar and milk relative to wheat and beef and veal in the CEECs, the observation in the EU is for lower protection for sugar, somewhat similar levels of support for milk and wheat, and higher protection for beef and veal. Support levels, however, are most similar for milk, sugar, pigmeat while they diverge vastly for the other commodities.

The differences and similarities between product groups and countries revealed by the commodity PSEs show that accession adjustments by the CEECs and the EU may be more a more difficult task than suggested by the aggregate figures alone. In addition, the ease that alignment is achieved will depend on the instruments used to transfer producer support.

Agricultural Policy Choice

The initial policy developments of the CEECs are broadly characterized by the removal of various agricultural producer supports and trade barrier instruments followed by the reintroduction of measures designed to protect producers or consumers. More specifically, in early transition, most consumer price subsidies and producer subsidies were phased out and eliminated along with most nontariff barriers to trade. Standard tariffs remained as the principle means of agricultural producer protection. Later, with increasing pressure for effective producer support, nontariff barriers were reintroduced. Nontariff export barriers also reappeared as governments sought to balance competing producer and consumer interests. After some time, greater agricultural market organization, characterized by deliberate and increased government intervention in agricultural markets, emerged that in many instances seems to reflect agricultural commodity regimes prior to the 1992 reforms of the Common Agricultural Policy (CAP) in Western Europe. However, budget constraints have in many instances limited the level of intervention or have required caps on programs that otherwise imply far-reaching intervention in commodity markets (USDA, 1996). Most recently, some countries have introduced or increased budgetary support measures, typically targeted to producers in less favored areas, such as in Estonia, the Czech Republic and Slovakia, but also for the purchase of agricultural inputs and services as in Romania.

External constraints, imposed by membership or commitments to regional trade associations and international trade agreements, have reduced the scope of government activity in selecting price and trade policy instruments. Among the most important are the Central European Free Trade Area (CEFTA), the Baltic Free Trade Area (BFTA), the Association Agreements (AA), and the World Trade Organization (WTO) Agreement on Agriculture.

Agricultural policy instrument choices of CEECs from 1989-96 can be described by a number of important developments, elaborated in Hartell and Swinnen (1998) and summarized as follows:

- After broad liberalization and subsidy cuts, the main instrument remaining was import tariffs.
- Gradually, a series of nontariff interventions emerged to protect producers and agricultural protection increased following declining terms of trade.
- In the Visegrad-4 countries, nontariff interventions evolved into a market organization system implemented to provide long run support to, and interventions in, agriculture (including variable import levies in combination with minimum guaranteed producer prices, mostly used in the milk, wheat, sugar, and beef subsectors).
- Production controls have been installed only after price support policies were implemented, and only in the milk and sugar subsectors.
- Quantitative export restraints have been used nearly permanently in Bulgaria and Romania, and intermittently elsewhere—especially in cereals markets.
- Uruguay Round Agreement (GATT/URA) implementation has converted variable import levies into tariffs.
- Policy regimes, particularly in the Czech Republic, Hungary, Poland, Slovakia and Slovenia, appear 'CAP-like' but their implementation and effective support level may be very different.
- Agricultural credit subsidies have become an increasingly important source of producer support and public expenditure, especially in Poland.

An emerging feature of CEEC agricultural policy is the greater use of direct budgetary measures to support producers. Some of these take the form of area or headage payments and are usually targeted to less favored areas (LFAs). Various subsidies are offered in a number of countries, some of which include fuel tax reimbursements, wage subsidies, capital investment subsidies, and production input subsidies. A notable example is Romania where a voucher system, first introduced in 1997, subsidizes producer input purchases. In addition, nearly all CEECs use budgetary resources for a variety of preferential credit subsidies and loan guarantee programs (Swinnen and Gow, 1999; Swinnen et al., 1998).

Bulgaria and Romania have recently liberalized their agricultural regimes: removing consumer subsidies, many producer subsidies, direct price controls, contract prices, registration regimes, and most quantitative restrictions on import and export. Others have simplified their means of intervention. However, many highly interventionist policies such as fixed or minimum guaranteed prices, intervention purchases, threshold triggering, and deficiency payments can be found throughout the CEECs. Export subsidies still play a prominent role in the policy regime of Hungary and to a lesser extent in the Czech Republic, Slovenia, and Slovakia.

Elements of Agricultural Protection

Even while the CEECs' choice of policy instruments are seemingly becoming more similar to each other and with the CAP, the actual implementation can vary substantially. The impact of the share of various policy instruments in agricultural support can be more easily analyzed by decomposing a country's overall commodity aggregated percentage PSE into its component parts (expressed as per cent of PSE) based on the classification of policy measures used by the OECD (1999).[4] This facilitates comparisons and assessment of policy convergence/divergence between groups of countries over time. The PSE is first decomposed into two components useful for understanding the general direction of agricultural support policy, market price support (MPS), and payments.

Table 8.2   Summary of policy instrument developments in selected CEECs, 1998-99

Country	Market and Price Support	Domestic Support	Credit Programs
Bulgaria	• Import duties, tariffs and tariff rate quotas • Export constraints liberalized • Price intervention abolished • Intervention purchases of grains for market stabilization • Temporary import ban on vegetables; ban on meat cuts for processing as a public health measure	• Direct payments (financial support and investment stimulation under numerous programs) • Grain storage support • Temporary discount on freight costs for grains	• Preferential credit for production and harvest of wheat, maize, sunflower and sugar • Interest subsidies on loans
Estonia	• Effectively none • Limited export marketing credits • Removed system of import quotas for grain • Food import licenses fee increased • Announced: customs tariffs to be introduced in 2000; policy reforms planed to bring farm policy in line with the EU	• Direct payments: dairy cow and arable crops; allowances for hardship • Subsidies: capital investments, fuel tax and liming • Subsidized premiums for new crop insurance program	• Long term interest rate credits and loan guarantees

Czech Republic	• Import tariffs and tariff rate quotas
	• Price regulation: intervention and guaranteed prices subject to quota for wheat and planned for pork; minimum prices for milk
	• Export subsidies: direct for milk; export credit subsidies for pork purchased at min. price and some other commodities ad hoc
	• Nonautomatic export licensing: major commodities incl. wheat, oilseeds, isoglucos; export quota: rapeseed
	• Contingency import protection introduced, includes:
	  - additional duties effective for one year
	  - import quotas for up to four years
	  - minimum import prices
	• Planned: sugar production quotas and minimum guaranteed prices
		• Direct payments: area and headage payments (beef cattle, sheep, suckler cows) in LFAs; support for organic farming; and 'highland' countryside support
		• Cattle herd maintenance and revitalization subsidy for most areas starting in 2000
			• Credit subsidies and loan guarantees for both working capital and investment

Table 8.2 Continued

Hungary	• Import tariffs and tariff rate quotas • Guidance price system with intervention: milk, beef, pigmeat with subsidies to processors • Minimum guaranteed prices with some state purchasing: wheat and maize • Deficiency payments for those not receiving orientation prices • Export subsidies: milk, pigmeat, poultry, wine • Target price with import surcharge: sugar • Retaliatory duties on imported Polish food products	• Direct payments: area payments for LFAs • Quality payments for pigmeat • Wage subsidies for promotion of agricultural employment • Fuel tax subsidies • Various production subsidies	• Interest rate subsidies • Capital investment grants • Interest relief for land purchases
Poland	• Import tariffs and tariff rate quotas • Intervention purchases (some with min. prices): wheat, rye, milk, pork; ad hoc intervention purchases and selling for others • Price support, production quotas and export subsidies: sugar; gradual introduction for tobacco, hops, fruit, vegetables. Plans to introduce quotas in milk and grains sectors in 2000 • Threshold system for import quantity or price triggering additional import levies: most crops and livestock • Ad hoc (temporary) import levies: wheat, maize, sugar, pork	• Subsidies for productivity enhancing inputs and field liming • Direct aid based on output to grain producers • Rural development action planned: - traditional forms of support - support for organic farming - improved access to credit - restructuring and enlargement of farms - export support program	• Subsidies on loans for inputs
Slovakia	• Import tariffs and tariff rate quotas • Administered prices and quota: milk • Minimum prices: sugar • Intervention prices: wheat, maize, slaughter bulls; ad hoc interventions in other commodities • Export subsidies: milk, sugar, malt, tobacco, others ad hoc • Nonautomatic import licenses: wheat • Nonautomatic export licenses: wheat, barely, maize • Import ban: Czech potatoes; import quotas: Czech pigmeat, sugar, beer • Surcharge until 2001 on most imports	• Direct payments: area payments for LFAs • Various input subsidies • Dairy cow subsidies for: - breeding stock and breeding activities - construction of buildings for cattle	• Interest subsidies, guaranteed loans and payment of interest • Operational credit

From Central Planning to the Common Agricultural Policy 197

Table 8.2 Continued

Country	Market and Price Support	Domestic Support	Credit Programs
Slovenia	• Tariffs and tariff rate quotas • Fixed prices: wheat and sugar • Price regulation: milk • Intermittent intervention purchases: pigmeat, wine • Temporary special import levy: wheat • Policy reform proposed: align market systems with the EU and include area payments for environmentally friendly farming, subsidies for sustainable farming, special subsidies for LFAs	• Direct payments: (headage payments for cow and sheep in LFAs) • Area payments for wheat (1999) • Input subsidies • Export promotion	• Credit subsidies for working capital and investments
Romania	• Import tariffs and tariff rate quotas; additional duties ad hoc • Import licensing only under preferential tariff quotas • Export licenses only under EU preferential tariff quotas • Export subsidy with quota: wheat, maize, pigmeat, poultry	• Voucher system for input purchases, since 1997 • Premia paid for wheat • Subsidized seed purchases for arable crop producers	• Subsidized interest: short-term for current production, medium-term for investment, machinery • Credits for purchase of live animals

Source: Compiled from AgraEurope, 1998, 1999; Cochrane, 1999; OECD, 1999.

The MPS component of PSE measures the transfers to producers that result from the price gap between domestic producer prices and border (world) prices that, ceteris paribus, is the effect of policy intervention working on trade borders. A change in the MPS (the price gap) however, is not always policy induced; world commodity price changes, currency devaluation, exchange rate adjustments, and production fluctuations are also reflected in MPS. The payments component of PSE is the aggregate of all other policy induced transfers made to producers individually from taxpayers.

Figure 8.5 shows the per cent share of MPS and payments comprising the PSE for the Czech Republic, Estonia, Hungary, Poland, and the EU for the periods 1991-93 and 1996-98. The aggregate per cent PSE for each period is also included. In addition, the decomposition of the aggregate payments of the last period, 1996-98, into more detailed categories is given.

In all countries represented during the period 1991-93, the MPS was the dominant form of support, except in Estonia where its large negative values, resulting primarily from currency devaluation, contributed to negative PSEs. Payments comprised at most 28 per cent of producer support among the countries including the EU. Poland's relatively high share of payments during this period is influenced by high negative MPS transfers during 1991 as a result of currency devaluation which overwhelmed all other support measures. The extremely high relative value for MPS in the Czech Republic reflects substantial reductions in payments to producers since 1990 which eventually became negative in 1992 due to land taxes. Most payments and the land tax were abolished by 1993. In Estonia, the low payments level reflects in part the gradual reduction and elimination of some sources of budgetary support from 1991 to 1993.

Estonia, the Czech Republic and Hungary have similar levels of support, around 10 per cent, while the PSE in Poland has substantially increased. The rising PSE in Poland has been mainly due to increases in MPS which have been proportionately larger than the increase in budgetary outlays to producers. In Hungary, the opposite happened; the reduction in some forms of payments was more than matched by reductions in MPS.

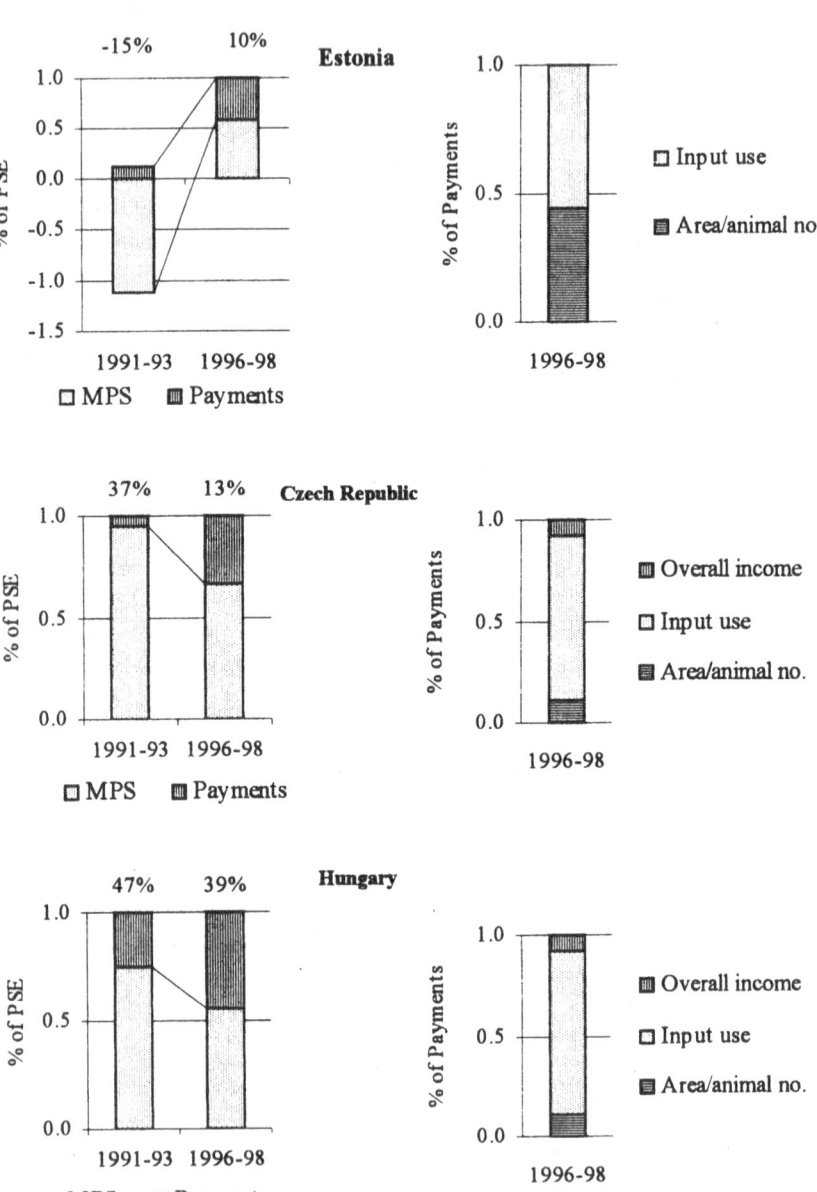

Figure 8.5 Decomposition of the PSE, 1991-93 and 1996-98

Source: OECD, PSE/CSE database.

From Central Planning to the Common Agricultural Policy 201

Figure 8.5 Continued

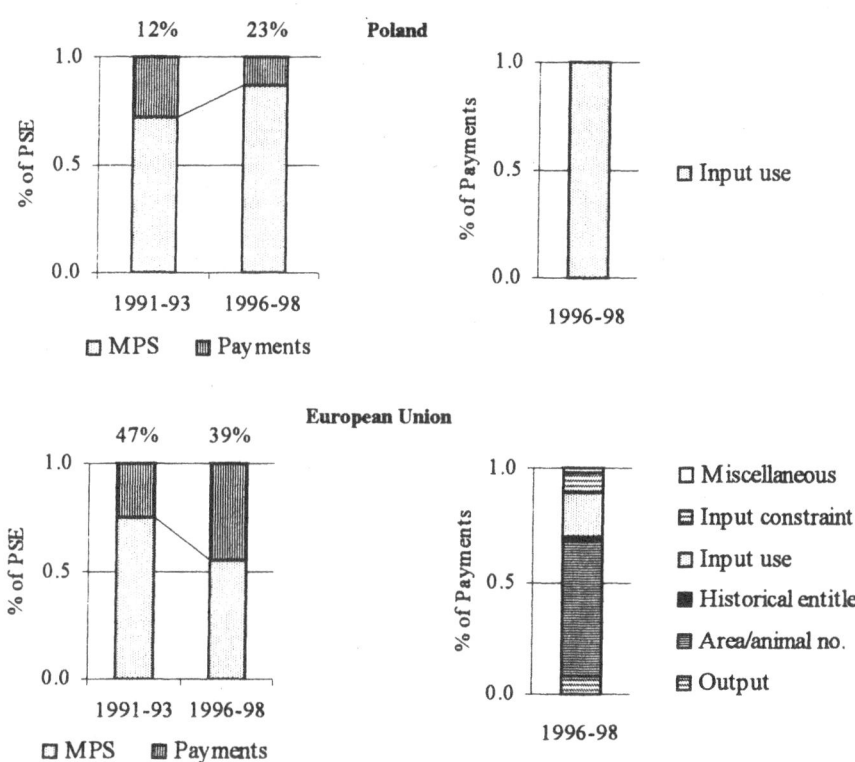

The proportion between MPS and payments has changed, often substantially, between the first period and the 1996-98 period. Except for Poland, all the CEECs increased their share of payments in producer support. The EU also experience a shift away from high MPS, reflecting changes in support mechanisms embodied in the 1992 CAP reforms and, more recently, restraints imposed by GATT/URA.

The second decomposition shown in figure 8.5 is of the aggregate payments component which will help convey a quantitative feeling to the relative importance of various budgetary related policy measures. Aggregate payments are classified into seven categories which include payments based on output, on area planted/animal numbers, on historical entitlements, on input use, on input constraints, on overall farming income, and miscellaneous payments.

While the proportion of payments has grown and is of similar relative size among countries, the source of each country's expenditures varies noticeably. Most strikingly, Poland's payments are exclusively for input use which has been the case since 1991. Much of this has been in the form of subsidized interest rates for working capital. Estonia's payment structure during the period is comprised of roughly equal payments for input use and area planted /animal numbers. However, the total value of payments for area and animal numbers occurred in 1998, the first year of implementation which, on a yearly basis, represents about 60 per cent of PSE transfers to producers. The structure of payments in the Czech Republic and Hungary appear somewhat similar; with the majority being payments for input use and smaller fractions for overall income, followed by payments based on output and area planted/animal numbers. The EU displays a somewhat more complex structure of payments but also one with much different emphasis than found among the CEECs. For example, payments for area and animal numbers are the most important component, easily 60 per cent of the total, followed by payments for input use, input constraints, output, historical entitlements, and miscellaneous.

These observations of the elements of agricultural protection show both emerging similarities and important differences in the source and share of support to agriculture. For instance, while MPS has generally declined, it remains the most important single source of support to producers in both the CEECs and the EU. However, other elements vary considerably such as the disproportionate reliance on payments for input use in many CEECs. Other features, including the presence of payments for overall income in some CEECs and not in the EU could potentially further contribute to the complexity of policy alignment since the policy choice set of one is not simply a subset of the other.

Political Economy Aspects of Trade and Policy

Notwithstanding that some elements of the EU's CAP are in flux, the preceding section has shown that, despite numerous similarities, there are still important differences in the choice of instruments and level of protection both between the CEECs and with the EU. In order to understand how CEEC policy has developed, and is likely to develop in the future when the concern is towards alignment, it is important to understand what elements are significant in determining the direction and form of agricultural policy. In this section, a political economy framework focusing on the distributional consequences of trade policy is elaborated to explain the previous observations and provide guidance in the direction of agricultural policy developments, given the structure of the economy and the existence of constraints to protection. Such insights should help policymakers anticipate obstacles and identify opportunities to improve the design and implementation of policy.

Political Economy of Trade Policies

Political economy is inherently linked with income distribution. The choice of trade policies and trade regimes has both efficiency and income distributional effects. The income distributional effects of trade policies therefor induce different preferences for trade policies for various interest groups. If trade liberalization will increase aggregate efficiency, but induce a decline in agricultural prices, farmers will oppose trade liberalization. This opposition will translate itself into political pressure for the government not to liberalize trade. The government will have to balance this opposition against the political pressure for trade liberalization from interest groups benefiting from the liberalization. The government's choice will be influenced by the balance of these pressures.

The same logic holds when a country has free trade, but external shocks (e.g. exogenously induced world market changes) induce political pressure for government intervention to offset the negative distributional effects of such changes. Many empirical studies show that agricultural protection was initially implemented as a reaction to falling world market prices in many countries (e.g. Tracy, 1989; Anderson and Hayami, 1986; Bullock, 1992; Swinnen and de Gorter, 1997; de Gorter and Tsur, 1991).

To understand why the government reacts to the pressure by some groups, and not others, it is illuminating to separate three factors affecting group influence on government: the income vulnerability of the interest group; the costs of protection on the rest of society; and the group's ability to organize effective political pressure.

The third factor is probably the most popular explanation.[5] For example, the high protection of farmers in western and northern Europe is often explained by the uneven political pressure from 'powerful and well organized farm lobbies' versus the 'dispersed, ill-informed and unorganized consumers'. Another argument in this category is that farmers, and small farmers in particular, are often represented in governments because their representation is typically taken up by Christian-Democratic governments or agrarian parties. As these parties tend to take center positions on many issues, they are often part of either center-left or center-right government coalitions. This political organization factor is also the most visible influence in day-to-day policy negotiations. However, empirical evidence suggests that while this factor has some influence it may be the least important of the three in explaining changes in agricultural protection. This factor also becomes less influential when explaining medium to long run evolution of protection. Therefore our discussion will primarily focus on the other factors.

The other two factors imply that the sectors most likely to gain protection, and most likely to be influential in opposing trade liberalization, are those sectors whose incomes are the most vulnerable (i.e. have most to lose from free trade) and where protection is less costly to the rest of society.

Income vulnerability is strongly related to comparative advantage. Domestic farmers will suffer when trade integration occurs with a country that has a comparative advantage in the production of the same and similar products.[6] The larger this comparative advantage, the more vulnerable they are and therefore, the stronger they are likely to oppose complete trade integration.

The costs of protection on the rest of society depend mostly on the structure of the economy. Important structural factors include the share of food in consumer expenditures; the impact of food price increases on inflationary pressures, wages, and industry profits; the share of agriculture in GDP and in trade; the share of agriculture in employment; and domestic and international demand and supply elasticities. Typically, opposition to agricultural protection declines:

- when food makes up a smaller share in consumer expenditures (lower costs for consumers);
- when food price increases have less effect on profits in the rest of the economy (lower costs for industry);
- when agriculture is a net importing sector (shifts part of the costs to other countries);
- when domestic supply is inelastic and total demand is elastic.

A structural change in the factors that cause a reduction in the costs of protection will make it more likely that governments increase agricultural protection or avoid trade liberalization. The cost factor explains, in combination with the growing vulnerability of agriculture which occurs with declining comparative advantage of agriculture, why agricultural protection typically increases with economic development and is higher in net importing countries of agricultural products (Gardner, 1987; Swinnen, 1994; Bullock, 1992; de Gorter and Tsur, 1991).

Numerous empirical political economy studies have found results consistent with these hypotheses and have concluded that governments adjust agricultural policies in response to changes in relative incomes and economic structural changes which affect the political costs and benefits of agricultural protection for the government (Swinnen et al., 1999; Crommelynck et al., 1998; Anderson, 1995; David and Huange, 1996; Lindert, 1991).

Similar patterns and evidence for support of these hypotheses are also found in the CEECs (Banse et al., 1999; Swinnen, 1996). Figure 8.6 shows higher PSE levels in countries with higher income levels which reflect less opposition from consumers and taxpayers. Figure 8.7 shows that agricultural protection in CEECs declines with higher net exports. An empirical investigation focusing specifically on six CEECs by Hartell et al. (1999) has also tested the hypotheses of agricultural protection. Their analysis found strong evidence that agricultural protection is higher in CEECs where the comparative advantage (vulnerability) is lower, where real exchange rate developments had negative impacts on farm profitability, where the share of agriculture in employment is lower and its share in GDP higher, and where agricultural products are net imports.

These results and observations have important implications for the direction of agricultural policy in CEECs as their economies develop. It also highlights the strong pressures and resistance from producers that governments are likely to encounter as a consequence of the income distribution changes resulting from the integration of structurally different, and differently competitive agricultural sectors.

Factors in Policy Instrument Choice

The choice of instrument or combination of instruments, in addition to their level of application, used to intervene in agricultural markets is important since each may generate different types of economic distortions, different distributions of costs and benefits, and entail different levels of

206 *Agriculture and East-West European Integration*

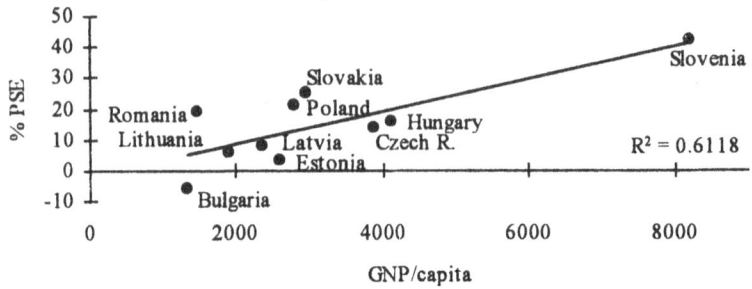

Figure 8.6 Agricultural support and economic development in CEECs, 1995*

* Producer subsidy equivalent

Source: Data from OECD, 1997, and World Bank, 1997.

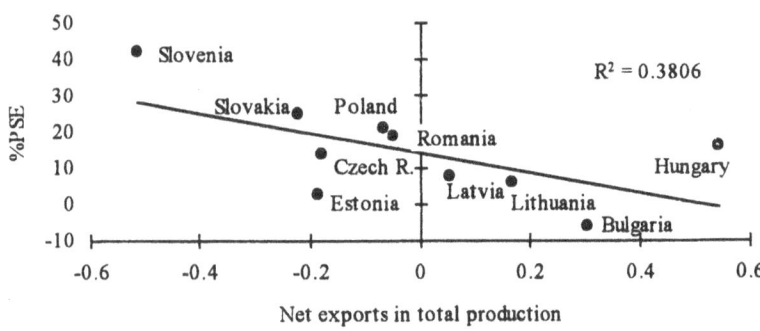

Figure 8.7 Agricultural support and value share of net agricultural exports in total agricultural production in CEECs, 1995*

* Producer subsidy equivalent

Source: Data from OECD, 1997, and World Bank, 1997.

administrative costs (e.g., implementation, monitoring and enforcement), distributional leakages, distortionary taxation costs, and deadweight losses (de Gorter, 1994). These costs and distributional consequences can be substantially different between, for example, a price support with a variable import levy/export subsidy system that was the core of the EU's CAP, and recent reforms that are beginning to place more emphasis on budgetary expenditures.

A normative literature of distortions and welfare has addressed the question of instrument choice in the interests of noneconomic objectives (Bhagwati, 1987). The objectives are considered noneconomic in that most trade policies are concerned with domestic income redistribution or concerns of 'food security' rather than addressing perceived market imperfections. In this sense, instrument choice is about how to optimally, or most efficiently, introduce distortions into the economy.

However, whether intervention is judged on the basis of direct targeting criteria or minimization of deadweight losses, observed agricultural price and trade policies regularly depart from efficiency based theory (Rodrik, 1986). The political economy literature offers an explanation for government policy choice which emphasizes that changes in the structural conditions of political institutions and economies have induced changes in the political costs and benefits of the use of various policy instruments (Campos, 1989; Rodrik, 1994; Swinnen, 1996).

As structural conditions and institutions change, so to does the optimum choice or mix of instruments, in much the same way that the politically optimum level of transfer also can change with the level of economic development (Kola, 1995). For example, implementation costs of farm programs have an important influence on governments' choice of policy instruments (Munk, 1995; de Gorter, 1994), and can vary considerably with farm size and structure (Sarris, 1994). A structural change which reduces implementation costs enlarges or alters the instrument choice set. This helps to explain a certain degree of path dependency often observed in agricultural policy. For example, Ray (1981) finds that among many OECD countries, the introduction of tariffs and non-tariff barriers is nearly always sequential which is exactly what is observed in the CEECs.

Exogenous factors often place limits on the scope, form, and operation of many support programs. This has certainly been true in the CEECs and can help explain why, even though policy choice during transition frequently appeared similar to the pre-reform CAP, it in fact often operated very differently.

Budget constraints have been the source of many reform proposals, such as in the recent experience of many OECD countries, and often limit the level of intervention. This has been the situation in many CEECs in early transition where, due to a lack of budgetary resources, minimum guaranteed prices were often set at or below the cost of production as well as below market price. The low threshold prices, in combination with the selective use of boarder controls, ensured that intervention was infrequently needed, and where used was always subject to specific quota limitations (Hartell and Swinnen, 1998).

Human capital may have been another limiting factor which likely contributed to the period of stopgap policy making just after liberalization and may have also impaired effective policy implementation. For example, despite the widespread use of minimum prices, variable import levies played a minimal role in maintaining internal producer prices. Unlike the administration of variable import levies in Western Europe, the 'variability' was not high with adjustment usually being made on a monthly or less frequent bases. In this sense they acted like an additional fixed import tariff. With experience, increasing sophistication, and increasing economic rewards to skill and education, this constraint is becoming less binding in policy instrument choice and implementation (Swinnen, 1996; Orazem and Vodopivec, 1997).

Institutional factors are important in policy choice and policy reform and are having an increasingly important role in developments in the CEECs (Swinnen, 1996). Institutional constraints include both domestic legislative and regulatory bodies and international agreements.

Domestic institutions greatly influence the type of regulation most obviously through (1) their ability to reduce transaction costs, (2) their different responses to political pressure, and (2) the degree to which each is able to alter trade law. For example, significant lobbying effort may be needed to elicit protection from a particular legislative body but may take on a semi-permanence that would not be forthcoming from a different agency. Domestic institutions can be an important source of hindrance to policy reform as well as a constraint to policy options because the path dependency characteristics of institutions tend to favor existing structures and behavior norms (North, 1993).

International trade law and associations have received a great deal of attention because they reduce the choice mix of interventions available to governments, alter government incentives in making decisions, and play a central role as a forum for policy reform (Tangermann, 1996; Giavazzi and Pagano, 1988). By entering into a trade agreement, governments are exogenously binding their actions, shielding them from domestic political pressure for protection and lending credibility and political acceptability to trade and price policies which diverge from the short run political optimum. Trade agreements, as external constraints to domestic policy, may also be especially durable in that the institutional nature of the commitments help prevent reversal by future governments.

In the CEECs as elsewhere, WTO negotiations have worked to reduce the level of tariffs, increase market access, and have prohibited certain instruments such as variable levies and quantitative restrictions. However, one unintended side-effect may be to encourage the greater and more creative use of non-tariff barriers (Ray and Marvel, 1984). Regional trade associations and agreements, such as CEFTA, also enforce rules and restrictions on the use of trade barriers and encourage greater regional policy coordination. CEFTA's institutional strength, however, may be weaker in that it's 'multilateral' coverage encompasses the least sensitive sectors and products and CEEC governments have repeatedly violate the spirit of the agreement by evoking national safeguard clauses in the face of extreme domestic pressure.

EU accession preparation is an increasingly important influence on CEEC domestic trade and price setting. This is formalized in the Association Agreements whereby the CEECs agree to align policy and fulfill the requirements of the aquis communitaire as a condition for membership. During the preparation phase, the EU is providing assistance for legal and institution building which further contribute to policy alignment.

Conclusions and Implications

The development of agricultural price and trade policies in the CEECs reveals significant variation in the level of protection between countries and commodities despite evidence of recent aggregate convergence. But the level of protection is still significantly lower than found in the EU with the exception of Slovenia and for milk in some countries. Recently, the composition of support in many CEECs has shifted significantly to greater use of payments in total PSE, similar to developments in the EU, with the main exception being Poland. However, the breakdown of the payments component shows that the CEECs place greater relative emphasis on payments for inputs, most predominantly credit subsidies. In addition, the relative pattern of food protection is also unlike that found in the EU. However, the degree of intervention and distortion is often less than implied by the choice of market regulatory instrument alone, which in many cases appear similar to CAP instruments.

Interest in the future development and factors influencing CEEC agricultural policy is heightened now that accession negotiations have commenced with a number of the applicants. This is important because the cost of accession will depend considerably on the degree of alignment of agricultural prices and policy. In the CEECs, domestic political economy, WTO constraints, and EU integration factors affect the level of agricultural protection and their policy choices.

Most CEECs have experienced economic growth in recent years, which is predicted to continue in the coming years (OECD, 1997). As the economy grows, a number of effects occur simultaneously, some with opposing effects on government policy incentives. On aggregate, political economy theory predicts domestic factors to increase political incentives for agricultural protection in the long run in the absence of credible constraints. Short run economic improvement in other sectors and macroeconomic stabilization have already enabled modest levels of protection to be applied to the most sensitive sectors.

The observations on agricultural policy outlined earlier can be understood as explicit choices that take into account the distributional asymmetries of various policy instruments, conditioned by the economic structures and institutional constraints, yielding them as the politically optimal although not necessarily economically efficient (Campos, 1989). The policies can change as the structural conditions change, implying a degree of path dependency which is widely observed elsewhere.

The common theme in political economy analysis is that agricultural price and trade developments are highly dependent on changes in the structural conditions in the economy but also on the evolution of institutional constraints. Institutional constraints such as the GATT/WTO, and regional free trade agreements that include agriculture have already had an important impact on the level and choice of agricultural polices in the CEECs. Now, with the certainty of EU integration, alignment in the choices of policy are more likely. Still, domestic political economy considerations continue to have an important impact on policy-making, particularly concerning the level of intervention.

Notes

1. The nominal protection rate is a measure of direct trade and price distortions evaluated at the nominal exchange rate by comparing domestic prices with world reference prices that are assumed to prevail in the absence of government intervention. See Bojnec and Swinnen (1997) for details of its construction, interpretation, and correction for exchange rates.
2. The OECD has calculated two series of PSEs: the first is the well-known producer 'subsidy equivalent' while the most recent series is a producer 'support estimate'. The main difference between the two series is how various policies are categorized and how general services provided collectively to agriculture are treated. In the 'support estimate', general services are categorized separately from the aggregate and commodity measures of support while in the 'subsidy equivalent', these values were in included in both measures and usually allocated among commodities on a production weighted basis. Thus, the 'support estimate' will normally always be somewhat lower than the 'subsidy equivalent'. In this chapter, we will report the 'support estimate' where data are available and reliable, otherwise the use of the 'subsidy equivalent will be noted.
3. For a detailed analysis of PSE developments for specific agricultural commodities along the agro-food chain in Bulgaria and Romania, see Gorton and Davidova, this volume, and Gorton et al. (1997).
4. Refer to OECD (1999) for a detailed description and definitions of the classification of policy measures included in the PSE and the allocation rules for assigning transfers to a particular component of support.
5. In political economy theory, Olson (1965) has analyzed how group characteristics affect their ability to organize effectively for collective action.
6. Of course, in the instance when trade integration occurs between countries who produce completely different commodities, there is no negative distributional effect, only benefits.

References

Agra Europe (1998), AgraFood East Europe (various issues),. Agra Europe Ltd, London.
Agra Europe (1999), AgraFood East Europe (various issues),. Agra Europe Ltd, London.
Anderson, K. and Hayami Y. (1986), *The Political Economy of Agricultural Protection*, Allen & Unwin, Sydney.
Banse, M., Bargel, T., Gorton, M., Hartell, J., Hughes, G., Köckler, J. and Münch, W. (2000), 'The Evolution of Competitiveness in Hungary's Agriculture from Transition to Accession', *MOCT-MOST: Economic Policy in Transition Economics*, vol. 10, no. 1.
Bhagwati, J.N. (1987), 'The Generalized Theory of Distortions and Welfare', in J.N. Bhagwati (ed), *International Trade: Selected Reading*, 2nd edition, MIT Press, Cambridge.

Bojnec, S., Münch, W. and Swinnen J.F.M (1997), 'Exchange Rates and the Measurement of Agricultural Price Distortions in CEECs and of CEEC-EU Accession Costs, Working Paper No. 3/5, Joint Research Project: Agricultural Implications of CEEC Accession to the EU', FAIR1-CT95-0029, Department of Agricultural and Environmental Economics, Katholieke Universiteit Leuven, Belgium.

Bojnec, S. and Swinnen. J.F.M. (1997), 'The Pattern of Agricultural Price Distortions in Central and Eastern Europe. An Update: 1990-1995', *Food Policy*, vol. 22, no. 4 , pp.289-306.

Bullock, D.S. (1992), 'Objectives and Constraints of Government Policy: The Countercyclicity of Transfers to Agriculture', *American Journal of Agricultural Economics*, vol. 74, pp. 617-29.

Campos, J.E.L. (1989), 'Legislative Institutions, Lobbying, and the Endogenous Choice of Regulatory Instruments: A Political Economy Approach to Instrument Choice', *Journal of Law, Economics, and Organization*, vol. 5, pp. 333-53.

Gardner, B.L. (1983), 'Efficiency Redistribution Through Commodity Markets', *American Journal of Agricultural Economics*, vol. 65, pp. 225-35.

Cochrane, N. (1999), 'Policy Response of Central and Eastern Europe to the Global Market Shocks of 1998', Presented at the OECD forum *Agricultural Policies in Non-Member Countries* in Paris, 23-30 April 1999.

Crommelynck, A., Kola, J. and Swinnen, J.F.M. (1998), 'Determinants of Agricultural Protection in Finland (1931-1990)', Working paper No. 14, Department of Agricultural and Environmental Economics, Katholieke Universiteit Leuven, Belgium.

David, C.C. and Huang, J. (1996), 'Political Economy of Rice Price Protection in Asia', *Economic Development and Cultural Change*, vol. 44, pp. 463-483.

de Gorter, H. and Tsur, Y. (1991), 'Explaining Price Bias in World Agriculture: The Calculus of Support-Maximizing Politicians', *American Journal of Agricultural Economics*, vol. 73, pp. 244-54.

de Gorter, H. (1994), *Assessing the Relative Transfer Efficiency of Agricultural Support Policies*, OECD, Paris.

Giavazzi, F. and Pagano, M. (1988), 'The Advantage of Tying One's Hand: EMS Discipline and Central Bank Credibility', *European Economic Review*, vol. 32, pp. 1055-82.

Gorton, M., Buckwell, A. and Davidova, S. (1997), 'Distortions and Inefficiencies in the CEEC Food Chains: A Comparative Analysis of Economic Transfers in Romania and Bulgaria', Working Paper No. 2/6, Joint Research Project: *Agricultural Implications of CEEC Accession to the EU*, FAIR1-CT95-0029, Wye College, University of London.

Hartell, J. and Swinnen J.F.M. (1998), 'Trends in Agricultural Price and Trade Policy Instruments Since 1990 in Central European Countries', *The World Economy* vol. 21, pp. 261-79.

Hartell, J., Bojnec, S. and Swinnen, J.F.M. (1999), 'Determinants of Government Intervention in Central and Eastern European Agricultural Markets: An Empirical Analysis', Working paper, Department of Agricultural and Environmental Economics, Katholieke Universiteit Leuven, Belgium.

Kola, J. (1995), *In Quest of the Best: Transfer Efficiency of Agricultural Policies*, Department of Economics and Management, University of Helsinki.

Krueger, A.O., Schiff, M. and Valdes, A. (1992), *The Political Economy of Agricultural Protection in Developing Countries*, Johns Hopkins University Press, Baltimore.

Lindert, P.H. (1991), 'Historical Patterns of Agricultural Policy', in C. Peter Timmer (ed), *Agriculture and the State: Growth, Employment, and Poverty in Developing Countries*, Cornell University Press, Ithaca.

MAFF (1997), Producer subsidy equivalent data, Ministry of Agriculture, Food and Forestry, Slovenia.

Munk, K.J. (1995), *Government Support to Sectors with Structural Adjustment Problems, A Public Finance Approach*, Center of Economic Studies, K.U. Leuven, Belgium.

North, D.C. (1993), 'Toward a Theory of Institutional Change', in W.A. Barnett, M. Hinich, and N. Schofield (eds), *Political Economy: Insititutions, Competition and Representation*, Proceedings of the Seventh International Symposium in Economic Theory and Econometrics, Cambridge University Press, pp.61-9.

OECD (1995, 1996, 1997), *Agricultural Policies, Markets and Trade in the Central and Eastern European Countries, the New Independent States and Chine: Monitoring and Outlook; Monitoring and Evaluation*, OECD, Paris.

OECD (1999), *Agricultural Policies in OECD Countries 1999 - Monitoring and Evaluation*, OECD, Paris.

Olson, M., Jr. (1965), *The Logic of Collective Action: Public Goods and the Theory of Groups*, Harvard University Press, Cambridge.

Orazem, P. and Vodopivec, M. (1997), 'Value of Human Capital in Transition to Market: Evidence from Slovenia', *European Economic Review*, vol. 41, pp. 893-903.

Ray, E.J. (1981), 'The Determinants of Tariff and Non-Tariff Trade Restrictions in the United States', *Journal of Political Economy*, vol. 89, pp. 105-21.

Ray, E.J. and Marvel, H.P. (1984), 'The Pattern of Protection in the Industrial World', *Review of Economics and Statistics*, vol. LXVI, pp. 452-58.

Rodrik, D. (1986), 'Tariffs, Subsidies, and Welfare with Endogenous Policy', *Journal of International Economics*, vol. 21, pp. 285-99.

Rodrik, D. (1994), 'What Does the Political Economy Literature on Trade Policy (Not) Tell Us That We Ought to Know?', CEPR Discussion Paper No. 1039, Columbia University.

Sarris, A. (1994), 'Implications of EC Economic Integration for Agriculture, Agricultural Trade and Trade Policy', in M. Hartman, P.M. Schmitz, and H. von Witzke (eds), *Agricultural Trade and Economic Integration in Europe and North America*, Wissenschaftsverlag Vauk, Kiel.

Swinnen, J.F.M (1994), 'A Positive Theory of Agricultural Protection', *American Journal of Agricultural Economics*, vol. 76, pp. 1-14.

Swinnen, J.F.M (1996), 'Endogenous price and trade policy developments in Central European agriculture', *European Review of Agricultural Economics*, vol. 23, pp. 133-60.

Swinnen, J.F.M and de Gorter, H. (1997), 'Agricultural Protection and Economic Development: An Econometric Study of the Determinants of Agricultural Protection in Belgium Since the 19th Century', Policy Research Group Working Paper No. 8, Department of Agricultural and Environmental Economics, Katholieke Universiteit Leuven, Belgium.

Swinnen, J.F.M, Gow, G.R. and Hartell, J. (1998), 'Political economy of agricultural credit subsidies in Central and Eastern Europe', Working Paper No. 3/7 for EU FAIR Project *Agricultural Implications of CEEC-Accession to the EU*, Department of Agricultural and Environmental Economics, Katholieke Universiteit. Leuven, Belgium.

Swinnen, J.F.M and Gow, H. (1999), 'Agricultural credit problems and policies during the transition to a market economy in Central and Eastern Europe', *Food Policy*, vol. 24, pp. 21-47.

Swinnen, J.F.M., de Gorter, H. and Banerjee, A. (1999), 'Agricultural Protection and Economic Development: An Econometric Study of the Determinants of Agricultural Protection in Belgium since the 19th Century', Working paper No. 20, Department of Agricultural and Environmental Economics, Katholieke Universiteit Leuven, Belgium.

Tangermann, S. (1996), 'Implementation of the Uruguay Round Agreement on Agriculture: Issues and Prospects' *Journal-of-Agricultural-Economics*, vol.47, no. 3, pp. 315-37.

Tracy, M. (1989), *Government and Agriculture in Western Europe 1800-1988*, Harvester Wheatsheaf, London.

US Department of Agriculture (1996), *Review of Agricultural Policies in Europe and the Former Soviet Union*, E. Jones, and J.Y Shend (eds), Agricultural Economic Report No. 733, Washington DC.

World Bank (1997), *World Development Report 1997*, Oxford University Press, New York.

9 Eastward European Union Enlargement and the Future of the Common Agricultural Policy

EWA RABINOWICZ

Introduction

As a starting point in negotiations, Agenda 2000 addresses the issue of eastward enlargement in addition to reform of the Common Agricultural Policy (CAP) and Structural Funds. Agenda 2000 can be interpreted as an opening bid on the behalf of incumbent members of the European Union (EU) in the enlargement negotiations. In short, the bid is as follows: no direct payments, production quotas, capping Structural Funds at 4 per cent of Gross Domestic Product (GDP), and firm adjustment to the *acquis*. However, a lot of ambiguities remain with respect to direct payments. While there is a solid commitment that those payments will not be initially paid to new members there are also suggestions that such conditions are only temporary, indicating a possibility of extending payments to the CEECs in the future but with no definite or clear commitment. Hence, the issue remains of what kind of CAP the Central and Eastern European countries (CEECs) will face in the long run.

This chapter examines several likely outcomes of the accession negotiations with respect to direct payments. This issue is highly contentious and at the heart of future development of the CAP as well as European integration in general. The topics involved relate to the high share of the payments in the common budget, the functioning of the common market, and equal treatment of member countries etc. The chapter will examine three different options: full application of the CAP, exclusion of direct payments, and a compromise involving a partial renationalisation of the CAP and reorientation towards the environment and rural development. It will be argued that the third option is most likely. It will also be investigated whether the decision on payments can be avoided by postponement. The outline of the chapter is as follows. In the next section the methodological framework of the study is presented. Then experiences from past enlargements are analysed. In the following section, the economic and geopolitical implications of enlargement are discussed. This analysis intends to identify the gainers and losers in accession. Pressure groups are then examined in order to understand formation of national preferences. Likely development of the CAP and pressures for further changes are analysed in the next section. Available options with respect to direct payments in the negotiation game are then identified and evaluated using the methodological framework outlined above. The final section contains conclusions.

Methodology

The chapter will not address the desirability of different options from an efficiency or equity point of view. Instead, an international political economy framework is used to analyse the likelihood of certain policy outcomes. International political economy focuses on phenomena that take on international dimensions, including interactions between states (Laursen, 1995). Moreover, the chapter analyses the future development of the CAP in a general negotiation framework rather than concentrating on the CAP alone.

The methodology used here applies two theories sequentially: the theory of national preference formation and the theory of interstate bargaining. Interstate negotiations are seen as a two-level game. The theory of national preference formation focuses on state-society relationships where governments are assumed to respond to shifting pressures from domestic social groups.

Negotiation Theory: A Two-level Game

The accession can be seen as a two-level bargaining process involving three players with different positions. The European Commission acts as the chief negotiator playing the role of central decision maker. However, the Commission must receive a mandate from the EU Member States that consists of a set of negotiating directives which the Commission has to respect in the international game. Thus, two-level negotiations are taking place between the Commission as the negotiator for the EU of external agreements with first Member States and, second, with the CEECs. This type of analysis is inspired by Putnam (1988) who claims that the politics of many international negotiations can be usefully conceived as a two-level game. The distinction between external and internal negotiations is an old concept in negotiation analysis (Raifa, 1982). Gugenbuhl (1995) provides an interesting application to the negotiation of the Association Agreements (AAs; see also von Hagen, 1996).[1]

There is a fundamental difference between bilateral and multilateral international negotiations. In the latter case, coalitions between groups of applicants may be formed. It could be argued that the enlargement negotiations should not be analysed independently, but rather be seen as interlinked bilateral negotiations. Even if each country applies individually for EU membership, they have similar interests and problems and could act collusively. The countries' similarities also impose some conformity in the treatment of candidates by the EU.

From a narrow perspective, accession negotiations are conducted only once. However, both the applicants and the incumbents know that once in the EU they will become involved in a continuous process of negotiation about emerging issues. Thus, enlargement negotiations could, to a degree, be treated as repetitive negotiations. Playing the same game with the same players will lead to a new and completely different equilibrium outcome (Siebe, 1991). Two implications follow. First, participants will become more cooperative. The 'shadow of the future is very long in the EU' (Calmfors et al., 1996) meaning that countries which are supportive to the CEECs can expect to be repaid (diffuse reciprocity) by later support of their positions by the CEECs. Second, some issues may be deferred for consideration in the future.

Formation of National Preferences

The theory of national preference formation focuses on state-society relationships. The pressure group model is most commonly used in this context (Becker, 1983). National preferences are a result of pressures exerted by competing groups and reflect a balance between winners and losers. A later section provides a detailed account of the pressure groups involved and their stakes in the accession. According to pressure group theory, small effective groups are considered more important for domestic policy formation because their comparative advantage in controlling free riding outweighs the relatively small numbers of votes these groups may deliver in an election. In addition, consumers are assumed to be rationally ignorant about specific policies, such as agricultural policy, which is only one of several items in the package they are voting for. Such ignorance lowers the cost of supporting special interests. Especially complex policies, such as the CAP, suffer less opposition because their costs are less well known. The confusion in the public mind about whether the Commission, the Council, or national governments are responsible for the agricultural policy relaxes political constraints (Winters, 1995).

However, the opportunistic approach to policy formation neglects the issue of how democratic political institutions constrain elected politicians to align their behaviour with voters' interests, (Persson et al., 1997). In particular, it is difficult to identify plausible social mechanisms through which small groups could compensate for their insignificant number of votes that would be consistent with the institutional framework and political culture of parliamentary democracies in Western Europe. Campaign contributions are not common and donations to individual politicians are often illegal in Western Europe. Instead, pressure groups tend to appeal to the general public invoking such issues as equity and the wider social benefits of policies for which they seek support. In particular, agricultural policy is facilitated by pressure groups appealing to several consensus-generating causes (equity, food security, rural amenities, environmental protection) in spite of the fact that the policy fails to deliver at reasonable cost, if it delivers at all. In view of the discussion above, the subsequent analysis in the chapter will consider the visibility of the effects of a policy and, especially, its legitimacy, as crucial for the success of lobbying activities of pressure groups.

Moreover, the institutional setting under which pressure groups operate plays an important role. Sectoral ministries are more prone to influence from special interest groups and will generally not be willing or able to advance liberal trade policies (Winters, 1995). Accordingly, the institutional arrangements surrounding the accession negotiations will be decisive since the influence of pressure groups will depend on how the negotiation process will be structured. Sedelmeir and Wallace (1996), argue that the Copenhagen package on trade concessions to the CEECs could be agreed to only after a political decision was made to charge a high-level group of senior officials with the task of obtaining comprehensive concessions, horizontally across a range of sectors, rather than relying on technical experts at the working group level (see also Smith et al., 1996). In our analysis we will argue that compromises across sectors will be possible.

Lessons from Past Enlargements

Analysing the outcome of past enlargements can provide useful inductive generalisations about past behaviour of the EU in similar circumstances. The focus is on the two latest instances, i.e. accession of Spain and Portugal and the European Free Trade Agreement (EFTA).

The EFTA countries (Sweden, Finland, and Norway) had high per capita incomes as compared to the EU average and, with the possible exception of Sweden, noncompetitive and highly protected agriculture. The negotiation process was rapid. The agreement included several innovative elements, inter alia: a new objective within the Structural Funds (Objective 6) was created and defined in such a way (population density below 8 persons per square kilometer) that it cannot be applied outside Scandinavia; national support (100 per cent domestic financing) of agriculture north of the sixty-second parallel was introduced conditional on not exceeding present levels of production, etc.; and environmental support (regulation 2078/92) was used as a substitute for additional regional support to arctic (and alpine) agriculture.[2] In spite of the fact that all applicants but Sweden pressed for the application of a long transition period and on use of Accession Compensatory Amounts (ACA), this option was rejected. Thus, the unity of the market was preserved and introduction of new impediments to internal trade avoided. The final agreement on agriculture was similar between Finland and Sweden even though the emphasis on agriculture in the opening bids was much stronger in the former country than in the latter.

When evaluating the outcome of the negotiations, one observes that the CAP for the incumbents has hardly changed. This is consistent with findings by Preston (1995) who has claimed that the problems created by increasing the economic diversity of an enlarged EU are addressed by the creation of new policy instruments overlaid on existing ones rather than by a fundamental reforms. The EU was, nevertheless, able to absorb Finnish agricultural policies by increasing its degree of flexibility while still preserving some fundamental principles such as market unity. It is arguable that the outcome constitutes a big leap toward a renationalisation of the CAP and to some extent the Structural Funds (Rabinowicz and Bolin, 1998).[3]

It might be that the flexibility demonstrated in the EFTA enlargement is of little use for the CEECs since it was achieved by allowing the new members to keep and pay for their favoured causes. However, not all flexible solutions were achieved by relying on national financing, both Objective 6 and agro-environmental measures are cofinanced by the EU.

The accession of Spain and Portugal (as well as Greece six years earlier) was in several respects similar to the present accession. Both applicants were considerably poorer than the incumbents were. Moreover, strengthening of democracy in both countries was an important reason for the enlargement. Gradual adjustment and a long transition period (implying use of ACAs) were key strategies. Initially intended to take ten years, the transition period was shortened due to completion of the internal market. The flexibility of the process is underlined by the fact that Portugal was granted a sugar quota in spite of having no domestic sugar production in the past.

Analysing the Spanish experience, Patier (1997) claims that the negotiation process has not ended by signing the Accession Treaty. It was possible to renegotiate not only some specific transition arrangements but even important problems that were not satisfactorily resolved during the initial negotiations. A similar situation is observed for the EFTA countries. In the case of Finland, negotiations continued on the level of support paid to southern Finland; in the case of Austria, the sensitive issue of the alpine transit region was postponed thus allowing accession to go forward (Nicolaides and Close, 1995).

The following conclusions emerge as relevant for the next enlargement. The EU has demonstrated a remarkable degree of flexibility and has been able to absorb a wide range of national variability. The ability to create new constructions appears almost unlimited. Most issues appear to be negotiable (even quotas in the absence of domestic production). There is, however, a strong tendency not to upset past agreements resulting in a minimalist approach to change. Some contentious issues have been deferred for resolution in the future, supporting the view of the negotiations as repeated games. Finally, there has been a reasonable conformity of treatment of similar issues across applicant countries.

Economic and Political Implications of the Enlargement

The impact of the enlargement will depend to a large extent on conditions and timing, and, hence, on the outcome of the negotiations. Following the logic of a cooperative bargaining game and taking into account the possibility of compromises across sectors, the deal on the CAP will be dependent on gains and sacrifices achieved in other areas by the incumbents and the applicants. This section briefly examines first, the implications of the accession excluding the CAP and second, the effects of the enlargement on agriculture and the budget.

Two-level Game with Exclusion of the CAP

Major long term benefits from the enlargement follow from the theory of economic integration. Assessments of the benefits of enlargement vary considerably depending on the assumptions (see review in SOU, 1997:156).

Aggregate economic benefits for the EU from enlargement are rather small. The economic benefits include gains from increased trade and increased competitiveness as a result of access to less expensive resources. Moreover, the EU would benefit from the stabilisation of economic policy in the CEECs that will follow from membership as more discipline is introduced to domestic policy-making since the discretion of national policy makers will be considerably reduced (Bofinger, 1995). The willingness and the capacity of the newcomers to implement EU legislation may, however, create problems.

The economic benefits to the EU would be unevenly distributed (Baldwin et al., 1997). The CEECs have comparative advantage in traditional industries that are resource and energy intensive (SOU, 1997:156). Germany, the UK, and France have comparative advantage over the CEECs in science-based products. Spain, Portugal, and Greece share the comparative disadvantage in science-intensive products and comparative advantage in labour-intensive goods. Thus, the enlargement will expose southern members of the EU to stronger competition (von Hagen, 1996).

Geopolitical considerations were always important, if not decisive, in the decisions to enlarge the EU in the past.[4] Moving the CEECs out of the sphere of Russian dominance is obviously an extremely important element. Political interests in enlargement are not the same thorough the EU, however. From the German and Austrian perspective, eastward enlargement is an essential element of peaceful stability. For similar reasons Sweden and Finland are also strongly committed to the enlargement, in particular to bringing in the Baltic countries.[5]

Since both political and economic benefits are unevenly distributed, the prospect of enlargement creates distribution problems within the EU. Moreover, application of Structural Funds according to the present rules would result in excessive transfers of funds to the new members, most likely at the expense of the present beneficiaries, the southern countries.[6] Unsurprisingly, the intention of the Commission is to disarm the opposition of potential losers by retaining the Objective 1 and making it more rigorously defined as well as capping the transfers to the CEECs.[7] Some of those who will lose structural support (implicitly) stand to gain on accession in general.

Existing estimates point to the CEECs gaining more than the EU from integration (SOU, 1997:156). The question is, however, how such a message will be taken in the CEECs. The opinion that the integration so far has benefited the EU more than the CEECs is common (Kawecka-Wyrzykowska, 1996). Moreover, most of the estimated benefits are due to liberalisation in the CEECs themselves, i.e. to measures that the CEECs could apply independently. Accordingly, the beneficiaries may not fully appreciate them.

The major economic advantage of membership is potential improvement of the investment climate in the CEECs. Kawecka-Wyrzykowska (1996) argues that membership would increase the credibility of the CEECs and attract more investment. Similar views are held by Baldwin et al. (1997) who write, 'Joining the EU will make the CEECs substantially less risky from the point of view of domestic and foreign investors'. In particular, full membership would eliminate risk for contingent protection as there is no provision in the AAs specifying that antidumping duties will be abolished on EU-CEEC trade. However, as Guggenbuhl (1995) has shown, the associated countries also made use of protection, often in connection with pressures by large foreign firms. Messerlin (1995) argues that recent tariff increases in the presence of foreign direct investment (FDI) suggests that the CEECs are using trade policies as a way of attracting FDI. Sapir (1995) also points out that lobbying by foreign investors for protection is a quid pro quo for investment. Accordingly, the impact of membership on FDI is not as clearcut as argued by Baldwin et al., (1997) and Kawecka-Wyrzykowska (1996).

The motives of the candidate countries for wishing to become members of the EU are first and foremost a desire to 'return to Europe'. The CEECs also expect, however, that membership will benefit their security in case of external threat. With respect to political stability, the issue is different for those countries that are invited to join North Atlantic Treaty Organization (NATO). Those countries may attach more importance to the economic implications of accession.

Participation in distribution programs such as the Structural Funds would strongly benefit the CEECs. Capping the Structural Funds payments at 4 per cent of GDP is not a real problem for the CEECs who will hardly be able to absorb the funds more efficiently than previous newcomers.[8] The estimated cost of complying with the *acquis* appears, on the other hand, to be excessive in relation to the GDP of the CEECs. The cost of environmental legislation alone amounts to more than 1,000 ECU per capita totalling more than 100 billion ECU (approximately 8-12 billion ECU per annum; see SOU, 1997:149). Moreover, the standards that will be imposed are more demanding than those countries would have chosen themselves at their present level of GDP and may even stunt Eastern growth. According to Smith et al. (1995) the *acquis* is surely a suboptimal set of rules for nations at their stage of growth and development.

The opening bid of the Commission is based on an assumption that membership will be attractive enough to the applicants even without such pleasing features as direct payments (or full participation in the Structural Funds). However, the analysis above indicates that the benefits from membership excluding the CAP are probably not high enough to make joining the EU, regardless of the deal on agricultural policy, an attractive option. If the opening bid is rejected by the CEECs demanding a more generous offer, an increase of generosity is more likely to come at the expense of CAP/direct payments than by increasing the Structural Funds transfers. This is because the CAP (especially direct payments) is heavily biased towards northern European farm products while the northern Member States are likely beneficiaries of accession.

Agriculture and the Budget

Enlargement will have a substantial impact on food and agricultural production activities since these products are not included in the AAs and only subject to limited liberalisation (tariff quotas). De Frahan (1994) and Piskorz, et al. (1995), among others, have identified several problems related to the application of the AAs including the favouring of EU importers over CEEC exporters and a lack of correspondence between the quota allocation and comparative advantages of the CEECs. Moreover, agricultural policy measures not included in the liberalisation foreseen in the AAs, e.g. minimum price fixing, can be imposed without consultation or warning.

According to estimates by the Commission (Agenda 2000), the budgetary impact in the hypothetical scenario of all ten associated countries joining in 2002 and fully applying the CAP in its current form would be an additional cost to the Guidance Section of the European Agricultural Guidance and Guarantee Fund (FEOGA) by 2005 of approximately 11 billion ECU per year; in direct payments, arable and headage payments close to 7 billion ECU and 1.5 billion ECU in accompanying measures. Market support measures to the CEECs would cost up to 2.5 billion ECU, largely absorbed by the dairy sector. Buckwell (1997) observes that there is huge range of estimates of the budgetary impact, ranging from 4 to 44 billion ECU. A consensus seems, however, to have emerged and the range of more recent estimates has considerably narrowed.

Estimates by a Danish committee on enlargement (Rapport om de okonomiske konsekvenserne, 1997) that are based on a global general equilibrium model, GTAP, indicates that the application of an unreformed CAP to seven of the applicants would result in a net cost amounting to 12.3 billion ECU. The enlargement will cause a considerable welfare gain to the CEECs of 38 billion Danish kroner (DK) and a welfare loss to the EU-15 of 78 billion DK. The gain to the CEECs results from transfers and would be big enough to offset the efficiency losses caused by higher prices and other distortions related to the CAP.

Banse et al. (1998) arrive at an assessment of the budgetary effects of the present CAP for seven CEECs that amounts to 11 billion ECU, which is similar to the figure estimated by the Danish Committee (compare above) and reasonably close to the estimates by the Commission. Direct payments amount to 40 per cent of the total cost. Application of the reformed (according to Agenda 2000 proposals) CAP to the CEECs would not change the total costs significantly but the share of direct payments in the budget would increase to 70 per cent.

Consistency of the enlargement with the Uruguay Round Agreement on Agriculture is one of the most critical issues. Aggregation of EU and CEEC commitments adds to domestic support limits, increases export subsidy volumes and value limits, and results in harmonisation of tariff bindings. The enlarged EU will most certainly not be able to respect these limits. In estimates by the Commission for the main commodity markets, adoption of the *acquis* in its current form would tend to increase surpluses in most sectors, which would add to the growing market imbalances foreseen after 2000 in the existing EU. The estimates by the Danish Committee (Rapport om de okonomiske konsekvenserne, 1997) and Banse et al. (1998) also indicate considerable increases in net exports from the CEECs.

Formation of Domestic Preferences: Pressure Groups and Bureaucracy

This section examines the position of interest groups on enlargement and CAP reform. The relevance of the CAP is due to the fact that, unlike past enlargements, it may be difficult to reach an agreement on accession without changing the CAP for the incumbents.

The major benefit from enlargement, the contribution to peace and long term stability in Europe, cannot be meaningfully allocated to some specific interests, even if the economic consequences, including the peace dividend, may perhaps benefit taxpayers. It is more meaningful to see such positive effects as overall societal benefits.

Role of the Commission

The EU's own political institutions exert a considerable influence, both formally and informally. This is reflected in the way the agenda is set, how policy is formulated, and which decision-making processes are used (Laffan, 1996). In many cases the EU institutions play an independent role in political decision making. The Commission has a monopoly on submission proposals for new rules of cooperation that gives it decisive influence on the political agenda.

Obviously, the Commission has its own stake in the process of enlargement. Bureaucracy theories would suggest that the Commission should favour enlargement since this increases the size of its own activity. For the same reason, the Commission should also favour deepening European integration. Since the two motives are to some extent in conflict with each other, the Commission's preferences are not clear-cut. Moreover, failure to deliver common policies of sufficient quality within the EU will, nevertheless, be blamed on the Commission, even if they are result of lower administrative ability in the CEECs (von Hagen, 1996). However, once the process has started, as now is the case, failure to reach an agreement certainly will be blamed on the chief negotiator, the Commission. The duty of the Commission is to work out the bargains in order to remove deadlocks or stalled positions. Accordingly, the 'logic of regret' will push the process to a successful end. With respect to CAP reform, one would expect renationalisation of the CAP to be strongly opposed by the central EU bureaucracy.

Taxpayers and the Budget

Over the past years, European Community (EC) Member States' contributions to the common budget have expanded considerably, particularly during the 1980s, e.g. the increase of the value-added tax (VAT) from 1.0 per cent to 1.4 per cent and creation of the fourth resource (a GNP-based contribution). Simple extrapolation indicates that future distributional conflicts related to accession will be solved by increasing the burden on taxpayers. Such a prediction would also follow from pressure group theory, which postulates that taxpayers are a weak group unable to defend their interests due to difficulties in organising and controlling free riders.

Other circumstances point out, however, that budget problems will play a key role in the future of the CAP and enlargement. Financial prudence, as required by the Maastricht criteria, will limit the possibility of solving the problem by sending the bill to the next generation of taxpayers. At the same time, the aging population of Europe will demand more from, and pay less to, the national budgets. Such a scarcity of funds is likely to result in a declining willingness to increase contributions to the common budget. Taking a longer perspective, Sinn (1998) argues that increasing mobility of production factors will put the welfare state under increased pressure. Faced with the possibility that net contributors will move elsewhere, the welfare state will have to reduce the redistribution element by adjusting the delivery of public services to individual tax contributions. If less is redistributed to the poor at home, willingness to redistribute to the poor in other countries will decline as well.

Several net contributors to the budget, most notably Germany, have already signaled intentions to reduce their budget contributions. The importance of the budget issue is also highlighted by Laffan and Shacleton (1996) who argue that in spite of its small size, the budget has been one of the most intractable issues on the EU agenda. They state that protracted dispute about EC revenue and expenditure contributed significantly to the 'malaise and stagnation of the early 1980s.

Labour and Industrialists

A closer integration between the EU with its scarce labour and abundant capital and the labour abundant/capital scarce CEECs is, according to the Stolper-Samuelson theorem, likely to benefit capital rather than labour in the EU. The opposite is, however, the case in the CEECs. Accordingly, a likely implication of the closer integration between the EU and the CEECs is a downward pressure on wages, especially for unskilled labour in the EU which is also more exposed to competition.[9] Mobility of labour, one of the four freedoms, is not popular among representatives of the trade unions. However, an inflow of younger workers from the CEECs where the age structure of the population is much more favourable would be to the advantage of the incumbent members of the EU.

Pressure Groups and CAP Reform: Farmers, Environmentalists, and Rural Groups

An analysis of the positions on CAP reform usually includes farmers and consumers. However, a Bruges Group (1997) publication, *20 Political Platforms for the Future of Rural Society*, which contains short summaries of assessments and reform proposals from twenty organisations, most of them nongovernmental organisations active at international and national levels, clearly demonstrates that the number of stakeholders in agricultural policy has increased considerably. Quite a few of the new stakeholders are motivated by ideological rather than pecuniary motives. Such wide interest in the matter puts the legitimacy of agricultural policy at the top of the reform agenda (compare discussion on formation of national preferences).

Farmers are the main beneficiaries of the CAP and are, unsurprisingly, against its reform. While farmers are far from being a homogeneous group, the present distribution of support favours large farmers and fertile areas. FEOGA Guarantee spending in 1988 amounted to 127 ECU per hectare in Less Favoured Areas (LFAs) and 268 ECU per hectare in normal areas (CEC, 1993). In general, a small number of farms accounts for the majority of production and also receive a majority of the support. Taking Sweden as a case in point, the 4,513 farms above 100 hectares (4.8 per cent of all farms) account for 30 per cent of direct payments. Those farms received 390,000 Swedish krona (SEK) in direct payments and 1.8 million SEK in total support per farm. This amount is excessive relative to GDP per capita in Sweden the same year.[10]

As long as price support was the major agricultural policy instrument, large and small scale farmers shared the same interests. Faced with a choice between low prices and high prices, all farmers unanimously united behind demands for the latter even if price policy mostly benefited larger enterprises. Without higher prices the small scale farmers and/or weak regions would not have survived even while only marginally benefiting. Large scale farmers, who often already had high incomes, needed the small scale farmers to provide cover and to create consensus-generating causes such as concern about poverty in the countryside or the threat of depopulation of remote regions. Reinstrumentation of agriculture policy towards direct payments makes this coalition weaker and redistributional conflicts among different groups of farmers more pronounced. The question that then emerges is: which of the two groups is likely to be stronger?

Pressure group theory would indicate that large scale farmers should constitute a stronger group due to their better ability to control free riders (because of their smaller numbers). The use of pressure group theory as a theoretical foundation for explaining agricultural policy was, however, criticised by de Gorter and Swinnen (1994).

Large scale farmers are able to invest more in lobbying activities but they deliver very few votes and are hardly likely to evoke compassion among general public. Small scale farmers in LFAs are, on the other hand, more likely to be supported by other groups. Moreover, a coalition between small scale farmers, environmentalists, and rural groups becomes more likely. This results from the perception that a few large farms are unable to provide the feeling of traditional 'rurality' and are, furthermore, not interested in environmentally friendly production (Hamsvoort and Latach-Lohman, 1996). Because there is a considerable overlap (85 per cent) between LFAs and areas classified as high value nature (Agenda 2000), smaller scale farmers operating in these generally unfavourable production zones are thought to be producers of environmental benefits. For these small farms, farming income accounts for only a small share of total income (Hill, 1996) and, hence, are likely to benefit from rural development initiatives.

The environmental movement has been gaining momentum for decades and is now, at least in some countries, considered an important political factor. Several environmental organisations (i.e. WWF, Birdlife International, European Environment Bureau) have shown a keen interest in agricultural policy and have well defined positions on CAP reform (for a more detailed discussion and analysis see SOU 1997:74). The environmentalists strongly dislike intensive agriculture. They are also inclined to approve of protectionism ('trade is bad for the environment') and support to low intensity and environmentally friendly (or 'producing') agriculture. Some environmentalists figure that those farmers who currently receive the most support do not deserve any.

Rural development organisations (i.e. Society for Rural England, Ecovast) also have stakes in the development of the CAP and well-developed positions on the subject. These groups exhibit, to a large extent, ideas similar to the environmentalists and favour redistribution of support from agricultural production to other rural activities including the production of public goods by agriculture. Moreover, they favour support to small rather than to large scale farmers as well as a regional redistribution of support from prosperous regions to LFAs (SOU, 1997:74).

The discussion above indicates that a change in the balance of influence between different farm groups and an alliance between small scale farmers and environmental and rural groups may be likely. There are also indications that consumer interests are gaining increasing weight in policy decisions.[11] However, this is a possible long term development and the traditional large farm-dominated lobby is still sufficiently influential as indicated by the fact that the Cork declaration has not been officially endorsed.

Conditions are fundamentally different in the CEECs. Farmers in the CEECs, most notably in Poland, constitute a much larger share of the population than in the EU. The share of farmers in the labour force varies from 26.7 per cent in Poland to 4.1 per cent in the Czech Republic (compared to 5.1 per cent in the EU). Csaba (1995) argues that, after a period of brief disorganisation, the old lobbies have reemerged, such as those in agriculture and industry, supplemented and reinforced by new ones such as small private business and the clientele of the new elite which have taken over many of the crucial sectors of the economy. Particularly noteworthy is the resurgence of the bureaucracy, especially in sectoral ministries.

Agenda 2000: New Trends and Pressure for Further Change in the CAP

Past enlargements have resulted in amendments for the newcomers and a novel use of existing instruments. The CAP for the incumbents has hardly changed. It is questionable whether the same approach can be followed in the next enlargement. The enlargement is, however, only one of several pressures for change facing the CAP. Thus, those external pressures may interact with the process of negotiation and affect the outcome especially if the indicated direction of change is the same.

Obviously, a compromise on the CAP will depend on how the CAP will look like at the time of the accession. It is difficult to foresee the future of the CAP with any degree of certainty.

The Agenda 2000 Reform of the CAP

Agenda 2000 constitutes an extensive reform decision. The most critical and relevant components of the reform to this discussion are summarised here. The intervention price for cereals shall be reduced by 15 per cent in two equal steps. The basic price of beef will be reduced by 25 per cent. Intervention prices of butter and skimmed milk will be reduced by 15 per cent. However, the dairy reform will enter into force from the 2005-06 marketing year. The milk quota will remain in place and quotas for most Member States will be increased by 1.5 per cent. New direct payments will compensate for losses. However, the term compensatory payment has been replaced by direct payments. Moreover, full compensation is not offered. Compared with the original document, the modifications subsequently proposed provide more scope for national solutions by relying on an envelope model for both milk and beef. The essence of the envelope model is to leave the design of part of the payments to the discretion of Member States. National support can be paid either per animal or per hectare.

The proposal includes a number of horizontal measures: cross-compliance and modulation. Cross-compliance is left to the discretion of the Member States who may decide on appropriate environmental measures. Reduction or annualisation of direct payments is allowed. Member States can also enact additional modulation based on labour force use per holding. Member States shall impose measures that reduce direct payments to farmers who fail to demonstrate that they are actively maintaining rural areas through genuine farming activities. Funds made available from cross-compliance or modulation will remain available to Member States as additional support for agro-environmental measures. LFA payments will be granted on a per hectare basis with the condition that farming practices are compatible with environmental safeguards and countryside preservation.

New rural development regulation will replace the FEOGA Structural Fund Regulation, four Objective 5a regulations, the three accompanying measures regulations, and the regulation on structural forestry support. The fusion under a single legal framework for rural development support will constitute a simplification of Community legislation.

Agenda 2000: New Trends in the Development of the CAP?

The main thrust of Agenda 2000 is based on a continuation of the 1992 reform strategy: a further shift from price support to direct income support.

Otherwise, reform breaks with past trends in several important respects. Previously, the reforms have followed a minimalist approach focusing on one product at a time rather than on a general review of the policy in its entirety. The general rule has been very simple: no crisis, no reform.[12] Agenda 2000 is an extensive reform covering several commodities and areas (rural development, environment, modulation). What is more important, however, is that the reform appears not to be driven by an acute crisis. Another important difference is that the suggested direct payments do not fully cover producers' gross revenue loss calculated on the basis of price support cuts.

Moyner and Josling (1990) observed that past CAP reform implied ever-increasing complexity. An explicitly stated ambition in Agenda 2000 is to achieve simplification. The cereal regime has indeed been simplified but otherwise the opposite seems be the case. Direct headage payments that are based both on 'virtual' and real cows and include a national component hardly constitute a simplification. Cross-compliance and modulation will add additional complexity.

The motivating force behind the current reform seems to have changed when compared to past reforms, in particular the 1980s, when internal factors (unmarketable surpluses and the resulting budget crises) dominated while international considerations were nearly irrelevant. However, international pressures and competitiveness did start to play a more important role by the time of the 1992 reform of the CAP.[13] The key priority of Agenda 2000 CAP reform today appears to be improved price competitiveness of EU agriculture on the world market.

Another important driving force, which has not been present in the past, is policy legitimacy. The increased visibility of direct transfers is evidently the cause of the legitimacy problem. The decision to introduce cross-compliance and modulation are hardly efficient solutions to environmental problems of the CAP or to distributional inequality. The inclusion of those measures is an obvious sign, however, that the aforementioned phenomena are embarrassing for decision makers and that the legitimacy of the general policy is in danger.

Agenda 2000 also constitutes a fundamental institutional change with important political economy implications. With the creation of national envelopes, lobbying activities will move away from Brussels to national capitals. Moreover, conflicts over the distribution of transfers will be internalised within the farming community. Furthermore, by allowing saved funds to be retained at the national level, the incentive to apply modulation and cross-compliance increases. The formal possibility to apply those measures is also likely to alter the balance of power between farmers and environmentalists by making money transferred through direct payments contestable (to some extent) for other purposes.

Finally, Agenda 2000 establishes a further step in the direction of renationalisation of the CAP.[14] A strong tendency towards renationalisation was already visible in the 1992 CAP reform. Due to the use of national reference values for yields, base acreage, etc., payments to Member States from FEOGA have been transformed to national envelopes with an almost fixed content. A partial renationalisation occurred, moreover, in relation to the EFTA accession (compare previous discussion of earlier enlargements). Likewise, de facto renationalisation has also taken place with respect to the application of regulation 2078/92.[15]

The movement towards renationalisation is intriguing as it occurs at a time when all policy areas point in the direction of increasing European integration. One explanation is that renationalisation is a rational response to the changing nature of the challenges and objectives facing agricultural policy as well as to changing political constraints. With the latter, tighter budget constraints make it impossible to solve the problems brought about by increased diversity by summing up national demands. Instead, consensus has to be achieved by increasing the possibilities for national discretion.

Looking at the objectives, agricultural policy can be decomposed into market regulation, income support, environmental support, and rural development. The question emerges as to which of those four areas are suitable subjects for a common policy. According to the principle of subsidiarity, the EU 'shall take action only if and in so far as the objectives of the proposed action cannot be sufficiently achieved by the Member States and can therefore, by reason of the scale of effects of the proposed action, be better achieved by the Community' (Maastricht Treaty). Subsidiarity can be interpreted as a presumption to decentralise unless a clear case can be made for centralisation. Suitable criteria for analyzing if such a case can be made are efficiency, equity, and accountability (CEPR, 1993).

Market regulations must obviously be a common responsibility. Otherwise, when applying the above criteria to the remaining three policy areas, several arguments in favour of a decentralised approach are apparent, in particular in relation to income support. Diversity of economic, social, and environmental problems and preferences make it difficult to achieve efficiency gains by having common regional or environmental policies as well (for a detailed discussion see SOU, 1997:74). There is, however, an obvious need to coordinate policy to avoid competition distortions and to respond to international issues such as trade negotiations where, for example, environmental support policy is likely to be highly controversial. Hence, a reasonable case can be made for partial transfer of sovereignty from the EU to the Member States but not for complete renationalisation.

Long Term Pressures on CAP Reform

In the long term the domestic pressure on the CAP will be mainly related to policy legitimacy and increasing importance of nonfarm pressure groups. These factors are strongly related. Farmers are becoming an increasingly small group, outnumbered by the unemployed and others with stronger claims to public support.[16] In a fast changing society where all other sectors have been forced to adjust or vanish, continuous support to farming is possible only if farmers provide something that is indispensable for society. Accordingly, internal pressure on the CAP indicates a reinforcement of the new trends identified in the preceding sections including reducing large payments though ceilings and modulation, stronger ecological conditionality and transformation of direct payments to environmental support payments.

Current CAP reform is also exposed to increasingly strong external pressures. The reform strategy in Agenda 2000 is based on the assumption that the new direct payments will be allowed under the World Trade Organization (WTO) 'blue box' provision.[17] The continued existence of the 'blue box' cannot, considering the development of US agricultural policy, be taken for granted. Disguising producer subsidies as an environmental compensation mechanism, as seems to be the strategy of the Commission (Agra Europe, 1998), may make it easier to defend the payments but will hardly eliminate the problem. It is not likely that the present level of payments will be defensible in WTO regardless of what the payments are called. What is proposed in Agenda 2000, moreover, is not a detachment of subsidies from production but rather a decoupling of EU exports from direct subsidisation (Agra Europe, 1998). Even genuine environmental or structural measures are difficult to defend against charges of production stimulation. Accordingly, the next WTO round is likely to result in a reduction of total allowable support.

Options for the Future of the CAP with Enlargement

The Options for Direct Payments

Agenda 2000 envisages the direct application of the CAP with the exception of direct payments to new members. Four major options are possible with respect to direct payments in the context of the negotiated agreement. The two obvious candidates are the opening bids of the Commission and the incumbents: no payments and full payments respectively. The third option is postponement (delayed accession and extended transition). A final possibility is a compromise involving a partial renationalisation of payments as well as reorientation towards environmental and rural support.

In the next sections the four options will be evaluated in the framework of the two-level bargaining game suggested earlier and, for the sake of simplicity these options are discussed as mutually exclusive alternatives. For all options but postponement, it is assumed that there will be a short transition period. The arguments developed relate in those cases to the post transition situation. The analysis will start at the EU level. In the next step the acceptability of the options to domestic pressure groups will be analysed.

Exclusion from Direct Payments

EU level The position of the Commission on the issue of direct payments in Agenda 2000 reflects the belief that such an option is preferred by the incumbent Member States. Some complications may emerge, however. A permanent exclusion from direct payments would only be possible within a framework of differentiated integration and a 'second class membership'. Inequality of treatment would be further underlined by a need to create a special arrangement for Slovenia, where prices after accession may fall. A 'second class membership' for the CEECs would hardly facilitate the achievement of the geopolitical objectives of enlargement. Kumar (1996) argues that only full membership could secure economic development and strengthen new democracies. Rosati (1994) points out that 'second class membership' has a smaller potential for integration but larger potential for conflicts. Moreover, the willingness of the CEECs to implement and enforce EU legislation would be impaired. Furthermore, the CEECs could hardly be expected to fully contribute to the budget because direct payments constitute a sizeable share of it.[18]

Exclusion would also create complications in the relations between the incumbents. Direct payments create a disturbance of competition between receivers and nonreceivers if payments are not decoupled. Thus, the system of nonpayment of direct support could be sustained only if payments are completely decoupled. Decoupling all direct payments would, however, threaten the very foundations of a common agricultural policy since once the linkage to production is gone there is no justification for a common policy. Subsidiarity would hardly imply that member countries should pay for each other's social policies, especially as low income countries may end up making transfers to rich countries.[19]

Would the CEECs accept the CAP without participating in direct payments? From a purely pragmatic point of view the answer could be yes. Experiences from past accessions indicate that the process of negotiation of the terms of entry is not over at accession but some issues can be postponed and renegotiated from stronger position. What speaks against this option is the fact that humiliating options may not be supported in referenda in the CEECs. It should be remembered that during recent history the CEECs were 'second class nations' in the Soviet empire. Remaining 'second class members' in the EU may thus be refused even if this would produce an economic gain. Moreover, such a gain is not likely as the economic gain for acceding CEECs will come from direct payments as earlier argued.[20]

A nonpayment option would, moreover, not be a stable solution. The amount spent on new members, including preaccession aid would, according to estimates by the Commission, amount to 4.5 billion ECU compared with 48.6 billion ECU spent on the incumbents. Baldwin et al. (1997) claim that in a democratic body such as the EU, new entrants will use their newly granted political power to undo any accession terms they feel are unjust. Accordingly, terms of entry would be renegotiated. Such a process of renegotiation would, however, take some time.

Formation of domestic preferences Considering the political weight of farmers in the applicant countries, most notably Poland and Slovenia, it is understandable that those countries cannot accept the nonpayment option, particularly given that the payments were extended to EFTA countries acceding after the 1992 reform. Moreover, the same reasoning used to argue for not extending payments to the CEECs apply equally well to the incumbents (European Economy, 1996). If payments are seen as compensations, they should not be paid indefinitely and not to the successors of the present generation of farmers. If payments are paid as income support, many of the present wealthy beneficiaries in the EU should be excluded while poor farmers in the CEECs included. If payments are, finally, seen as a reward for stewardship of the land, all farmers should receive them. Consequently, any exclusion will be perceived as a discriminatory policy.

An additional complication for farmers in the CEECs is the fact that the structure of the support to agriculture after accession would be very unbalanced, ranging from zero for oilseeds (where direct support is the only form of assistance) to very high for sugar beets (where price support dominates). This would lead to the reallocation of production and a very uneven income distribution among farmers. The argument that prices will increase in the CEECs as a result of the accession is not universally valid for all countries and all commodities, especially after allowing for additional price reductions resulting from Agenda 2000 reforms.

Regarding the domestic preferences in the EU, the issue emerges of the political sustainability of direct payments if they are truly decoupled. A reformed welfare state that puts increasing demands on the poor in exchange for very modest support can hardly pay large decoupled sums of money to wealthy farmers. Such payments would most probably also be resented by rural groups and environmentalists who would demand that the money should be used for 'something useful' such as supporting the environment. Moreover, decoupling seems to be in direct conflict with cross-compliance, which is favoured by the environmentalists.

Full Payments

EU level The full payment option would probably be welfare decreasing for the EU. The overall level of transfers implied by the option is simply too large to constitute a mutually beneficial solution for both the incumbents and the applicants. Moreover, incompatibility of this option with the WTO commitments would threaten the next round of trade negotiations.

Countries that favour further reforms of the CAP, such as the UK and Sweden, would furthermore reject this option out of fear that it would facilitate the long term survival of the CAP. If payments are offered to the first wave of entrants, the expectation is created for extending them to the next wave as well.

Formation of domestic preferences Extending full payments to the CEECs is likely to be opposed by environmentalists and rural groups who fear that the long term survival of an unreformed CAP would be enhanced by creating a large number of new beneficiaries. More importantly, full extension of payments would be strongly resented by taxpayers. The amount required to extend the present CAP to the CEECs is not excessive in relation the budget availability, though. The budget proposal included in Agenda 2000 contains a margin for EU-21 of 6,570 million ECU. This would almost cover the cost of direct payments to the CEECs. That the money seems to be (almost) available does not mean, however, that it will be paid. Firstly, the process of reaching a compromise on Agenda 2000 has absorbed more resources than originally planned. Moreover, a possible budget reserve will not wait for the CEECs but will most likely be absorbed or repaid to Member States.

The budget issue is often dismissed arguing that the resources which would be required to ensure full participation of the applicants in the existing distributional programs are trivial in view of the historical significance of the event as well as in relation to total GDP of the incumbents. Kawecka-Wyrzykowska (1996) claims that this would amount of an increase of the budget from 1.2 per cent to 1.4 per cent of total GDP (see also Buckwell, 1997). This argument, as shown previously, is not valid.

A Compromise Involving Renationalisation of Payments

A classical compromise in a bargaining situation tends to lie somewhere 'in between' both opening bids depending on the relative bargaining power and the structure of the overall agreement. This could imply the payments are lower or that only some type of payments is extended to the CEECs. A simple reduction of payments by some percentage would however, not be *communautaire*. Even if interstate transfers are essentially side payments in bargaining games, they need to follow common principles and be dressed as common policies (Hooghe and Keating, 1994). It is worth noticing that the nonpayment option is justified by the Commission using the logic of 'no need for compensation'. Exclusion of some payments can more easily be motivated by general principles. A possible solution could include distinguishing between pure income support payments and payments for preservation of nature and the cultural landscape, which could cover a large share of the arable land in Europe (European Economy, 1998). This position also foresees direct income payments that are decoupled and temporary. One way of reducing redistribution without discrimination is to reduce the scope of a common redistributive policy. Accordingly, a compromise based on the above ideas would be likely to include movement of income support payments to the national level and extension of other policy components to the CEECs. Tailoring environmental (and rural) support to local and national conditions could also allow for differentiation of payments without creating explicit discrimination.

The term renationalisation is itself a contentious one since the CAP has been seen as a cornerstone of the integration process. But the CAP is not longer as central to the EU as it once was and its importance will continue to diminish. A sector that accounts for less than 3 per cent (and falling) of the GDP, can hardly remain a centrepiece of the Union. Moreover, the goal is not a full renationalisation but a rebalancing of national and supranational responsibilities.

This option could be accepted in the WTO context if total support were reduced, the income support component decoupled, and environmental support organised in such a way as to convincingly provide delivery of public goods where the market has failed.

Partial renationalisation would certainly improve efficiency. By vastly increasing the diversity of conditions in member countries, the enlargement will reinforce arguments in favour of moving policy discretion in agriculture towards national governments. The question is, however, whether such an option could be supported as a compromise bid on behalf of the EU. This will critically depend on whether the agreement will be reached on a sector by sector basis or whether a broad compromise across different sectors will be possible. The latter is a likely outcome because the possibility of retaining political control over pressure from EU-based interests is bigger in accession negotiations where geopolitics play a central role than is possible in a trade-led formula such as that used to negotiate the AAs. Hence, the interest of those groups who would gain on a speedy accession could be expected to dominate over those who defend the present agricultural policy.[21]

A proposal (October 1998) by the Commission regarding cofinancing of the spending under the FEOGA Guarantee lent support to the hypothesis that renationalisation, indeed, may be an important element of the accession agreement. With exception of accompanying measures, which have been introduced in conjunction with 1992 reform of the CAP, guarantee spending is at present fully financed by the EU. The idea has been rejected while reaching the compromise on Agenda 2000 CAP reform but can easily be reused.

Domestic preferences Analysing this option from a point of view of domestic preferences in the EU, a denationalisation of direct income support and a reallocation of money from income support to environmental and rural development measures would be strongly opposed by large scale farmers. However, a coalition of small farms and the rural/environmental lobby could certainly support such an option. As argued before, such a coalition is likely to emerge and gain strength due to common interests. To oppose WTO and free trade proponents, farmers need support from the environmentalists and rural groups. Such support is, however, not likely to be given at the present distribution of payments. Long term internal pressures on the CAP reform, which were argued as being related to fading legitimacy of the policy point also in the direction of reducing large transfers and reallocating the funds for other purposes such as rural development and the environment.

Postponement: Protracted Negotiations and Long Transition

Transition periods were, albeit to a different degree, always relied on for coping with past enlargements. However, the use of ACAs, a device for mitigating adjustment problems, was rejected in the last accession. Transition periods were also used as a way of postponing some conflicts, possibly in expectation of renegotiating the issue at some later stage.[22]

A postponement could result from protracted negotiations (seven years as in the case of Spain) or a very lengthy transition period. A ten year transition period was previously applied (Greece, Portugal, Spain) and has already been suggested by some countries for the upcoming accession due to concerns about labour migration. Labour mobility is an important issue for the incumbents who fear an exodus from the CEECs to Western Europe. Powerful labour unions will most certainly oppose unrestricted labour mobility as long as the gap in wages remains at a high level. Demand for compliance with the *acquis*, in particular with the rules directly affecting the functioning of the market, could be used as leverage by the EU to curb demands by CEECs on transfers through direct payments. This could result in exclusion from payments during the transition period.

Major disadvantages of a long transition would include the postponement of integration, hence foregoing the integration benefits for some time, as well as costly arrangements for partial integration. Free trade for industrial goods will materialise as a result of the AAs while maintaining border controls only for agricultural products would be costly. A long transition period would also risk provoking a backlash in the

CEECs. Accordingly, this option would be opposed by industrialists who prefer rapid accession.

A long transition would solve the problem of direct payments if high cost to the budget were the only major obstacle. However, some groups and countries may oppose extending payments to the CEECs not because of the cost involved but to avoid prolonging the CAP. A long transition period will, moreover, not resolve all the contentious issues. Furthermore, it is not likely that the transition could be used to postpone decisions on crucial issues such as direct payments. In particular, farmers in the CEECs will demand, before voting in referendums, to know what kind of CAP will apply in the long run.

Conclusions

The enlargement is likely to produce both economic and political benefits. Admission would anchor the CEECs in the market economy and support democratic political institutions. However, only a membership on equal terms would facilitate the achievement of the geopolitical objectives of the enlargement.

Seeing the accession negotiations as repetitive games should cause the incumbents, who may expect future reciprocity, to be more favourably inclined to the needs of the applicants. Because benefits of enlargement are unevenly distributed with southern countries obtaining less of both the economic and political advantages, the demands from the CEECs for a better deal will be accommodated by sharing the CAP money rather than by increasing the Structural Funds.

Denying direct payments to the CEECs would eventually undermine the very foundation of the CAP for the incumbents. A common policy of supporting farm incomes would not be credible if the poorest farmers were excluded. However, budget constraints will certainly prevent the extension of direct payments to the new members. It has been argued in this chapter that the solution to this problem will involve a partial renationalisation of agricultural policies, in particular of income support, as well as reorientation of the CAP towards the environment and rural development. By allowing more flexibility and reliance on subsidiarity, a compromise to the enlargement problem could be achieved.

The arguments for (partial) renationalisation being an important part of the accession agreement may be summarised as follows: National considerations have always played a significant role in the history of the

CAP. In critical moments, intergovernmental considerations dominated over the supranational ones. Renationalisation was an important problem-solving device in the previous accession. A strong tendency towards renationalisation of the CAP has been observed in recent years. This tendency is an efficient response to changing objectives and constraints. All mechanisms so far responsible for renationalisation will be reinforced by eastward enlargement. CAP is, furthermore, no longer an indispensable element of European integration.

Arguments for reorientation towards rural and environmental support can be found in the changing balance of power between taxpayers and farmers as well as the changing balance of power between rural/environmental groups and large scale farmers. Fading legitimacy and external pressures for CAP reform also point in the same direction.

It is hardly possible to offer a detailed prediction of the design of the compromise on the CAP. Such a compromise will have to involve a lot of creative engineering. The flexibility demonstrated by the EU in coping with past accessions makes such creativity likely to materialise. Likewise, Laffan (1996) emphasises the importance of seeing the EU's development as an evolutionary process recognising it is not a frozen institution. Moreover, it is an experimental process that is not unidirectional (Wallace, 1996).

Notes

1   Guggenbuhl (1995) argues that, with reference to the outcome of the negotiations on the AAs, the arrangements have been imposed on the Associated countries by the Community as the stronger party. Guggenbuhl also illustrates the role of side payments in reaching the agreement: Portugal, who long opposed textile concessions to the CEECs, received commitments that it would benefit from structural assistance to regions heavily dependent on the textile industry. This benefit was also extended to Greece. Under these conditions, the Commission's proposal to remove the EC's tariffs on textiles in six years could be accepted. France's position was to avoid further concession for products already in surplus within the Community. This was partly resolved by relying on triangular operation, by which foodstuffs imported from Poland, Hungary, and the Czech Republic would be sold to the former USSR.
2   Consequently, the share of environmental support is considerably higher in Sweden and Finland than among previous members of the EU.
3   The EU now contains countries with permanent and considerably higher levels of support than found among previous members. This higher level of support is to substantial degree paid by the new members themselves and involves instruments that are not used elsewhere in the EU.

4   This was certainly the case for Greece. An evaluation of economic consequences of Greek accession made by the Commission came to the conclusion that the accession should be postponed indefinitely (Nicolaides and Close, 1995).
5   An assessment of the implications of the enlargement for Sweden's security, commissioned by the government and conducted by one of the most experienced Swedish diplomats, came to the conclusion that the enlargement would substantially increase Swedish security (SOU, 1997:143).
6   Application of Structural Funds according to the present rules would imply a net transfer to the CEECs amounting (in 2005) to 32.7 billion ECU (Tracy, 1998).
7   Objective 1 of Structural Funds covers regions of the EU that have GDP per capita below 75 per cent of the average for the EU.
8   The experience of Spain in the early years of the accession indicates that transfers amounted to roughly 1 per cent of GDP, rising to 1.5 per cent after six years (Kwiecinski, 1995).
9   Highly regulated labour markets in Western Europe may, however, prevent such adjustment and see unemployment rise instead.
10 Calculated by the National Board of Agriculture, Sweden, 1997.
11 Following the BSE scandal and the critique of the Commission's handling of the issue, food safety questions have been moved away from DG VI. This transfer of responsibility is implicitly based on the assumption that it makes a difference who in the Commission is handling an issue. In other words, institutions matter.
12 In 1984 and 1988 it took a failed summit to force Member States to agree on a compromise (Moyner and Josling, 1989).
13 The design of the 1992 reform of the CAP was strongly affected by the ongoing GATT-process. The move to direct payment and the possibility of placing the payments in the 'blue box', as a result of the Blair House agreement, were decisive for a successful completion of the Uruguay Round.
14 An important caveat applies. National envelopes proposed for milk and beef in Agenda 2000 are commonly financed. Hence, only the policy discretion has been renationalised and not the funds.
15 This environmental regulation is arranged as a menu resulting in substantial variability in the application of regulation 2078/92 among the member countries.
16 A simple comparison may illustrate the disparities: 10 per cent of the French population lives below the poverty line. The monthly allowance for the long term unemployed amounts to 2445 French francs which gives an annual income comparable to direct payments from 13 hectares.
17 The 'blue box' measures were created as a result of the Blair House agreement (between the US and the EU). 'Blue box' measures include production-limiting programmes (deficiency payments and area and headage payments).
18 In case of the new members in the latest accession, contributions to the budget followed eligibility for benefits.
19 Several of the net beneficiaries of the CAP are also above average-income countries including Denmark, France, and The Netherlands.
20 Moreover, poverty in the CEECs, which is a result of the legacy of communism, creates a feeling of historical injustice and an implicit claim to 'compensation'. An additional source of such claims is the Marshall Plan which helped many of the present EU members rebuild their economies after World War II but which never reached Eastern Europe.

21 A good example of such tensions is provided by Mr. Barnevik, managing director of ABB, a Swiss/Swedish company, which moved decisively into Eastern Europe and Russia. He made several statements urging a quick CAP reform for the purpose of facilitating the enlargement.
22 The ban on antibiotics in animal feed in Sweden is a good example of the latter use of transitory arrangements. Sweden was allowed to keep the ban for a period of four years. The issue was discussed again but Sweden was not successful in extending the ban. The EU has, however, introduced a ban for four types of antibiotics for the whole union.

References

Agenda 2000, CEC, Brussels.
Agra Europe (1998), January 30.
Baldwin, R. (1994), *Towards an Integrated Europe*, CEPR.
Baldwin, R.E., Francois, J.F., and Portes, R. (1997), 'The Costs and Benefits of Eastern Enlargement: The Impact on the EU and Central Europe', *Economic Policy*, April 1997, CEPR.
Banse, M., Munch, W., and Tangermann S. (1998), 'Accession of the Central European Countries to the EU: Implications for Agricultural Markets, Trade, Government Budgets and the Macro-economy in Central Europe', ACE Project.
Becker, G. (1983), 'A Theory of Competition Among Pressure Groups', *Quarterly Journal of Economics*, vol. 98, no. 3.
Bolin, O. and Rabinowicz, E. (1992), 'Would We Get a More Reasonable Agricultural Policy in the EU', only available in Swedish as 'Ur askan i elden får vi en förnuftigare jordbrukspolitik i EU', in O. Bolin and B. Swedenborg. (eds), *Mat till EG-pris*, SNS, Stockholm.
Bolinger, P. (1995), 'The Political Economy of the Eastern Enlargement of the EU', CEPR Discussion paper no. 1234.
Bruges Group and European Network of Experiences in Sustainable Development (1997), *20 Political Platforms for the Future of Rural Society*, September 1997.
Buckwell (1997), 'Economic Transition in Central and Eastern Countries and the Former Soviet Union: Implication for International trade', International postgraduate course, Wageningen Agricultural University, unpublished.
Calmfors, L., Flam, H., Gottfries, N., Haaland Matlary, J., Lindahl, R., Nordh Berendsson, C., Rabinowicz, E., and Vredin A. (1997), *EMU- A Swedish Perspective*, Kluwer Academic Publishers.
CEC (1989), *Farms in Mountainous and Less Favoured Areas of the EC*. Brussels.
CEPR (1995), *Flexible Integration: Towards a More Effective and Democratic Europe*, Monitoring European Integration 6, CEPR.
CEPR (1993), *Making Sense of Subsidiarity: How Much Centralisation for Europe*, Monitoring European Integration 4, CEPR.
Csaba, L. (1995), 'The Political Economy of Trade Regimes in Central Europe', in L.A. Winters (ed.), *Foundation of Open Economy*, London, CEPR.
de Gorter, H. and Swinnen, J.F.M. (1994), 'The Economic Polity of Farm Policy', *Journal of Agricultural Economics*, vol. 45, no. 3, pp. 312-26.

de Frahan, B.H. (1995), 'What to Expect from Association Agreements', *Food Policy*, vol. 19, no. 4, pp. 397-402.
European Economy, No 2 (1996), 'The CAP and the Enlargement, Economic Effects of the Compensatory Payments', European Commission, Directorate General for Economic and Financial Affairs, Brussels.
European Economy, No 5 (1997), 'Towards a Common Agricultural and Rural Policy for Europe', European Commission, Directorate General for Economic and Financial Affairs, Brussels.
Guggenbuhl, A. (1995), 'The Political Economy of Association with Eastern Europe', in F. Laursen (ed.), *The Political Economy of European Integration*, Kluwer Law International.
Hill, B. (1996), *Farm Incomes, Wealth and Agricultural Policy*, Avebury, Aldershot.
Hooghe, L. and Keating, M. (1994), 'The Politics of European Union Regional Policy', *Journal of European Public Policy*, vol. 1, no. 3, pp. 367-93.
Kawecka-Wyrzykowska, E. (1996), 'On the Benefits from Accession for Eastern and Western Europe', in L. Ambrus-Lakatos and M. Schafer (eds), *Coming to Terms with Accession*, Forum report of the Economic Policy Initiative No. 2, CEPR, Institute for East-West Studies.
Kumar, A. (1996), 'The CEEC Countries' Aspirations for Enlargement', in L. Ambrus-Lakatos and M. Schafer (eds), *Coming to terms with Accession*, Forum report of the Economic Policy Initiative No. 2, CEPR, Institute for East-West Studies.
Kwiecinski, A. (1995), 'Structural Funds and the European Union: Benefits for Poland', SAEPR, Warsaw.
Laffan, B. (1996), 'Economic and Monetary Union: A Political Project', Report written for the Swedish Government Commission on the EMU, SOU 1996:158.
Laffan, B. and Shacleton, M. (1996), 'The Budget', in H. Wallace and W. Wallace (eds), *Decision Making in the European Union*, Oxford University Press.
Laursen, F. (1995), 'On Studying European Integration: Integration Theory and Political Economy', in F. Laursen (ed), *The Political Economy of European Integration*, Kluwer Law International.
Messerlin, P.A. (1995), 'Central and East European Countries' Trade Laws in the Light of International Experiences', in L.A. Winters (ed), *Foundation of Open Economy*, London, CEPR.
Moyner, M.W. and Josling, T. (1990), *Agricultural Policy Reform: Politics and Process in the EC and the U.S.A.*, Iowa State University Press, Ames.
Nicolaides, P. and Close, A. (1995), 'Accession to the European Union: The Ultimate Bargain', in F. Laursen (ed), *The Political Economy of European Integration*, Kluwer Law International.
Patier E. (1997), 'An Experience of Accession to the EU in the Agricultural Sector: Spain and Portugal', International postgraduate course, Wageningen Agricultural University, unpublished.
Persson, T., Roland, G. and Tabellini, G. (1997), 'Comparative Politics and Public Finance', Institute of International Economics, unpublished.
Piskorz, W., Krzyzanowska, Z., Dabrowski, J., Guba, W., Leszko, D., Romanowska, K. and Tylawska, H. (1996), 'Evaluation of Effects of European Agreements for Polish Agriculture and its Integration with the EU as Regards the Real, Institutional, Regulatory and Commercial Spheres', FAPA, Warsaw.

Preston, C. (1995), 'Obstacles to EU Enlargement: The Classical Community Method and the Prospects for a Wider Europe', *Journal of Common Market Studies*, vol. 33, no. 3, pp. 451-63.
Putnam, R.D. (1988), 'Diplomacy and Domestic Politics', *International Organisation*, vol. 42, no. 2, pp. 427-60.
Rabinowicz, E. and Bolin, O. (1998), 'Negotiating the CAP: The Nordic Experience', *Swedish Journal of Agricultural Research*, no. 28, pp. 5-15.
Raiffa, H. (1982), *The Art and Science of Negotiations*, Harvard University Press.
Rapport om de okonomiske konsekvenserne af den fremdide falles landbrukpolitk set i lyset af EU's udvidelse (1997).
Rosati, D. (1995), 'Impediments to Poland's Accession to the European Union: Real or Imaginary', in E. Kawecka-Wyrzykowska and T. Roe (eds), *Polish Agriculture and Enlargement of the European Union*, Warsaw School of Economics, Warsaw.
Sapir, A. (1995), 'The Europe Agreement: Implications for Trade Laws and Institutions' in L.A. Winters (ed), *Foundation of Open Economy*, London, CEPR.
Sedelmeier, U. and Wallace H. (1996), 'Policies Towards Central and Eastern Europe', in H. Wallace and W. Wallace (eds), *Decision Making in the European Union*, Oxford University Press.
Siebe, W. (1992), 'Game Theory', in V. Kremenyuk (ed), *International Negotiation. Analysis, Approaches and Issues*, Jossey-Bass Publishers.
Sinn, H-W. (1998), 'European Integration and the Future of the State', forthcoming in Swedish Economic Policy Review.
Smith, A., Holmes, P., Sedelmeir, U., Smith, A., Wallace, H., and Young, A. (1996), *The European Union and Central and Eastern Europe: Pre-accession strategies*, Sussex European Institute Paper 15, Sussex.
SOU (1997:74) (Official Reports of the State), 'Common Agricultural Policy, The Environment and Regional Development', only available in Swedish as 'EU:s jordbrukspolitik, miljön och regional utveckling'.
SOU (1997:156) (Official Reports of the State), 'Economic Implications of EU Enlargement' only available in Swedish as 'Samhällsekonomiska konsekvenser av EU utvidgningen'.
SOU (1997:149) (Official Reports of the State), 'Environment in the Enlarged EU', only available in Swedish as 'Miljön i ett utvidgat EU'.
SOU (1997:143) (Official Reports of the State), 'Bigger the EU: Safer Europe', only available in Swedish as 'Större EU–säkrare Europa'.
Tangermann, S. (1979), 'Germany's Role Within the CAP: Domestic Problems in International Perspective', *Journal of Agricultural Economics*, vol. 30, pp. 241-56.
Tracy, M. (1998), 'Structural Funds', proceedings from a World Bank Policy Workshop in Lithuania, April 1997, forthcoming.
von Hagen, J. (1996), 'The Political Economy of Eastern Enlargement of the EU', in L. Ambrus-Lakatos and M. Schafer (eds), *Coming to Terms with Accession*, forum report of the Economic policy Initiative No. 2, CEPR, Institute for East-West Studies.
van der Hamsvoort, C.P.M. and Latacz-Lohman, U. (1996), 'Auctions as Mechanism for Allocating Conservation Contracts Among Farmers', LEI-DLO, The Hague.
Wallace, W. (1996), 'Government Without Statehood: The Unstable Equilibrium', in H. Wallace and W. Wallace (eds), *Decision Making in the European Union*, Oxford University Press.
Winters, L.A. (1995), 'Trade Policy Institutions in Central and Eastern Europe: Objectives and Outcomes', in L.A. Winters (ed), *Foundation of Open Economy*, London, CEPR.

10 The Impact of Central and Eastern Europe Joining the Common Agricultural Policy on Agricultural Protection in the European Union: A Political Economy Perspective

HARRY DE GORTER AND JÁN POKRIVČÁK

Introduction

The Common Agricultural Policy (CAP) of the European Union (EU) has protected European farmers while distorting world markets and creating a major problem for the European Community's budget. The rise in agricultural output generated in part by generous increases in price supports was not matched by an expansion in demand. With world prices not keeping pace with domestic prices, the percentage producer subsidy equivalent (PSE) for the EU has risen from 36 per cent in the early 1980s to 48 per cent in the late 1980s and has stabilized at this level (OECD, 1996a). In the meantime, the EU has accommodated new members from north and south, like Spain, Portugal, Greece, Austria, and the Nordic countries. Austria and the Nordic countries have high cost agriculture with national support prices above that prevailing in the CAP at the time of their accession. On the other hand, the budgetary implications for the EU of taking in Spain and Portugal were dampened by phasing these countries into the CAP over time (whose comparative advantage were in nontemperate crops anyway and so did not directly compete with existing EU member agriculture).

The situation will be different when any of the Central and Eastern European countries (CEECs) join the CAP. Not only do several of these countries have comparative advantage in their major livestock and crop enterprises (like the Czech Republic and Hungary), these countries subsidize farmers less now and in some instances even tax agricultural production (Swinnen, 1996).

The question addressed by this chapter is: will the inclusion of additional countries increase the overall support in European agriculture? In other words, will the weighted average agricultural support of the existing CAP and those additional countries poised to join be higher or lower than the adjusted CAP support after the EU's CAP has been expanded? To answer these questions we have to analyze how the institutional structure of the CAP alters preferences for agricultural protection of individual countries and aggregates them to arrive at common agricultural policies.

Several papers argue that the institutional structure of the CAP decision-making process results in an increase in overall protection to agriculture. The 'supranational' characteristic of the CAP is identified as the critical factor whereby common financing results in an upward bias on individual country support price preferences (Hill, 1984; Pearce, 1983). Schmitt (1984), Runge and von Witzke (1987), and others refer to this phenomenon as the 'restaurant table' effect. As each member of the EU allegedly share the 'bill' of agricultural support costs, they have an incentive to 'order' relatively 'expensive' policies when they meet at the 'dinner table' (the annual EU price-setting process). The resulting average level of protection is deemed to be higher than if the CAP did not exist and if each country decided on its own protection level, i.e. would pay the cost of their own meal.

If the supranational character of the CAP is the cause of high agricultural protection in the EU, the inclusion of the CEECs would increase the overall protection to European agriculture. In other words, protection to agriculture in a new and expanded EU would be higher than in the current EU.

The analysis in this chapter is based on a political economy model of economic integration and agricultural protection (Pokrivčák et al., 1999) to determine how the extension of the EU with countries from Central and Eastern Europe is likely to affect agricultural protection in the EU. We conclude that the most likely scenario for the EU with respect to the CEECs accession is that the overall average agricultural protection is *lower*.

Our model explicitly deals with the setting of common support prices. Price support is not, however, the only mechanism to transfer income from the nonfarm sector to farmers. The CAP has become complex. Major changes have been made since 1993. These changes resulted in lower weight being placed on price support while increasing the importance of direct income payments not directly related to price levels. There is, however, a straightforward extension of our model to incorporate income payments. There is a one-to-one and increased mapping from support price preferences to preferences for direct income transfers to farmers.

The chapter is organized as follows: the next section provides a brief introduction to the stylized policy mechanisms of the CAP while the following section evaluates the agricultural situation and policies in the CEECs. The fourth section develops a political economy model of agricultural support prices in the EU. The model assesses each country's price preferences (within and outside the EU) and the EU's common price determination. The fifth section evaluates the alleged 'restaurant table' effect and determines the conditions under which EU CAP prices would be higher or lower than otherwise would have been the case (i.e. does the 'restaurant table' outcome actually occur or not). The chapter ends with some conclusions regarding CEEC's accession to the EU.

Background

The primary objective of the CAP is to redistribute income from the nonfarm sector to farmers. Commodity price supports with import barriers and export subsidies (along with output controls) have been the most common means used by the CAP to achieve this objective. A common support price to all countries is the cornerstone of the CAP. The EU's price support mechanism implies two types of income transfers to farmers: a transfer from consumers and taxpayers to farmers and a transfer from one country to another. The former type of transfer is accomplished through transfers to farmers from consumers who pay higher prices than they otherwise would with import levies and sometimes alternative forms of production controls, and from taxpayers who finance production and export subsidies and other policy instruments dealing with excess production. Intercountry transfers occur indirectly because of the 'financial solidarity' in financing the CAP with the common budget and of net positive and negative trade positions between countries. Contributions to the common budget consist of revenues from import duties, producer levies, and contributions from Member States as a per cent of their value-added tax (VAT) base. After 1988, budget revenues are determined as a factor of gross domestic product (GDP), depending on the amount needed to balance the budget. An individual country's benefit from the CAP depends on the sectors obtaining subsidies, the country's net trade position (reflecting consumer transfers from one country to farmers in another) and the relative size of that country's production relative to total production in the EU.

It follows that net food importers and relatively rich countries transfer income to net food exporters and relatively poor countries, ceteris paribus. The United Kingdom (UK), for example, imports a high proportion of its food from abroad and therefore contributes a relatively high amount to the common budget in the form of import duties. The UK's relatively small agricultural sector means that it receives relatively less from the common budget and common prices than many other EU Member States. In regard to off-budget (consumer) transfers to farmers, the UK contributes to farmers in the rest of the EU because it is an importer. However, the contributions of the UK to the common budget are low on account of the country's relatively low VAT base (or per capita GDP). Due to the principle of financial solidarity adopted in the EU, Member States with relatively low GDP per capita contribute disproportionately less to the common budget than do the richer countries.

The supranational CAP produces a continuum of beneficiaries and losers among interest groups and countries. The extent to which countries gain or lose depends on two exogenous factors: the level of comparative advantage/disadvantage in agriculture and GDP per capita. The countries that have comparative advantage in agriculture (net exporters) and are relatively poor (low GDP per capita compared to the EU average) benefit the most from the CAP. On the other hand, the biggest net contributors to the common budget of the CAP are relatively rich countries with comparative disadvantage in agriculture (net importers).

Farmers in all EU countries benefit from the CAP. The biggest winners are low cost farmers or those farming sectors with the highest comparative advantage in a low cost country (relatively low GDP per capita). These farmers gain on two accounts: their productivity is high compared to other sectors in the economy, and their support price is higher than the country's politically optimal price would have been outside the CAP. The least gains from the CAP are realized by relatively inefficient farmers in relatively rich countries.

The level of protection for EU farmers is decided in the annual price review which can be broken into two stages: First, the European Commission makes proposals based on social, economic, financial, and environmental aspects. Second, ministers of agriculture (the Council of Ministers) negotiate prices, giving the decision process a fully political nature (Pearce, 1983). Each government comes to the price review with clearly defined national preferences for what it would like the CAP prices to be. The different national preferences have to be accommodated and trade-offs are made in reaching a compromise (Wallace, 1983). This often results in lengthy negotiations. The decision is reached by a vote, and qualified (weighted) majority rule is the commonly used voting procedure.

The CEECs and the CAP

Many of the CEECs have voiced their desire to join the EU and the EU has decided that these countries shall become members of the European Union in the future. Their full membership will have far-reaching implications for their own agricultural sectors, as well as for agriculture in the EU and the rest of Europe (Swinnen, 1996). The agricultural sector has a more important role in economies of the CEECs than in those of the EU countries (see table 10.1). However, agriculture's role in the economy for these CEECs is expected to decline as comparative advantage of these countries gradually moves towards manufacturing (Anderson, 1993).

Table 10.1 Importance of agriculture for the CEECs

	Agricultural Employment (% total employment)	Agricultural Trade (% total imports)	Food expenditures (% household income)
Poland	25.6	11.1	30
Hungary	10.1	7.4	31
Czech Rep	5.6	9.6	32
Slovakia	8.4	9.3	38
Slovenia	10.7	8.2	28
Romania	35.2	9.9	60
Bulgaria	21.2	10.6	48
Lithuania	22.4	10.8	58
Latvia	18.4	na	45
Estonia	8.2	16.7	39
CEEC-10	26.7	na	na
EU	5.7	9.5	22

Source: Commission of the European Communities, 1995.

Policy instruments to intervene in agriculture differ between the CEECs and between years (see Hartell and Swinnen, 1998, for a survey). Of the policy instruments price support is extensively used in all the CEECs. Minimum and guaranteed prices are set for major commodities and government interventions like purchasing or selling commodities or border measures are conducted to avoid the falling of market prices below the prescribed levels. Where consumer purchasing power is an issue guaranteed prices serve as a price ceiling that is supported by export bans. Some of the CEECs avoid the accumulation of surpluses caused by high guaranteed prices by supply control. Slovakia, for example, uses a milk quota system combined with guaranteed prices. If undesired surpluses are created anyway, export subsidies install the balance. Export subsidies are often utilized by Poland, Slovakia, Hungary, and Czech Republic, rarely by Rumania or Bulgaria. Declining agricultural profits and high interest rates make access to commercial loans by farmers difficult. To remedy this situation credit subsidies are introduced in many of the CEECs. Some countries, like Czech Republic and Slovakia, rely on input subsidies to stimulate technological progress.

Swinnen (1996) observes common trends in the development of agricultural policies in CEECs in the post-1989 period. After an initial liberalization ad hoc protectionist measures were introduced in the second phase of development. These measures alleviated the pressure on decline of agricultural production and income. Ad hoc measures are being replaced by comprehensive CAP-like market organization in the third phase.

Compared with the EU, protection of agricultural producers is significantly lower in the CEECs. For example the aggregate percentage PSE in the Czech Republic fluctuated between 28 per cent in 1992 and 20 per cent in 1994. The Hungarian percentage PSE did not reach 20 per cent during the same period of time (OECD, 1996b).

There are several studies quantifying the consequences of enlargement of the CAP to Central and Eastern Europe (see Tangermann, 1996, for a survey). The assumptions made by these studies differ as do the structures of the quantitative models, thereby producing a wide range of results. Assuming no reform of CAP price levels, these studies by and large argue that EU enlargement to include the CEECs would increase agricultural production and income, but cost taxpayers and consumers more in these CEECs. Ignoring economic inefficiency (deadweight costs), the CEECs would clearly be net beneficiaries of the CAP. The contributions of the CEECs to the common budget would be relatively small due to their relatively low GDP per capita and their net agricultural export status. The cost to current EU Member States of income transfers is expected to increase sharply after the accession of the CEECs. Mahé and Roe (1996), for example, estimate intercountry transfers of income arising from pre- and postenlargement of the CAP (table 10.2).

Table 10.2 Intercountry balance of payments transfers due to the pre- and post-1992 CAP (billion ECU)

	1991 (1)	1996 (2)	Enlargement Impact (3)
UEBL	-318.5	-495.4	-504
Denmark	782.2	764.3	-216
France	1 565.4	2 195.2	-2 246
Germany	-2 715.1	-3 965.1	-3 628
Ireland	1 669.0	1 448.1	-96
Italy	-2 875.5	-3 173.3	-1 766
The Netherlands	211.9	-348.0	-756
United Kingdom	715.0	417.7	-1 429
Greece	1 043.4	1 841.1	-156
Spain	349.8	1 419.3	-1 033
Portugal	-445.5	-157.8	-180
EU	-	-	-12 000

Source: Mahé and Roe, 1996, pp. 1314-23.

The Model

The purpose of this section is to develop a formal political economy model that determines the impact of EU enlargement on the CAP's support price and if the weighted average support price of current members and of the CEECs increases or decreases as a result (i.e. does the equivalent of the 'restaurant table' effect hold or not?). The result hinges critically on each country's ideal support price when they are members ('inside') the EU compared to the ideal support price when they are on their own (or 'outside' the EU). Of course, both of these ideal support prices are hypothetical for each country in the EU because we observe the CAP's 'common' agricultural support price. For individual countries currently outside the EU, their observed support prices are a good indication of their ideal support price outside the EU but no measure is currently available of their preferred price support if they were to be members of the EU.

Before Integration or 'Outside' the CAP

To determine politically optimal domestic support price, consider a political market of rational, self-interested politicians and fully informed citizens. Using tax and subsidy type policies, politicians maximize support from citizens who provide them support if the policy helps them and reduce their support if the policy hurts them. Different marginal utility of incomes among different income groups allows politicians to increase their votes through redistribution of income. Optimal redistribution occurs when the marginal decrease of support from the taxed group equals marginal increase of support from the subsidized sector (de Gorter and Swinnen, 1994, 1995; Swinnen, 1994).[1] The support price that maximizes political support is identified as P_j^*.

After Integration or 'Inside' the CAP

The supranational CAP is created. There are two salient features of the CAP: common prices and financial solidarity. Agricultural prices are the same in all Member States. Due to the principle of financial solidarity the balanced budget equation does not have to hold for each Member State. It is only the overall EU balanced budget equation that has to be satisfied.

Let $P_j^\#$ denote politically optimal support price ($s_j^\#$ is politically optimal per unit subsidy) for a country 'inside' the CAP, given the other countries would accept it. The politically optimal price support for a country outside the EU would be higher for a net contributor to the CAP than its politically preferred price support when it is a member of the CAP. The reasoning is as follows: a net contributor transfers income from its consumers and taxpayers to foreign farmers. Without these intercountry transfers, the income of domestic taxpayers and/or consumers would be higher for a given level of income transfer to the agricultural sector A. Hence, in our political model, the political outcome would be such that politicians would have a higher price support preference outside the CAP than if their country was inside the CAP and at the same time was a net contributor to the CAP. This holds whether the country's price preferences are above or below the chosen (observed) common price in the EU. This case of net contributors is depicted in figure 10.1 for the case of two countries with different price preferences. The reverse holds true for net beneficiaries of the CAP.

There is a politically optimal transfer of income from taxpayers to farmers or vice versa for a country both inside and outside the CAP. Moreover, there is a unique politically optimal agricultural protection that maximizes domestic political support. The political preferences of a Member State inside and outside the CAP do not necessarily coincide. The politically optimal agricultural protection for a net contributor to the CAP 'outside' the EU would be higher than its politically preferred agricultural protection when it is a member of the CAP. Any deviation, whether positive or negative from the politically optimal support, reduces domestic political support, i.e. countries have Euclidean preferences over a policy space. In a single-dimensional case when agriculture is treated as a whole, the preferences are single-peaked because the further away the actual outcome is from the politically optimal level, the less support the politicians of country j can expect.

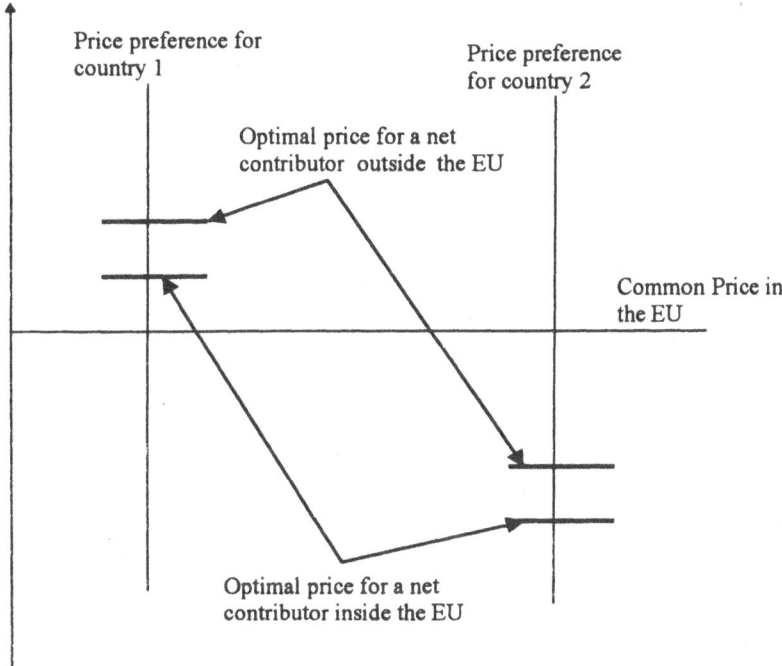

Figure 10.1 Examples of the price preferences for a net beneficiary of the CAP inside versus outside the EU

The actual EU outcome (equilibrium policy or observed CAP price support implemented) is a function of the array of ideal policies of each Member State, the European Commission's price proposal (itself dependent on the former), and the legislative procedure in the EU of making the final price support decision. A simple consultation procedure applies to most agricultural policy issues (at least within the framework of the CAP).

Under this procedure, the Commission makes a proposal that is 'free from political bias' (Fearne, 1991), and the Council decides thereon, after receiving a nonbinding opinion from the European Parliament. Decision making in the Council proceeds by a vote.

The decision concerning the level of common prices adopted by the CAP in the end is made in the annual EU price review process. By assuming self-interested entrepreneurial politicians that maximize their *domestic* political support, we consider the annual price review process as a forum for advancing national interests. Because each country has a different ideal preference for the level of the common CAP support price, the final compromise is determined by a bargaining process which depends on the voting system adopted by the EU. This automatically rules out the notion that the Commission or Council maximizes its political support like national governments do. This is a reasonable assumption given that neither the Council nor the Commission is elected directly but rather have their members nominated by national governments. Therefore, each member represents the interests of his or her national government which results in the bargaining process indicated above.

Integration and Protection

Does integration into the CAP cause the average level of protection to go up. The result depends on three key factors:

- the support price adopted in the Council: P^{EU}
- the optimal domestic transfers for each country *outside* the CAP: P_j^*
- country j's proportion of total EU agricultural production: Q_j/Q

In the previous section, we have established how the price preferences are determined. The ideal price of the Member State depends on the income gap between the agricultural sector (A) and all others (B) after the intercountry transfers are realized (after the Member State pays its contribution to the common budget and receives its benefits from the common budget). The Member States that are net contributors to the CAP prefer higher prices while outside the CAP than they would prefer inside the CAP. The reverse holds true for net beneficiaries. As there are both beneficiaries and contributors, the intercountry transfers do not push common support prices up. Financial solidarity, the first salient feature of the CAP, does not cause higher protection for agriculture in the EU.

Because the countries have single-peaked preferences for the common support price, both positive and negative deviation from the country's ideal price reduces domestic political support. Positive deviation (common support price being higher than the ideal price) also diminishes domestic political support. The situation is symmetric with respect to the deviation of the common intervention price from the ideal price. Bearing in mind this symmetry, there is no inherent tendency in either a qualified or simple majority to push price supports up rather than down. The decision in the Council's price review is equally likely to be blocked by countries not willing to increase prices as by the countries not willing to reduce price support. The decision rule can equally likely push price support up or down. Adoption of a common EU intervention price creates no institutional pressure for higher protection of agriculture. Therefore, using simple majority in the following discussion will not alter the results.

In a single-dimensional issue, if all voters (members of the Council) have single-peaked preferences defined over the issue, then the median voter cannot lose under simple majority rule. Therefore, the price preference of the median country, $P^{\#}_{MED}$, is to be adopted as the common price. In a single-dimensional case such as this under consideration, the existence of single-peaked preferences of each representative of a country in the Council assures that no voting cycles occur. Furthermore, the optimal price preference of the median country is the equilibrium result for the CAP under majority rule. In reality, however, the Council seldom decides on a change of a single common price. Rather a formulation of package deals, where each country 'loses' on one commodity and 'gains' on other, is used as a procedural rule. In this multidimensional case, the necessary and sufficient condition for existence of a dominant point under majority rule requires that it be a median in all directions (Mueller, 1989). But there is no guarantee that a median in all directions will exist for any preferences of individual representatives of EU countries in the Council. However, the cost of indecision over a prolonged period of time makes the stability of the outcome more likely (Plott, 1967).

Higher protection to agriculture in the EU due to the supranational character of the CAP than otherwise would have been the case depends on the relationship between the sizes of each country's agricultural sectors as measured by the Q_i's and their price preferences. If we assume that all Member States have agricultural sectors of the same size, then the supranational feature of the CAP causes higher protection to the EU's agriculture only if there is a particular distribution of politically optimal prices across countries. Indeed, assuming the same size of the agricultural sector across countries, the supranational nature of the CAP produces higher agricultural protection in the EU if countries with high preferred prices are clustered closely to the median and countries with low preferred prices are far below the median level (an example is depicted in figure 10.2). In this case, countries with efficient agricultural sectors and low support price preference are 'forced' to accept high support prices by the supranational CAP. If the reverse is true, then the CAP generates lower protection to agriculture than the weighted average of all individual country protections outside the CAP.

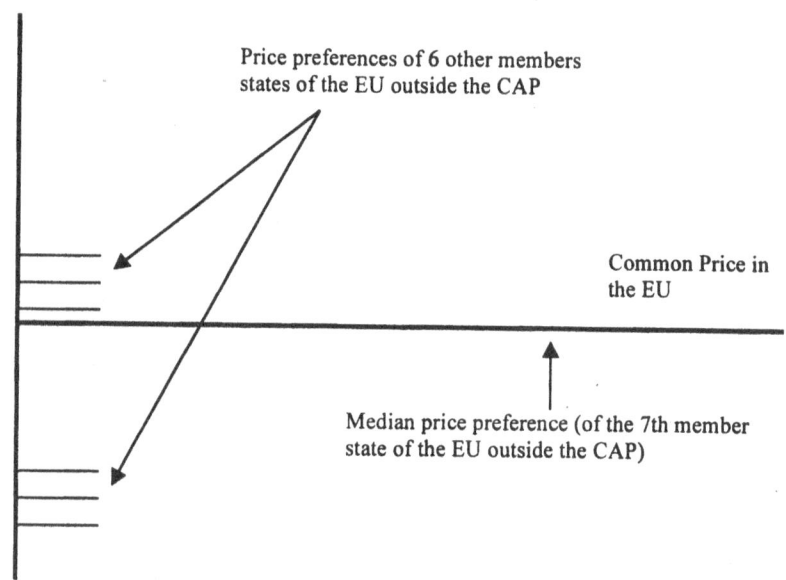

Figure 10.2 An example of the CAP resulting in higher price supports (analogous to the 'restaurant table' effect) assuming all 7 countries' agricultural sectors are of equal size

Another situation under which the 'restaurant table' effect does not hold is when countries with large agricultural sectors, relative to total agriculture in the EU, prefer prices above that of the median country. In this situation, one can show that the supranational nature of the CAP does not cause higher overall protection for agriculture in the European Union. Figure 10.3 depicts this situation. Country 1 is depicted as a relatively large agricultural producer (represented by a large Q_i/Q reflected by the distance OG in figure 10.3), country 2 as a medium size agricultural producer (distance GH), and country 3 with a small agricultural sector relative to the EU total. The actual CAP transfer (represented by the optimal CAP transfer preferred by the median country), is area $P^{\#}_{MED}DIO$ (assuming that the median country is a net contributor to the CAP because its ideal support price inside the CAP is lower than that outside the CAP). The politically optimal transfer for country 1 if there were no EU is area P^{*}_1AGO, area BCHG for country 2 and area EFIH for country 3. It is possible in figure 10.3 that the sum of domestic politically optimal transfers outside the CAP is higher than that with the CAP. In such a situation, the 'restaurant table' effect does not hold.

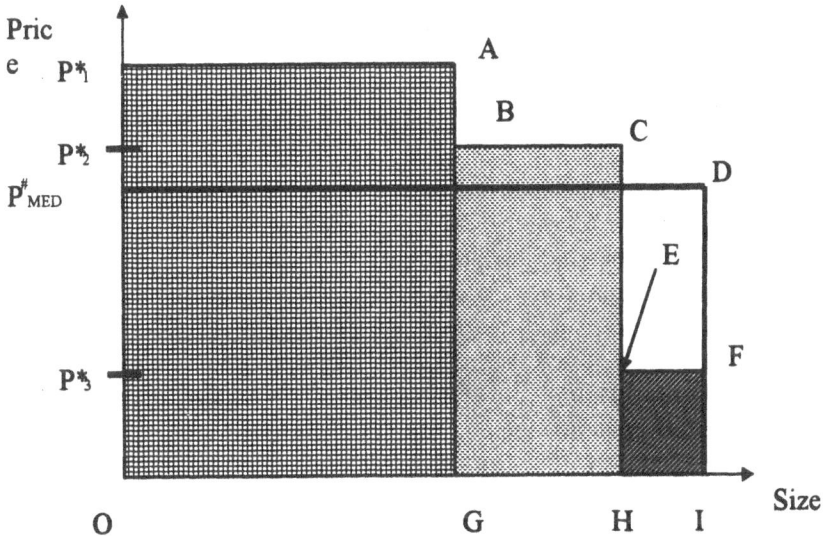

Figure 10.3 Size of production and the 'restaurant table' effect

In conclusion, our model states that there are unique ideal support prices for a country both inside and outside the CAP. Deviation from these ideal support prices reduces domestic political support. In the EU, if one country or a compact coalition of countries is a net beneficiary of a commodity regime, there is automatically a country or a compact coalition of countries that is a net contributor to the commodity's regime. If net beneficiaries have a vested interest in increased price support, net contributors have a vested interest in not to increasing price support.

Unlike in Mahé and Roe (1996), our political model does not lead to a 'restaurant table' effect because it considers not only countries that have vested interest in increasing prices (net beneficiaries) but net contributors too.

The supranational nature of the CAP causes higher protection for agriculture in the EU only under very specific conditions.[2] The 'restaurant table' effect is more likely to occur in the CAP when relatively small domestic income transfers are politically optimal for relatively large countries. The possibility of the 'restaurant table' effect is even higher if these countries are net beneficiaries of the CAP. However, evidence for the EU is such that the 'restaurant table' effect is not very likely to occur. Germany, as the largest EU member, has a preference for the highest agricultural support price. German dissatisfaction with low support prices within the CAP was openly manifested in 1985 when the country vetoed a decision of the Council to lower target prices for cereals. This is a good indication that German support prices would increase as well as the weighted protection for European agriculture if Germany was outside the CAP.

Moreover, some Member States with relatively small agricultural sectors compared to the EU total, like the Benelux countries and Denmark, need not oppose reductions in support prices or trade liberalization because their agricultural sectors are efficient and therefore the countries export farm commodities to both EU and third countries (Tracy, 1996). If there were no CAP, these countries would decrease agricultural support, compared to current common EU agricultural support. However, weighted average protection to European agriculture would decrease rather insignificantly as these countries have a relatively small agricultural share of the EU total. On the other hand, relatively large countries with high price preference (Germany, France) would increase the weighted average of protection a great deal.

Countries do not share the 'bill' of the CAP as people do in a restaurant. For example, Germany pays more (as a wealthy net importer) for the CAP than most other countries and vice versa for the UK (as a net exporter with lower per capita GDP). Yet the UK is a proponent of 'less expensive meals' (i.e., wants lower support prices) while Germany calls for each country in the CAP to 'order more expensive meals' even if it costs Germany proportionately more.

Moreover, notice that several West European countries that are not members of the CAP confer higher protection for agriculture than the EU. Switzerland, for example, with an inefficient agricultural sector relative to the rest of the economy, has an aggregate percentage PSE of approximately 80 per cent while Norway's is about 75 per cent. Protection for agriculture has also decreased for Austria and the Nordic countries that recently joined the CAP. The high protection of agriculture in the EU is due to other factors like relative income parity with the rest of the economy (see Swinnen and de Gorter, 1993; Swinnen, 1994; and de Gorter and Swinnen, 1994, 1995). The 'restaurant table' effect is not necessarily the central reason for high agricultural protection in the European Union.

Implication for the CEECs Joining the CAP

The accession of the CEECs into the EU's CAP will alter preferences for agricultural protection both in the current EU countries and in the CEECs. Preferences for agricultural protection in the current EU countries will be lowered. The reason is straightforward. The current EU countries will become larger net contributors to the common agricultural policy (table 10.2). There will be intercountry income transfers from the current EU members to the CEECs. For a given transfer of income to domestic farmers costs to current EU taxpayers and consumers will be higher in the expanded CAP. Politicians of the current EU members will have lower preferences for agricultural protection in the new and expanded CAP than in the current CAP. The overall median preference for agricultural protection of a coallition of current EU members will therefore be lower.

The CEECs, on the other hand, will prefer higher agricultural support inside the CAP than outside the CAP. Inside the CAP the CEECs will enjoy the status of net beneficiaries. Because the CEECs have small GDP per capita relative to the EU's current Member States and a relatively large agricultural sector they would greatly benefit (neglecting deadweight costs) from joining the CAP. Some of the income going to farmers of a net beneficiary of the CAP comes from foreign consumers and taxpayers. Ceteris paribus, a net beneficiary prefers higher income transfers through the common budget. Moreover, we can predict that the preferences of the CEECs for agricultural support inside the CAP would on average be below the current EU median preference.

The CEECs have efficient agricultural sectors relative to the rest of the economy. The relative income gap between farmers and the rest of the economy are expected to be lower in the CEECs than among current EU members (Swinnen, 1996). Because of this comparative advantage in CEEC agriculture, the relative urban/rural income gap is low leaving little room for politicians to strive for higher common prices unless they impose higher taxes on agriculture relative to other sectors of the economy.

What will happen to the overall level of protection to agriculture in a new and expanded EU? There will be a decline of politically optimal agricultural protection for current EU countries and the politically optimal agricultural protection for the new members of the EU will be below the current EU median level.

These two forces then result in a lower common agricultural support for the CAP in the expanded EU. This expected effect of CEECs' accession to the EU on CAP prices is depicted in figure 10.4. With a view to accession of the CEECs to the EU's CAP, there is demand from politicians of Member States for the CAP reform, lowering support prices. This demand stems from lower price support preferences of current Member States due to expected worsening of the net contribution position of the current Member States after the accession.

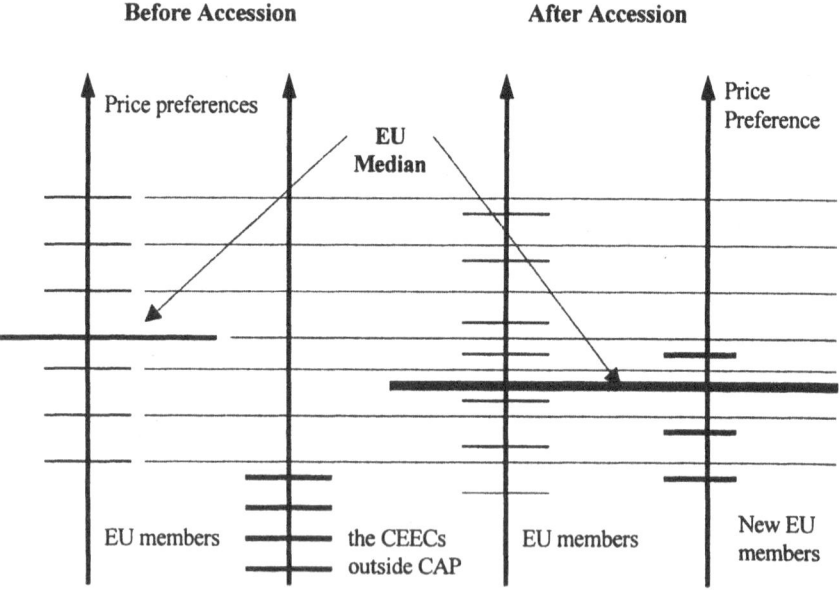

Median Price Preferences of the EU Declines for Two Reasons:
- price preference of current members declines because of increased costs of CEECs
- new countries price preferences inside the EU are relatively lower than those of incumbents

Figure 10.4 Median price preferences and the accession of the CEECs

In conclusion, our political economy model does not confirm the 'restaurant table' effect of the CAP as proposed and accepted as the conventional wisdom in the literature on this subject, due to the supranational character of the EU. The institutional pressure for 'high' common prices is not a general effect of the CAP itself, but it can occur, as when large countries prefer low prices and/or countries with preferences for high prices are clustered closely to the median position while optimal preferences for low price supports are farther below the median position.

Even if the CAP remains unreformed, the Eastward enlargement of the EU would decrease the level of agricultural protection in the EU. The impetus will be provided by the current EU members because of a deteriorating effect of the accession on their net contribution position.

Notes

1 Dead weight cost (DWC) is not considered here. For how to incorporate DWC in the model see Swinnen and de Gorter (1993).
2 The above analysis of the 'restaurant table' effect in the EU can be extended to a multidimensional case. In such a case, one would have to compare optimal weighted vectors of commodity prices for each country outside the EU with the actual price vector outcome in the EU. The analysis becomes more complex because voting over price packages is more conducive to voting cycles.

References

Anderson, K. (1993), 'Intersectoral Changes in Former Socialist Economies: Distinguishing Initial from Longer-Term Responses', in I. Goldin (ed), *Economic Reform, Trade, and Agricultural Development*, Macmillan, London and St. Martin's Press, New York, pp. 291-321.
Commission of the European Communities (various years), *Report on the Agricultural Situation in the Community*, Office for Official Publications of the EC, Luxembourg.
De Gorter, H. and Swinnen, J. (1994), 'The Economic Polity of Farm Policy', *Journal of Agricultural Economics*, vol. 45, no. 3, pp. 312-26.
De Gorter, H. and Swinnen, J. (1995), 'The Economic Polity of Farm Policy: Reply', *Journal of Agricultural Economics*, vol. 46, no. 3, pp. 403-14.
Fearne, A. (1991), 'The CAP Decision-Making Process', in C. Ritson and D. Harvey (eds), *The Common Agricultural Policy and the World Economy*, C.A.B International, Wallingford, pp. 101-16.
Hartell, J. and Swinnen, J.F.M. (1998), 'Trends in Agricultural Price and Trade Policy Instruments Since 1990 in Central European Countries', *The World Economy*, vol. 21, no. 2, pp. 261-79.
Hill, B.E. (1984), *The Common Agricultural Policy and Past, Present and Future*, University Press, Cambridge.

Mahé, L.M. and Roe, T.L. (1996), 'The Political Economy of Reforming the 1992 CAP Reform', *American Journal of Agricultural Economics*, vol. 78, pp. 1314-23.

Mueller, D.C. (1989), *Public Choice II*, Cambridge University Press, New York.

OECD (1996a), *Agricultural Policies, Markets and Trade in OECD Countries*.

OECD (1996b), *Agricultural Policies, Markets and Trade in Transition Economies*.

Pearce, J. (1983), 'The Common Agricultural Policy: The Accumulation of Special Interests', in H. Wallace, W. Wallace and C. Webb (eds), *Policy Making in the European Union*, Wiley, Chichester.

Plott, C.R. (1967), 'Notation of Equilibrium and Its Possibility Under Majority Rule', *The American Economic Review*, vol. 57, pp. 787-806.

Pokrivčák, J., de Gorter, H. and Swinnen, J.F.M. (1999), 'Economic Integration and Agricultural Protection: Does There Exist a Restaurant Table Effect in the Common Agricultural Policy?', Policy Research Group Working Paper, Department of Agricultural and Environmental Economics, Katholieke Universiteit Leuven, Belgium.

Runge, C.F. and von Witzke, H. (1987), 'Institutional Change in the Common Agricultural Policy of the European Community', *American Journal of Agricultural Economics*, vol. 69, pp. 213-22.

Schmitt, G. (1984), 'Warum die Agrarpolitik ist, wie sie ist, und nicht, wie sie sein sollte', *Agrarwirtschaft*, vol. 33, pp. 129-36.

Swinnen, J.F.M. (1996), 'Endogenous Price and Trade Policy Developments in Central European Agriculture', *European Review of Agricultural Economics*, vol. 23, pp. 133-60.

Swinnen, J.F.M. (1994), 'A Positive Theory of Agricultural Protection', *American Journal of Agricultural Economics*, vol. 76, no. 1, pp. 1-14.

Swinnen, J.F.M. and de Gorter H. (1993), 'Why Small Groups and Low Income Sectors Obtain Subsidies: The "Altruistic" Side of a "Self-Interested" Government', *Economics and Politics*, vol. 4, pp. 285-93.

Tangermann, S. (1996), 'Reforming the CAP: A Prerequisite for Eastern Enlargement', Paper prepared for the Kiel Week Conference *Quo Vadis Europe?*.

Tracy, M. (1996), 'Agricultural Policy in the European Union and Other Market Economies', APS-Agricultural Policy Studies, Brussels.

Wallace, H. (1983), 'Negotiation, Conflict and Compromise: The Elusive Pursuit of Common Policies', in H. Wallace, W. Wallace and C. Webb (eds), *Policy Making in the European Union*, Wiley, Chichester.